IN SEARCH OF SILVESTR

ABOUT THE AUTHOR

Jan Beránek is a director and organizational strategist at Greenpeace International.

A Czech ecological activist and energy expert, he was a former member and chairman of Czech Green Party.

He is a keen astrophotographer.

The Czech edition of *In Search of Silvestr* (*Pátrání po Silvestrovi*) was published in 2020.

Copyright © 2025 Jan Beránek

All rights reserved. No part of this publication may be reproduced or transmitted in any format by any means, electronic or mechanical, including photocopy, recording or any information storage and retrieval system, without prior permission in writing from the publisher.

Published by
Landmark Books Pte Ltd

Landmark Books is an imprint of
Landmark Books Pte Ltd

ISBN 978-981-94-1919-7
Printed in Singapore

A gripping and moving account of the author's search for the fate of his granduncle Silvestr Němec who arrived in Singapore in 1939 as a 22-year-old employee of the Bata Shoe Company. The story of Němec, who died in action during World War II as a volunteer, is embedded within the history of Bata which started as a small Czech family company and expanded into a global corporation with a branch in Singapore. This makes *In Search of Silvestr* a fascinating insight into not only the last battle for Singapore on Pasir Panjang Ridge and Bukit Chandu, but also the shoe company many of us grew up with.

Kwa Chong Guan
Adjunct Assoc Prof (Hon.), History Department,
National University of Singapore
Co-author, Seven Hundred Years, A History of Singapore, *and editor,* Shipwrecks and the Maritime History of Singapore.

In Search of Silvester is not a historical monograph, but a historical reportage reminiscent in places of the works of the late Miroslav Ivanov. The fact that Beránek is an amateur does not diminish the book in any way. Quite the contrary, the text shows what the publications of professional historians so often lack: passion for the subject.

Petr Zídek
Czech historian and journalist

Thanks to honest and persistent work with archival sources (personal correspondence, memoirs, official reports, etc.) from archives in the Czech Republic, London and Singapore, and even contacts with descendants of memoirists, the author, with his keen approach, reconstructs not only the life of his granduncle until almost his fateful end, but also the fate of Singapore during World War II.

    The author presents and analyses four possible hypotheses about the death of his granduncle Silvester Němec who defended Singapore as a volunteer. This factual historical whodunit thus has no definitive solution (yet), but sometimes, as is the case here, the search itself (for the author, certainly, and for the curious reader, almost certainly, too) is exciting enough.

Roman Mocpajchel
Slovak military historian

"First to Bata then to school" was an advertising mantra known to many Singapore schoolchildren. But few realise that Bata was a Czech company that set up business in Singapore on North Bridge Road in the 1930s.

Even less are aware that Bata employees ended up dying in the Battle for Singapore and in internment camps during World War II.

Jan Beránek reveals the history of Bata and the fate of the Czech community in war-time Singapore in this deeply personal and objective work of committed research.

Lee Geok Boi
Author, Syonan: The Japanese Occupation and Its Legacy

Fascinating context and range of topics, fascinating plight. It would be possible to comment at length positively on everything, but there is no need. Thank you and congratulations on a great job.

Michal Hora
Specialist, National Library of the Czech Republic

IN SEARCH OF SILVESTR

Unravelling my granduncle's fate,
Bata, Czechoslovaks and
World War II in Singapore

Jan Beránek

◊LANDMΔRK◊BOOKS◊

To my grandmother, Františka, in memoriam.

"Our dead are never dead to us until we have forgotten them."

George Eliot

CONTENTS

Prologue 13
I   Inheriting the Family Archive 17
II   Weaving from the Web 26
III Discovering Bata in Zlín 33
IV Tracing Roots in Vémyslice 56
V   Czechoslovaks in Singapore 70
VI Troubles Within the Community 96
VII Silvestr's Vocation 108
VIII From Zlín to Singapore 117
IX Volunteering for the War 130
X   Invasion of Malaya 153
XI Battle of Singapore 176
XII Czechoslovaks During the Occupation 201
XIII Scenarios of Silvestr's Fate 212
XIV Tracing Silvestr in Today's Singapore 238
Epilogue 249

Appendix I: Dramatis Personae 252
Appendix II: Tools for Research 272
Bibliography 275
Acknowledgements 285

- Prologue -
An Eight-Year Quest

IN 2017, I started my research on the fate of my granduncle Silvestr Němec, a young Czech employed by the Bata Shoe Company in Singapore, who volunteered to fight the Japanese when they invaded Singapore during World War II and went missing in 1942.

I had no idea then where this search would lead me. Over time, the quest produced a whole collection of stories that spanned a century and across continents, covering not just Silvestr's life but also the Bata company in the Far East, other Czechoslovaks who lived in Singapore before and during World War II, as well as my own journey of discovery.

This is an excerpt from my blog, written back in March 2017:

> *A few weeks ago, I decided to launch a quest for information and documents related to the life and death of my granduncle Silvestr Němec.*
>
> *In 1938, the Bata Shoe Company sent Silvestr from its home base in Zlín, Czechoslovakia, to its newly established branch in Singapore. This is also where the war eventually found him at the end of 1941, shortly after the attack on Pearl Harbour. Silvestr volunteered and was mobilised to defend Singapore against the Japanese invasion. Then, around mid-February, during the fall of Singapore, he [...] went missing, and never resurfaced after the war.*
>
> *For his family living in the town of Vémyslice, in the southern Moravia region of Czechoslovakia, it was a deeply traumatising situation. His parents had not only lost their youngest son, but even after the war, did not know much about his fate. Silvestr was formally*

declared dead by the British government in July 1947, nearly two years after the Japanese surrender.

In 1951, the British government awarded the family a small compensation based on the estimated value of Silvestr's lost property in Singapore. However, at the end of the complicated bureaucratic process – perhaps also because Silvestr's family were country folk with limited education and no knowledge of foreign languages, and Czechoslovakia by that time was isolated from the world by the Soviet Iron Curtain – only a fraction of the promised amount eventually reached his parents. The feeling that they had been robbed of the small legacy left by their missing son only deepened their wounds and despair.

I think that this is one of the reasons why hardly anyone talked about Silvestr in the family. The traumatic story was almost entirely pushed out of their minds.

My mother never had a chance to meet her uncle Silvestr: he had disappeared three months before she was born, and more than six thousand miles away. I, myself, can only vaguely recall a few times when Silvestr was mentioned. This was mostly when my grandmother – Silvestr's older sister – went to lay flowers and tidy up the small war memorial in the centre of their hometown. Silvestr's name is engraved there, among about a dozen other local citizens who lost their lives during World War II.

Although I spent a great deal of my childhood at my grandmother's place – almost every weekend and summer vacation, enjoying a magical time on the farm I loved so much – Silvestr Němec had been nothing more to me than a name attached to a vague story of my grandmother's brother, whom I knew had disappeared in a battle in the war. It meant nothing to a young boy more interested in enjoying outdoor adventures in a beautiful countryside.

From a larger historical perspective, the story of Silvestr is barely noteworthy. There were millions of people who perished during the hell of World War II. Silvestr, who joined the volunteer defence units in Singapore with the rank of Private, fought a short futile battle; his role was most likely negligible, with no outstanding achievement or heroism.

Had I begun my search for the facts and evidence 20 years ago, I might still have had a reasonable chance of finding some living witnesses and capturing their firsthand accounts of those events, *perhaps even their memories of my granduncle. But 75 years have passed and it's too late for that.*

Yet, I have decided to embark on this journey, determined to discover and collect whatever I can. I wish to do that in order to honour the memory of Silvestr Němec, whose tragic story has almost slipped our memory, and to recover it for my family and for those interested to learn about how Czechs ended up fighting in a war far from their own homeland.

I do not claim that my efforts provide a full picture of the events of the past. However, I believe that the exploration itself – based on scattered evidence from archives around the world – may be an intriguing story of its own.

In retrospect, I must say that not even in my wildest dreams did I expect that my research would take me so far. It's fascinating how much can still be recovered from the forgotten past, how many directions the research can expand into, how many surprises and miracles one can encounter during such a project and most importantly, how many remarkable people one can get to know along the way.

This book traces my research journey – each step of my quest to find out more about Silvestr, what happened to him, as well as the other Bata Czechoslovaks in Singapore.

On many occasions – such as when I was studying how Baťa organised his business or the 20th century history of Vémyslice or what other Batamen captured in their diaries, letters and articles about their work and life in Singapore in 1930s – I was vividly picturing Silvestr in those contexts and situations, and trying to imagine how he might have thought or felt about them.

Initially, I had not considered the possibility of publishing a book based on my research. What changed my mind was the growing readership of my blog and the number of people encouraging me to capture the whole story in print. Perhaps, by providing an insight into my research process may also help those interested in embarking on their own family history research.

My book about my granduncle Silvestr was first published in Czech in October 2020, and now its English version has found its way into the hands of readers like you. However, this is not the end of my journey. My research carries on, although at a slower pace, and I continue to come across new details and fragments of information every now and then.

PROLOGUE

In the meantime, I would like to express my gratitude to those who have encouraged and supported me on this project, for their interest and kindness. You will find a proper acknowledgement section at the end of the book.

Finally, more than 80 years have passed since the dramatic events described in this book took place, during which my granduncle disappeared at the age of 22. I hope that these pages will help to resurrect the stories of Silvestr, and the many others who found themselves in the middle of the brutal war in the Far East.

- I -
Inheriting the Family Archive

MY PIECING TOGETHER of Silvestr's story began in February 2017. I realised only later that it was just a few days from the 75th anniversary of his presumed death. This coincidence would become the first of many during my research journey.

It was late February. I was visiting my motherland again. My family and I had been living in the Netherlands for many years, and several times each year, we would make a trip back to the Czech Republic. During that visit, my mother showed me a box of old family documents. She knew that I had recently been trying to trace our ancestors and construct a family tree.

I've heard that interest in family history often surfaces at around my age – in one's late 40s or 50s – perhaps because we've already travelled a fair bit on life's journey and are curious to view our lives in the context of something bigger, like where we come from or what our ancestors were like.

In my case, the final push was when old Czech parish registers were made accessible online, and as I was working full-time in Istanbul at the time, away from my family, I suddenly found myself with some spare time in the evenings. As I browsed through the scanned pages of sometimes hard-to-read records from the 17th to 19th century, it almost felt as if I was holding those very old documents in my hands. And by randomly reading through these records, I got little glimpses into the everyday lives, as well as dramatic moments, of people long forgotten.

As I was sharing my excitement about this experience with my family, my mother felt that a box of old marriage, death and land purchase certificates she'd been a guardian of would interest me.

That box also contained about two dozen papers related to

Silvestr Němec. They included a letter from Silvestr upon his arrival to Singapore in March 1939, and some post-war correspondence with Silvestr's friends and colleagues from the Bata Shoe Company in Singapore. The latter provided his parents with recollections of their missing son and accounts of how the Bata men had searched for Silvestr after the liberation of Singapore.

Those papers marked my starting point.

When Hope Floats

The earliest letter, dated December 1945, is from Pavel Ambrož:

> I was, together with your son Silvestr Němec, employed by the Bata Shoe Co. Ltd. in Singapore. We were friends. Both of us joined the Singapore Volunteer Forces and when the war started, we were mobilised and attached to the British Army in Singapore. I was a machine gunner, your son served with the armoured cars.
>
> About three days before the occupation of Singapore by the Japanese, Silvestr was wounded and moved to a field hospital. After the fall of Singapore (15 February 1942), I searched for him in all the hospitals but did not find him. Now that the British have taken over Singapore again, I went through the military records and found that he has been listed as missing.
>
> It is possible that he had left on one of the ships that evacuated the Europeans from Singapore, got captured at sea by the Japanese war ships and was interned in one of the many prison camps on Java, Sumatra and various places in Indonesia. There are still about 250,000 prisoners on Java and there are no comprehensive lists of all their names as yet. The fighting is still going on there.
>
> After the Japanese took over Singapore, I went to look at your son's apartment and mine. Both were pillaged [...] I am very sorry that I cannot give you any more details. I do, however, hope that once the Allies accomplish the liberation of Java, they will find him in one of the prison camps there.

I don't know what, if any, information had reached Silvestr's parents earlier. It is quite possible that this letter was the very first factual report they received from the Far East about their son. We can only imagine the anxiety of his parents, desperately clinging on to the hope offered in

Pavel Ambrož's letter – that Silvestr could still be alive in a prisoner-of-war camp somewhere in Indonesia.

During my research in the Czech National Archives in Prague, I found a file from the Repatriation Department of the Czechoslovak Ministry of Work and Social Care created in September 1945. The subject under reference number K-12837 read "Sylvestr Němec – enquiry – Singapore". The file contained just a single sheet of lined paper. On it was this handwritten entry:

> Sylvestr Němec, born on 19 October 1919, worked for the Bata company in Zlín until 1941, then left for Singapore with several other colleagues. Contact: František Němec, Vémyslice 23, near Moravský Krumlov.

At the back of that sheet was a short, typewritten note: "19 November 1945 – Enquiry form sent to Singapore". That was it, nothing more. It is obvious that the Czechoslovak authorities did not search very hard.

Sadly, Silvestr's parents did not progress much further either. This is understandable, considering they were living in a small town in the Czechoslovak countryside and did not speak any foreign language.

The family archive, however, contains a copy of their reply to Pavel Ambrož, sent to Batanagar on 12 January 1946. Batanagar was a small town built by the Bata company on a bank of the Hooghly River in India in 1934. It was the first centre of the company in the Far East, serving the needs of its newly opened leather shoe production factory there. Today, Batanagar is part of the larger suburban area around Calcutta.

In their reply to Ambrož, Silvestr's parents wrote:

> Your kind letter brought us great joy, both because we have learnt more about our son, as well as because you poured at least some hope into our hearts that he might still be alive [...] We are grateful for the photograph you sent us and, hopefully, you won't mind if we ask you to send us five more copies, so that we can share them with the family and his friends.

Silvestr's father also asked for additional information and invited Ambrož, should he be to the region, to visit the family in Vémyslice, so that they could talk about Silvestr in person.

A reply from Ambrož followed shortly, dated 21 February 1946.

He sent four additional photographs and the original negatives – unfortunately, I have not been able to find any of them in the family archives. The short letter includes a sweet note worth quoting:

> Please, forgive me for writing you these letters in a business style, but I have no talent to write personal letters. My mother keeps criticising me for this all the time.

Silvestr's father also sent an inquiry to the Bata company's headquarters in Zlín. Their reply arrived just before Christmas 1945:

> We have received your letter, and we share your pain due to the loss of your son. We understand perfectly that you wish to obtain some object from his property, for the family's remembrance. Because the postal service to Singapore has only just been restored, we have not yet managed to obtain more information about your son. If you wish to write directly to the Singapore branch of Bata, here is the address [...] Yours faithfully, Bata Zlín.

The family wrote to Singapore on 2 January 1946, addressing their plea to Antonín Jugas, the head of Bata in Singapore. In their letter, Silvestr's parents mentioned the possibility that Silvestr might have been killed, and begged for more information:

> You will hopefully be able to understand us, old parents, who do not want to believe in such a horrible possibility. We therefore grasp this opportunity and beg you that such a prospect [that Silvestr died] be either confirmed or pronounced as false.

Before the end of the month, Jugas responded with a detailed letter that gave new information on Silvestr's role in the Singapore Volunteer Force. In it, Jugas also mentioned some steps he himself had taken to search for Silvestr:

> Dear Mr Němec,
> I received your letter yesterday and I am terribly sorry that it has to be me to give you a report that is sad not only for you, but also, for all of us. The barbarian war had claimed eight lives from our Bata family here in Singapore.

I will try, as much as I am able, to give you a true picture about what happened since he [Silvestr] was mobilised. I apologise if some details that you would be interested in are not included, I will gladly answer if you write to me again with more questions. We, all the Czechoslovaks here, were interned by the Japanese and went through tremendous suffering until we were liberated by the British Army.

Your son was mobilised on 4 December 1941 and was assigned to the armoured vehicles (Company B) as a Private, number 13779. Some of our other staff also volunteered.

Up till the end of January 1942, we were receiving regular information about everyone, but after the fight for Singapore island started, all reporting stopped. It was only after the capitulation that we learned from our people that your son was injured and taken to a hospital. Since then, nobody has heard of him. A true hell stormed over Singapore at that time. It took about a week until [our boys] emerged, one by one – dirty, ragged, exhausted – but not all of them, as we had hoped.

In early September 1945, as soon as we were liberated by the British Army, we searched for information on everyone from our family who were still missing. On the day of 12 November 1945, we sent a written inquiry about your son to the main command in Singapore, and we received a written reply that they cannot provide us with any information until they obtain a formal army report.

As a result, I am not able to give you any information, either positive or negative. We are however tracking the fate of all of our people, and I will not forget to inform you once an official army report arrives.

We had also taken steps to take care of all the assets of your son, particularly the financial matters, with the banks and the post office. As for the personal property in his apartment, there is almost no hope. All the houses were occupied by the Japanese, who took what they liked and destroyed the rest. We lost all our personal belongings, except for a few small pieces that we kept with us at all times. However, I will make an attempt to see whether anything can still be recovered.

Please find attached one photograph, which I took from his [Silvestr's] record in our files; I think it might be his last photograph and you may appreciate it.

Although I have no official information, I am writing to you so that you are not kept in uncertainty for too long. I know how it feels; my whole family was evacuated to India for three-and-a-half years, and I did not get any single line from them for the whole period. My wife kept writing to me every month, but the Japanese probably threw all the correspondence into the sea.

As I have already informed you, we have a complete register of all the Czechoslovaks here, and I will share every detail immediately with you.

With my deepest sympathies, A. Jugas.

What I find interesting in this letter is not only the very kind tone of Jugas, but also how the Bata company took great care of its Czechoslovak employees – Jugas referred to them as "our family".

What a contrast this is to the bureaucratic style of the Czechoslovak Ministry of Defence. Their reply to Silvestr's parents in May 1946, four long months after their enquiry, was:

> *The British Ministry of War – in order that it can investigate your case, requests from you more information about the military unit at which your son had been serving. Therefore, provide all known information to the Czechoslovak Ministry of Defence, especially about which military unit your son was attached.*

When Hope Sinks

While the exchange of letters in 1945 and 1946 bears witness to the desperate attempts of the Němec family to find out about the fate of their son, the letters a year later were more resigned – Silvestr had not emerged after the liberation of Singapore and the earlier seeds of hope were proving to be barren.

The first letter of 1947 came from Downing Street, and was addressed to Františka Němcová, Silvestr's mother. The British Under-Secretary of State informed her "with regret that no information is available in the Colonial Office other than the fact that he [Silvestr] was reported missing on 15 February 1942".

Silvestr's father forwarded this letter, written in English, to Josef Vyhnálek, another colleague and friend of Silvestr's from Singapore. Vyhnálek was particularly helpful to our family with translating correspondence from abroad and settling official matters in Czechoslovakia.

A pencilled handwritten note by Silvestr's father is on the back of this letter. The despair and sorrow of his last sentence brings me to tears every time I read it:

> Mr Vyhnálek, we are sending you our warm greetings along with this letter that we have received from London. One professor who came to Vémyslice helped us to read it. We are supposed to write to the Governor, you can see this, and other things we ought to do in the letter. Mr Vyhnálek, all is lost, this search of ours, and writing is futile, our dear Sylva is certainly dead!!!"

And indeed, less than two weeks later – on 17 July 1947 – the Social Welfare Department of Singapore filed an official Certificate of Death for Silvestr Němec. We cannot be sure if it was in response to the inquiries from London and Vémyslice, or if it was done simply because nearly two years had passed since the liberation of Singapore in September 1945, and Silvestr had not been seen or reported to have been seen anywhere.

The authorities in Singapore did not have any further knowledge regarding Silvestr's death. These uncertainties were clearly captured by the wording on the Certificate of Death: "It has been presumed... [that Silvestr] died in or around Singapore... on or about 15 February 1942".

In the summer of 1947, the family received a letter from Vyhnálek. It appears that he might have been the last person to see Silvestr alive, and it was during the fierce fighting on Pasir Panjang Ridge along the southern coast of Singapore.

Vyhnálek refers to Silvestr's Certificate of Death, and adds:

> That is information from the official record. I can only add that the chances of him being still alive are very small, because it's almost two years since the war and he has not reported yet. It is a very sad message. I wish to share with you details of his death, if only they were known to me. Unfortunately, I do not know more than I have already told you during your visit to Zlín.
>
> I remember vividly how we were attacking the Japanese, he [Silvestr] was very pale, so it seemed to me that he might have felt that something would happen to him. It was when we were attacking the hill CAP [correct reference is Gap Hill] near Pasir Panjang in Singapore and was about halfway up the slope when thousands of airplanes

spotted us, and we were heavily bombed and fired upon by machine guns. During that bombing, we ran and scattered into the rubber plantations and that was the last time I saw your Silvester. During all the time of my captivity, I thought he might have escaped to India or Australia, but after the liberation, I have unfortunately learnt that nothing is known about his fate.

In Memoriam

This is all Silvestr's parents ever learnt about the fate of their son. With nothing else to grasp onto for hope, the family focused on settling his affairs overseas. With the help of Silvestr's friends and colleagues from the Bata company in Singapore – namely Josef Vyhnálek, Matěj Bohman and Josef Zuna – they compiled a list of lost property from Silvestr's apartment.

What really caught my attention was that at the bottom of the list of ordinary items such as furniture and clothing, was mention of a Leica camera. It seems that Silvestr, like me, was a keen amateur photographer. Just one small detail like that and I suddenly felt an instant personal connection with him; I imagine we would've had a common topic to discuss had he survived and returned home. Such a shame that none of his photographs survived the war!

A copy of the property list was sent to the War Damage Claims Commission in Kuala Lumpur. After exchanging several documents and questionnaires, the Commission finally awarded the family a compensation of 1,550 dollars in 1951. It took another three years before the compensation reached the family, but by that time, it was only a fraction of the established value. I can only speculate on the reasons: some of it was perhaps lost during the complicated delivery from the Far East to socialist Czechoslovakia which was, by then, already behind the Iron Curtain; part might have fallen through due to the family's limited ability to deal with all the foreign formalities; and whatever was left, was massively devalued by the sudden 'reform' of Czech currency in June 1953 – a secretly prepared plan of the Communist government to give the national economy a boost at the expense of its people. Overnight, they introduced a new currency with incredibly bad forced conversion rates, which effectively wiped out most of the cash and savings of Czechoslovakians.

From what I have heard from my relatives, what was eventually received by the family was just enough to buy several balls of imported wool. So, it was fortunate that the British colonial government sent the family a more lasting symbol of appreciation: two war medals and two stars awarded to Silvestr in memoriam. These are the 1939-1945 Star, the Pacific Star, the Defence Medal, and the War Medal 1939-1945.

Millions of these medals and stars were awarded around the world, but I am glad that we have a set of them at home too as they represent the permanent memory of Silvestr. The Pacific Star has become more meaningful to me after I learnt what the coloured stripes of the ribbon it is attached to symbolise: the yellow in the centre represents the sand of beaches and the green stripes the jungle. They now trigger my imagination of the landscapes in which Silvestr spent the last three years of his life.

Another letter in the box of family documents which my mother showed me, dated October 1947, was from Vyhnálek. In it, he recollects the horrors and chaos that followed the occupation of Singapore:

> I don't know if you will ever be able to learn more detailed information, because the disorganisation in Singapore around the time of surrender was incredible. There were lots of corpses scattered around the streets, and nobody was taking care of them. When, months later, we were sent as prisoners of war to clean up the city, we were only finding nameless skeletons lying around.

It struck me, after reading the whole set of letters, that if it was not possible to discover more details about Silvestr's fate in the years immediately following the war, then my chances now – 75 years from his death – would be virtually non-existent.

Others would probably stop here and be satisfied with the few facts and the rough outline of the story: Silvestr fought as a volunteer, was wounded and had gone missing during the fall of Singapore to the Japanese. Presumed dead. Clear. Done. End of story.

However, to me, these fragments of information had exactly the opposite effect. They ignited my curiosity and desire to find out more. Each little fact led to a chain of new questions which drove me to seek and uncover the bigger picture.

And so, my journey had only just begun.

- II -
Weaving from the Web

FROM THE FAMILY ARCHIVES, I did have a handful of leads: specific information that Silvestr was attached to the Armoured Cars unit of the Singapore Volunteer Corps; a first-hand account that he was last seen in a battle at Pasir Panjang, where he was wounded and taken to a hospital; and four names of his colleagues from Singapore who were likely to know more.

But what were the chances that any of them could provide me with new information? If they were 22 years old – as Silvestr was – at the time of the Japanese Occupation, it would mean they were now be over 100 years old. Even if I was lucky enough to find one of them alive, could he reliably recall the distant past?

If I had begun my research a few decades earlier, I might have met people who remembered the events I am trying to investigate, but researching in this digital age had a different kind of advantage: the Internet. It enabled me to connect with a number of historians around the world, as well as to tap into relevant digitised archives in several countries. Search engines enabled me to retrieve some valuable information hidden in the remote corners of the World Wide Web.

Initial Internet Links

When I typed "Silvestr Němec Bata Singapore" on the search bar, the first relevant piece of information I found was a reference to Silvestr Němec on a website run by *Spolek pro vojenská pietní místa* (Czech Association for Military Graves). There was an entry for Silvestr because his name was engraved on a war memorial in Zlín, together with others who had fallen during World War II.

This was a great discovery for me because, until then, I had no idea that my granduncle's name was on a memorial anywhere other than in his hometown of Vémyslice. Realising that he is also remembered in Zlín made me very happy and compelled me to visit Zlín sooner.

But there was more information on the webpage next to Silvestr's entry, a whole paragraph of exciting details:

> On 2 February 1942, most of the volunteer units were sent to the front to help stop the Japanese advance. Several Czechs were wounded in the first fights that took place under continuous artillery fire: Kožušníček, Vítek, Němec [...] During the siege of Singapore, a Private Silvestr Němec lost his life along with many other wounded soldiers and personnel at the Alexandra Hospital.

This paragraph references a historical essay, *Krajané na Dálném východě během 2. světové války* (Compatriots in the Far East During WWII), written by Ivan Procházka and published in a Czech military history magazine in 1996. It was a hot new lead, and I pursued it. With the help of the magazine's chief editor, I got in contact with Procházka. We agreed to meet in Prague, where he lives.

I also used my trip to Prague to visit the Czech National Library located in the beautiful historical building of Klementinum. There, I was able to read the original essay. To my delight, it included several sources: many of the key facts were based on *Batanagar News, October 1945*, and there was also mention of unpublished memoirs, letters and interviews conducted by the author.

What I hoped to find in the library was more information on the Czechoslovak volunteers in Singapore, as well as details about the Pasir Panjang battle. There were about two dozen generic books on the Battle of Singapore, all Czech translations of largely English texts – a testament of the interest of many Czechs in military history, and in particular, that of World War II. Another potentially useful discovery was a catalogue of periodicals that the Bata company published in Zlín during the 1930s and war years – I was hopeful that there might be mention of the Bata operations in Singapore and perhaps even some hints about the Czechoslovak employees working there, so I added those to my reading list.

After I left the library, I met up with Ivan Procházka. Our meeting was not only an enjoyable experience but a breakthrough moment in my search. He was, like me, about 50 years old then. Historical research, with a focus on World War II, is his passion. Although Procházka is a locksmith, not a historian by education or profession, he dedicates his personal time to incredibly meticulous research in various Czech archives. Once every few years, he summarises his findings and publishes them in the form of an essay or a book. The 1996 essay about the Czechoslovak volunteers in the Far East was his first published work. His two most recent books are a monograph about Czechoslovak women serving in the British Army during World War II and a detailed history of a special reconnaissance unit that was formed as part of the Czechoslovak legion army in France in 1940.

Procházka had spent years excavating the archives of several Czech institutions, many of which I had not even heard of. He thus provided me with extremely useful tips and personal contacts. In addition, as a follow-up to our meeting, he sent me excerpts from his collection of documents pertaining to wartime Singapore. These included the sources he used for his 1996 essay, as well as some valuable extras like part of a collection by Dr Emil Máčel. It was in this collection that I found the authentic memoirs of Josef Vyhnálek – a key witness of the dramatic war events in Singapore and Silvestr's colleague and friend – as he wrote them on a typewriter in 1966. Imagine my thrill when I found all these treasures in my email inbox!

The only thing Procházka asked in return was that I publish my research in some shape or form. This request made me feel a bit uneasy: I was not sure how far I'd be able to go in my quest, and therefore, whether there would be anything worth publishing. While I was actively blogging about the progress of my research at the time, and my blog posts were reaching a growing audience (some of whom even contacted me personally with tips or leads), publishing a print article – let alone a book – was a far stretch for me at that point in time. As such, I am now very pleased to have fulfilled my promise to him with this book.

The Serendipitous Chain

Another lead I followed, which turned out to be very important, was provided by my friend Jana Lutonská. She suggested that I contact *Paměť národa* (The Memory of the Nation), an organisation that collects Czech citizens' personal stories about events in the 20th century.

Although they did not show much interest in Silvestr, explaining that their focus is on the totalitarian era of Czechoslovakia, they did put me in touch with Judita Matyášová.

Matyášová is a freelance journalist who has been documenting forgotten stories mostly from the first half of the 20th century – in particular, she was very interested in the first two decades of modern Czechoslovakia, that is, the period before the First and Second World Wars. She has published several books, including *Přátelství navzdory Hitlerovi* (Friendship Despite Hitler), a story about 80 Jewish-Czech children who were sent by their parents from Nazi-occupied Prague to Denmark, thus saving their lives. She not only tracked them down individually and documented their stories, but also organised a reunion for them some 70 years after their flight.

My inquiry about Bata in Singapore excited her because she had worked on several stories about Bata employees in Batanagar, the company's first branch in the Far East. One of these stories was about Josef Kramoliš, a pioneer of the Bata company in Singapore, who was sent there from its Zlín headquarters in 1932. I was impressed by how familiar Matyášová was with the literature and documents in relation to the pre-war history of Bata. More importantly, she had established direct contact with a number of descendants of the former 'Bata families' from Batanagar who are now scattered around the world, from Canada to Australia. One of these contacts turned out to be a true miracle.

Within two days of our initial email exchange, Matyášová had sent me a link to download a large file. An accompanying note said that she had just met a descendant of a Batanagar family who might have something that was of interest to me. I remember opening the document on my mobile phone and staring at it in disbelief. It was an image of a document with this headline summary:

> *Remembering Private Nemec – 1st Btn., SSVF, Salesman, Bata Shoe Company, Singapore. A 75th Anniversary Memorial Document to the Bata Czechoslovaks in Singapore and Malaya during The Fall of Singapore in February 1942.*

Several days later, I received the contact of its author: Olek Plesek from Australia. I wrote to him immediately. His reply came overnight, due to the difference in our time zones, and this would mark the beginning of a lasting cooperation. He was as shocked by this unexpected connection as I was. The subject line of his email read "The Miracle of Silvestr Němec" and this was followed by these first lines of his message:

> Hi Jan. You have no idea, absolutely no idea, what your email has done for me. It has brought me the greatest feeling of satisfaction over the two years or so that I have been working on this document. To get such a result is beyond the realm of expectation.

Imagine what his reply did for me too! I recall shivering with excitement, due in part to the new facts contained in Olek's work, but even more so, to this new connection we had established.

Attached to the email was an updated version of his document. Olek also shared some background information about himself: Olek (an English version of his Czech name, Oldřich) was born in 1943 in Batanagar, where both his parents worked for the Bata company. The family moved to Calcutta when his father was promoted in 1950. Olek later settled in Australia, where he married Vera, daughter of another Czechoslovak couple, the Bodas, who worked for Bata in its Klang factory in Malaya. When the Japanese army advanced through Malaya in December 1941, they had fled to Singapore. It dawned on me then that it was very likely they met Silvestr there!

Olek, who is now retired, spent several years researching the Czechoslovaks from Bata in the Far East. He began by documenting his native Batanagar, which has largely disappeared after being developed into high-rise apartments, a golf course and a commercial centre in 2005.

The scope of Olek's research later extended to Singapore – first, when he traced the history of his wife Vera's family, and later, when he contacted Michael Pether, a historian from New Zealand. Olek was helping Pether reconstruct the passenger list of the *SS Redang* that was sunk by the Japanese navy when it was used to evacuate civilians from Singapore in February 1942. It appears that a group of Czechoslovaks working for Bata were among its passengers. Sadly, several of them had not survived the tragic sinking.

The information that Olek was gathering motivated him to conduct more systematic research, and this was compiled and sent to me. His 30-page document highlights three Czechoslovaks working for Bata, who joined the Singapore Volunteers and did not survive the war:

Silvestr Němec, Rudolf Janeček and Karel Vítek. The paper goes on to outline the fate of several others who met their death through attempted evacuation, all likely aboard the *SS Redang*: Bedřich Heim, Klement Plhoň, Oldřich Smržák, Josef Strangfeld and Eugen Straussler.

It may be noteworthy that Eugen Straussler was the father of Tomáš Straussler, who was born before the war in 1937. After the war, Tomáš' widowed mother remarried a British officer named Kenneth Stoppard, and Tomáš went on to become the famous theatre and screenplay writer, Tom Stoppard.

Finally, Olek's document summarises the wartime life of the Czechoslovak Bata survivors who were interned in the infamous Changi prison and later at Sime Road Camp. This group included Růžena Mizia and her two small children. She was the only one among the wives of Batamen who did not evacuate.

As for specific information about Silvestr Němec, Olek's document contained one reference that was new to me:

> Marus Bohman's memoirs note that Larry Kent, formerly Ladislav Kvapil, recalled that a Czech boy was among those who were cold-bloodedly bayoneted in their hospital beds.

Although the memoirs of Marus Bohman were eventually published as a book, this quoted sentence was not included in the final version. How lucky it was then for me to have access to Olek's research.

But why did Olek dedicate his paper to my granduncle Silvestr, whom he did not know at all? Here is his answer:

> I believe it is more attention-getting than some [titles] such as 'History of the Batamen in Malaya'. I want people to read this document. I specifically chose Silvestr Němec because of his young age, and the horrific alleged circumstances of his brutal death at the Alexandra Hospital. This does not diminish in any way the lingering deaths of those in POW camps, the horrors of dying at sea on a boat that has been bombed, or the traumatic three-and-a-half years in Changi and Sime Road internment camps. Silvestr Němec epitomises the very worst outcome in a tragedy we will never be able to comprehend. On 15 February this year, we commemorated the 75th Anniversary of the surrender of Singapore. I wonder how many from Bata, especially Bata Singapore, paused to remember those that

had died, or suffered terrible privation, as a result of trying to defend Singapore and protect Bata assets in the region.

I discovered all this in my initial correspondence with Olek Plesek. The next step for us was to work together to map the wartime history of Bata and its Czechoslovak employees in Singapore. A comprehensive list of all of them, with key biographical data, is in Appendix I of this book – the fruit of our joint efforts.

But first, my research would take me to the birthplace of Bata, the famous shoe brand and company that employed my granduncle Silvestr and dispatched him fatefully to Singapore – Zlín, in the Czech Republic.

- III -
Discovering Bata in Zlín

ZLÍN IS A CITY that many probably have not heard of. It is the regional capital of an eastern province in the Czech Republic and the city where the Bata shoe enterprise was originally established in 1894. Back then, in the late 19th century, Zlín was a small town of less than 3,000 inhabitants. It served as one of the centres of guilds and craftsmen scattered around the mountainous region, where people made a living mostly by farming. Many of the shepherd families supplemented their seasonal income by making shoes by hand. Shoes therefore became one of the distinctive products of Zlín, where dozens of families established small cobbler workshops in what we would call 'start-ups' today.

In 1894, one of these workshops, registered under the name 'Antonín Baťa' obtained a license for tanning and shoemaking. This little enterprise was run by three siblings of the Baťa family: Anna, Antonín and Tomáš. Although shoemaking could be traced back to seven generations of the family, the siblings decided to try and do things differently. In fact, Tomáš Baťa had – three years earlier, in 1891 – tried to set up his own shoe production workshop in Vienna when he was just 15 years old. Unfortunately, that attempt failed.

Tomáš would eventually succeed in growing a leading global shoe brand in the 1930s, but he faced no shortage of challenges in his trial-and-error approach, and the company narrowly avoided bankruptcy several times.

The first critical moment for 'Antonín Baťa' happened just a year after its registration. At a time when the young company was facing ominously growing debts, the elder brother, Antonín, was drafted into the army and Anna left for a job in Vienna. Tomáš, thus thrust into leadership, switched the production to much cheaper canvas shoes with leather soles, and managed to rescue the company which, at the time, already had 50 employees.

Six years later, after Anna opted out, the two brothers transformed their firm into a public company named 'T. & A. Baťa' and operated out of a small factory. In 1908, when Antonín died, Tomáš became the sole owner of the enterprise. By then, he was already running a major factory located in a new three-storey building in Zlín. Tomáš had been inspired by modern factories when he visited England, Germany and the United States to study innovation.

In 1914, during World War I, Tomáš Baťa travelled to Vienna and succeeded in securing a major contract for shoes for the Austrian army, thus preventing the army from conscripting his workers. The contract also opened the door to more military orders – that gave their business a major boost and allowed it to grow stronger than most of their local competitors.

By the end of the war, he employed 4,000 workers. Thanks to the introduction of modern machinery, he was already able to produce two million pairs of shoes annually. The company attracted many workers from the poor mountain settlements around Zlín, and the city grew rapidly. However, after World War I, the Austrian Empire fell apart and became a number of independent states. One of them – the newly created Czechoslovakia – suffered from a prolonged economic crisis and inflation, resulting in many of the shoemaking companies in Zlín going bankrupt.

In those difficult times, Tomáš Baťa made another courageous move: he decided to cut the prices of his shoes by half, using the famous slogan: "Baťa crushes costliness". This attracted thousands of new customers, and the brand quickly expanded its market. Such a price reduction was possible because Tomáš convinced his employees to voluntarily take a 40 percent cut in salary. The company, on its part, provided housing and supplied all their basic needs, from food to clothes, at half the usual prices. Once again, the unorthodox and visionary thinking of Tomáš rescued the firm.

Just a decade after World War I, the number of Zlín citizens increased fivefold, and most were employed by the Bata company. Tomáš Baťa, determined to drive the city's urban development to suit his ambitious plans and vision, ran in the municipal elections and succeeded in becoming the mayor of Zlín in 1923.

The 1920s saw another massive growth of the Bata business,

expanding into other industrial sectors: first, those related to shoemaking like rubber, leather and chemical production, and fabrication of socks and stockings; then later, to construction, transport, healthcare, education, printing, film studios and aviation. I was surprised to learn that a Bata factory in Zlín produced and sold a total of 200 airplanes during the 1920s and 1930s, before the company was closed by the Germans after Nazi occupation in 1939.

During the 1920s, Tomáš Baťa also began to spread his business overseas, establishing shoe factories across Europe and the United States, along with export and sales networks. Finally, in 1931, the firm became a joint-stock company: Bata, a.s.

By the time Tomáš Baťa died in a tragic airplane accident in Zlín in July 1932, his company had over 31,000 employees. It was active in nearly 40 different sectors, including scientific research, sales and services. It was producing 36 million pairs of shoes annually – 80 percent of overall shoe production in Czechoslovakia. It had factories in five countries as well as some form of presence – like warehouses and shops – in 40 countries across four continents. It also ran a network of 2,500 stores, 700 of which were overseas.

After Tomáš' tragic death, the transition of the company's leadership to a management group – led by his stepbrother Jan Antonín Baťa and a team of talented directors from Zlín – turned out to be a success. The Bata company entered what I would consider its Golden Era, building on the tremendous success of Tomáš, and further expanding and strengthening its operations globally during the 1930s. This was when it began to establish its presence in India and the Far East, a phenomenon we will explore later.

But let's return to my search for Silvestr in Zlín.

Traces of Silvestr in Zlín

My attempt to follow the Bata lead began with me sending an inquiry about Silvestr to Bata Zlín's generic email address. I was surprised to receive a reply from them the next day. Mrs Rajchová from Customer Service wrote to me to say that she had considered my unusual request and would recommend that I try to find information about former employees in the Czech State Archives in Zlín. She also suggested that I contact the Tomáš Baťa Foundation, which is also based in Zlín.

Following the advice of Bata's Customer Service, I wrote to the state archives in Zlín to inquire about Bata company documents from the 1930s and 1940s. Of course, I was keen to find specific information about my granduncle Silvestr. It took more than a week before I received a reply, but it was worth the wait. In the detailed response, Dr Martin Marek diligently described all the relevant documents of the archives he found. Unfortunately, he did not find anything related to my granduncle, except a wartime document which stated some basic facts:

> Name and Surname: Silvestr Němec
> Date of Birth: 20 October 1919
> Marital Status: Single, no children
> Education: Business school
> Employed at Bata from: 21 September 1936
> Position before departure: Seller
> Date of departure and destination: 31 December 1938, Singapore, Str. Settlements
> Position in the destination: Pedicurist
> Family contact: Father Němec Sylvestr, Vémyslice 23, Moravský Krumlov county

Marek offered to prepare these documents for me, should I wish to visit the archive in person. He also suggested additional documents which I could further research on. Up until then, I had no information about what work Silvestr did in Bata company, so having all these details, including the exact date of his departure for Singapore, was very thrilling.

Following another lead, I also searched online for copies of *Batanagar News* which Prochazka referred to in his essay about Czechoslovaks in the Far East during World War II. I found that this very rare publication was available at the Tomáš Baťa Foundation in Zlín. While I was scrolling through the list of publications in their inventory, another item caught my eye: *The Fight and Fate of the Batamen in Singapore and Malaya*, published in 1945 by Jan Baroš.

It now became clear to me that I had to grab the first opportunity to travel to Zlín, schedule an appointment with the Tomáš Baťa Foundation, pay a visit to the local branch of the Czech State Archives, as well as check the city library for the local periodicals from the 1930s and 1940s. This would also be an opportunity for me to pay my respects to my granduncle Silvestr at the Zlín war memorial, where his name had been inscribed.

Eventually, I realised that due to my limited time in Zlín, I could not squeeze in a visit to the local library. Thankfully, the library's manager, Mr Kaňka, was kind enough to grant me unrestricted online access to the library's resources for several weeks, which allowed me to study the periodicals from home. From that period of research, I found several highly relevant articles which I will touch on in the chapters on Bata in Singapore and the wartime events there.

Two of these texts, however, need to be mentioned right here as they directly refer to Silvestr Němec. The first article was published in the newspaper, *Tep noveho Zlína* (The Pulse of the New Zlín), in May 1946. Entitled "*Tři roky v japonském zajetí*" (Three Years in Japanese Captivity), the full-page article describes the war experience of Josef Vyhnálek and contains this reference:

> *Several Czechoslovaks were captured by the Japanese just a day before capitulation: Rudolf Janeček, Karel Vítek, J. Sinkievicz, J. Vyhnálek and wounded Silvestr Němec, whom we have not seen ever since, and he is still missing.*

This clearly says that Silvestr was wounded and captured, as opposed to having been murdered in Alexandra Hospital, as some other sources suggested. What a potential turn of events! Of course, this opened up possibilities in my mind, like the scenario where Silvestr might have endured captivity and survived, and perhaps started a new life with a family somewhere, far from Czechoslovakia. I knew this was incredibly unlikely, but *what if* – and the truth is that his body was never found to confirm his death.

This is one of the possible scenarios regarding Silvestr's fate, and we will explore it in greater detail – together with other scenarios – in the penultimate chapter, checking each against the official records and personal accounts I have collected.

The second article is titled "*Zapomenutí baťovci na Dálném východě ve 2. světové válce*" (Forgotten Batamen in the Far East During World War II). It was published in December 1993 in a regional daily, *Zlínské noviny* (Zlín Newspapers). The author, Emil Máčel, wrote:

> *The volunteer units were eventually relocated from the coastline to the bushes on the fighting front. The volunteers were attacked by well-*

trained and well-equipped Japanese soldiers. In the heavy fighting that commenced, several Czechoslovaks were wounded: Kožušníček, Vítek, Němec [...] When the Japanese stormed a hospital full of wounded soldiers, they mercilessly and brutally murdered them all. This is how Silvestr Němec met his end.

Máčel stated that the article was based on materials provided to him by a Mr Jedovnický from Australia and memories of several other Batamen whom he contacted with the assistance of Mr Hrabica. As mentioned, I had already obtained part of Emil Máčel's personal archives from Procházka, and it indeed contained documents and correspondences between Máčel and Hrabica, and several others.

I discovered that Máčel had passed away in November 2014. He was an active member of the local branch of *Český svaz bojovníků za svobodu* (Czech Association of the Freedom Fighters) in his hometown of Malenovice near Zlín. After the Velvet Revolution – the liberation of Czechoslovakia from the Soviet socialist regime in 1989 – he dedicated a lot of time and work to reconnect with the former Bata employees who decided to stay in exile after the Communists took over Czechoslovakia in 1948 and who then ended up being scattered all around the world. Using the information he collected, Máčel wrote several articles summarising their stories. These were published by the Zlín regional press during the 1990s.

Although there was no new information about Silvestr in Máčel's articles, the documents in his collection became another valuable source of information on the Czechoslovak Bata employees in Singapore.

Treasures of Baťa Villa

When planning my visit to Zlín, I connected with my friends Pavel and Věra Stojar who live there. They offered to let me stay with them, as well as to take me on a tour around the city, which allowed me to see and explore more.

My first stop in Zlín was the Tomáš Baťa Foundation, where my inquiry was promptly answered by Ms Zvolská. She confirmed that, indeed, their library had complete volumes of the *Batanagar News* from 1938, 1945 and 1946, as well as some other resources which I could study on-site in their office at Baťa Villa.

The villa was built from 1909 to 1912 to serve as Tomáš Baťa's new home. It was a modern building at the time, designed by an architect from Prague Academy of Arts. It is surrounded by a big garden, with a spacious terrace out front. When you step into the building, you are greeted by a hall with a double-height ceiling, and custom-designed wooden interiors. Back in the day, the villa was located in a quiet area, separated from the city centre by a river, yet offering a great view of the complex of buildings forming the main Bata factory.

Today, Tomáš Baťa's former home houses his foundation and I was there on a specific mission: to access a rare collection of *Batanagar News*, which turned out to be a weekly newsletter published by the Bata factory in Batanagar for its workers. As I already knew, its 6 October 1945 edition featured a long article entitled "The Story of Batamen in Malaya". Here is how the article starts:

> Just this week, the first batch of Batamen from Malaya arrived in India after three-and-a-half years of internment in the Japanese prison camps. They arrived in such a condition that the authorities sent them to a hill station to at least partly restore their shattered health and over-strained nerves before they could see their friends and families at Batanagar. Only two of the group were able to undertake the tour from the port of Madras to Batanagar. They are Mr Bohman and Mr Jedovnický, both graduates of the Bata School of Work, who gave us first-hand information about life under the Japanese in Southeast Asia.

The text further describes in detail the dramatic wartime events experienced by the Czechoslovaks from Bata in Singapore. The account starts with the mobilisation in December 1941, and goes on to cover the last-minute evacuation of civilians on ships, the fall of Singapore in February 1942, the horrors and death tolls of the prison camps, some stories of sabotage by Bata employees when they were tasked to produce shoes for Japanese soldiers, and ends with the liberation of the internment camps at the end of August 1945.

My granduncle is mentioned twice. First in a paragraph describing the intake of the Czechoslovak volunteers to the defence forces:

> In the beginning of December, complete mobilisation was ordered all over Singapore. The Czechoslovak Batamen who were of military age and healthy, all joined the SSVF (Straits Settlements Volunteer Force) and the FMSVF (Federated Malayan States Volunteer Force). The

training was quick and hard, but they, and all the others who joined, undertook it with the greatest earnestness, as they felt the gravity of the situation. Matuš, Bohman, Kožušníček, Ambrož, Jedovnický were in Machine Gun Units; Vítek, Janeček, Němec were with the Rifle Corps; Čepka, Mráz in Bomb Disposal Units; Zamara and others in some other, and so on. These units were posted for beach defence all along the coast.

The second time Silvestr is mentioned is in the paragraph about the last battles:

> Casualties – yes, there were many. It cannot be ascertained now who and how many were wounded; so far as we know, Kožušníček, Vítek and Němec were wounded. Němec was sent to the military hospital, and when the Japanese later captured it, in the rage of animal brutality, they mercilessly killed all the wounded soldiers lying in beds. Here Němec met his end.

This text – along with the private letters from Pavel Ambrož and Antonín Jugas – is another document that places the death of Silvestr at the Alexandra Hospital during the massacre by Japanese soldiers on 14 and 15 February 1942.

The question remains: who, or what, is the primary source of this recurring information? It's quite obvious that neither Ambrož nor Jugas were present in Alexandra Hospital during that tragic day. Therefore, they could not have witnessed Silvestr being murdered there.

Could an answer be found in *The Fight and Fate of the Batamen in Singapore and Malaya* by Jan Baroš, published in Canada in 1945? Reading the copy held in the library of Bata Villa, I realised that it was just an expanded version of the *Batanagar News* article. Its additional sections dealt with the setting up of the Bata branch in Singapore in 1931 and the details of life in the internment camps. There was also a lengthy section about the methods of torture used by the Japanese on their prisoners. There was, however, no additional information about Silvestr, nor about the last days of the battle for Singapore.

But at least this extended version confirmed that it was based on the stories of Bohman and Jedovnický, as told by them to Jan Baroš, shortly after their arrival at Batanagar from Singapore. Where they got the information about Silvestr's murder in Alexandra Hospital remains unknown. The story must have been told and spread among the civilian internees in the camps. But what was its origin?

It could have been that Vítek or Kožušníček – wounded during the fights, according to this post-war testimony – was also admitted to Alexandra Hospital. Thus, the massacre was witnessed and later told to the other Czechoslovaks in the Japanese internment camp. That is certainly a plausible scenario.

Would it be possible to find their first-hand accounts somewhere? Vítek had not survived the war, having died of malaria in the Batu Lintang prison camp in Kuching, Borneo, on 18 March 1945. Kožušnícek, however, was among the lucky survivors. Perhaps he recorded his accounts, or someone else captured his memories elsewhere. Finding those would be a real breakthrough.

All I had at that stage were the two versions of the 1945 text about Batamen during the war. Both were written by Jan Baroš, who clearly had a talent for storytelling. But this raised another potential problem. Reading his articles, I noticed a certain over-dramatisation, exalted heroism and simplification of the story. I am not saying this to criticise Jan Baroš – after all, we should be grateful that he recorded and published the stories told to him by Bohman and Jedovnický, as otherwise their eye-witness accounts would probably be entirely lost. My point is that we need to read his texts and described details with a critical mind and a healthy dose of scepticism. For example, his tendency to exaggerate is apparent in this description of the Alexandra Hospital massacre:

> ...when later the Japanese captured it, in the rage of animal brutality, they mercilessly killed all the wounded soldiers lying in beds.

The merciless brutality of the Japanese, as they stormed through the hospital, is well documented; but as a matter of fact, we know not all the patients were murdered – it is estimated that some 300 out of more than 800 unarmed men present (both medical staff and patients) were massacred by the Japanese troops.

Putting that aside, I think it may help to know more about Jan Baroš to better understand where he is coming from. I found out that Baroš was Chief Editor of *Batanagar News*. As recorded in his personal diary, he flew to India from Zlín in 1936 in a Bata airplane, while a printing press was shipped to Batanagar via sea. His mission in India was not just to publish the factory weekly, but also to manage relations with the Indian and British press, to organise Bata advertisements in other media, to lead cultural and charitable activities, and to promote the company and Czechoslovak culture. In today's terms, it would be called 'public relations'.

Baroš was a prolific writer. He authored several books documenting the early years of the Bata company in India. The most famous one is a detailed chronicle called *Čechoslováci na březích Gangu* (Czechoslovaks on the Banks of the Ganges). Another which piqued my curiosity was his biography of Mahatma Gandhi, whom he knew personally.

As a result of his literary ambitions, the *Batanagar News* became much more than a weekly factory bulletin. Although practical information and company announcements dominated its pages, there were also travelogues and reflective essays. One that really captured my attention, "Masaryk and Gandhi", explored the similarities between the two statesmen who won independence for their respective countries, Czechoslovakia and India.

While browsing through various editions of *Batanagar News*, something else caught my eye: a full-page illustrated advertisement for Bata shoes. It featured a dramatic drawing with a headline in Bengali that, when translated, read: "Beware of Tetanus, even a small injury can be dangerous – so wear shoes". The caption of the picture said: "The above illustration is a real picture of an unshod peasant and the working class whom the skeleton threatens at every moment with fatal consequences of not wearing shoes. In the illustration there is one of our attractive rubber shoes – costing eight annas a pair – best suited to the conditions in which the masses live and work".

Finds at the State Archives

My second stop in Zlín was the regional branch of the Czech State Archives. It is located in the nearby village of Klečůvka and housed in a former chateau. I had exchanged email with its historian, Martin Marek, who was not just the custodian of the archives but also a historical researcher who is considered by some in the circle of Bata enthusiasts as controversial because he also documented some of the darker aspects of the Bata company. An example is that one of its factories used Jews from the infamous Auschwitz concentration camp as forced labour.

I, however, greatly appreciate Marek's critical approach to history. It is not the role of a researcher to construct a romanticised, idealised picture of the past, but to discover and document its complicated, multifaceted nature. This is also the approach I decided to adopt in my own exploration.

Since my first research trip to Zlín, I have visited the archives in Klečůvka several times, spending dozens of hours in their reading room, pouring over various historical documents of the Bata company. As such, I was able to collect a wealth of information, including several unique photographs, some of which are reproduced in this book.

Perhaps the most important document is a catalogue of Bata employees dispatched to foreign countries before the Second World War. It is a large hardcover book, leather-bound, and with its title printed in gold, *The List of Employees Overseas*. It weighed several kilograms, and I had to be careful when turning its pages, but what an amazing feeling to hold such an artefact in my hands!

The List was created in September 1944 (as indicated on the first page) during the occupation of Czechoslovakia by Nazi Germany. It contains personal details of over a thousand Bata employees who were sent abroad from Zlín. Germany was not included as it was obviously not considered 'being abroad' at the time.

While the Bata company had previously sent selected employees overseas for shorter missions, it adopted a different approach in the 1930s by arranging long-term transfers. For the latter arrangement, employees' contracts in Zlín were first terminated. Bata then funded their travel costs overseas and re-hired them locally at the destinations. Personal files were thus transferred with them and not kept in the Zlín headquarters. Sadly, as a result, some of the personal documents – including those of my granduncle Silvestr – were lost during the war in Singapore.

Marek explained to me that a number of employee records were deliberately destroyed by the company's management at the beginning of World War II so that they could not be used by the occupying Germans. Another wave of shredding old archival records took place after the war. This makes *The List of Employees Overseas* – which contains data (albeit summarised) for each employee sent abroad – a particularly precious source of information.

The first several pages of the list provide overall statistics on how many employees were sent overseas during the first half of 1939, and to which destinations. This period is interesting because it covers the period when Czechoslovakia ceased to exist as an independent country after it was partitioned, and when Czech lands were occupied on 15 March 1939 by the Nazi German army under Hitler, thus establishing the 'Protectorate of Bohemia and Moravia'.

From the List, we can see that 502 people were sent abroad by Bata in the first half of 1939. Most were transferred to the United States and Canada. Only 30 headed to British India while 22 left for Singapore in early 1939. We also learn that at the time of creating the List in September 1944, a total of 50 employees were stationed in Singapore.

Other research papers by Marek state that these overseas transfers of Bata employees started around March 1938. They were scaled up after September 1938 when Czechoslovakia was forced by the Munich Treaty to surrender significant parts of its territory to Nazi Germany. It is obvious that the management of Bata wanted to send as many of its talented people abroad as possible before the borders would be completely closed. This was in response to the fact that most of Bata's factories were located in Czechoslovakia and its neighbouring countries, which were gradually being controlled by Nazi Germany.

Some of its key markets, however, were in different parts of the world, often in countries under British dominion. Bata's strategic solution was therefore to relocate its production accordingly. This was done by establishing 'core teams' consisting of several dozen talented people whose combined skills covered all that was necessary to establish shoe production, distribution and sales in the destination countries from scratch.

These core teams were required to function autonomously. In some cases, they were accompanied by shipments of the full production lines, dismantled in Zlín, so that a new factory abroad could be assembled quickly. This was also the case of the Bata factory in Singapore, as we shall see later.

There are 1,029 Bata employees catalogued in the List, with nearly half of them transferred abroad in the first half of 1939. It is interesting to note that, of these, 79 were "non-Aryan people" – that is, Jews. Their departure from Europe, on the very eve of World War II, almost certainly saved their lives. It is sometimes said that Jan Antonín Baťa had intentionally sent his Jewish employees abroad to save them from Nazi persecution, that he was a Czech version of Oskar Schindler. However, while it is true that those Jews were brought out of Nazi Germany, there is no evidence that they were given special treatment over other staff.

Jan Antonín Baťa was first and foremost a pragmatic businessman who sent selected talents overseas regardless of their backgrounds, religious or otherwise. There are several well-documented cases where Bata managers terminated the contracts of their Jewish employees to avoid trouble with the German authorities. It is also a fact that the Zlín management allowed the factory in Chelmek, Poland, to use the Jews from Auschwitz in its workforce. However, I do not think their intentions were evil – the Bata company just wanted to avoid antagonism with the Nazi regime and the German managers of that factory.

The main priority of Bata's management, even before the war, had been to protect the overall efficient operation of the company. One of the principles driving the company, as laid down by its founder Tomáš Baťa, was to avoid politics.

Yet, the List includes a small table that summarises so-called 'enemy property' – listed were assets of 447 employees, with a combined value of 48 million Czechoslovak crowns. My guess is that these 'enemy' employees were those who refused to declare their obedience to the Nazi Empire. We can be quite sure that this group included employees in Singapore who not only maintained relations with the Czechoslovak exiled government's embassy in Mumbai, but who also volunteered in the British military forces. There can be no doubt that this made them traitors in the eyes of the Nazi authorities who were occupying Czechoslovakia at that time.

An overwhelming majority of staff recorded in the List were men: 594 of them single and 401 married. Most were between 20 and 30 years old, with only 36 who were 40 or older at the time of their departure. Silvestr was only 19. As for women, there were just 34, of which only one was registered as married. There is, however, an interesting note in the table: "The List does not include female instructors who married overseas, and therefore probably no longer work for the company." So, it appears that more women had been transferred abroad but had left Bata after they got married.

Marek told me that this was probably an intentional policy of the company: Bata sent young women to its foreign hubs so that its male employees – who were mostly young and single – could marry them. This was because it was probably harder for them to court local women, and mixed marriages were not preferred then. Another custom (if not rule) in those times, was that once a female employee got married, her contract was terminated. This was so that she could focus on maintaining the household and eventually raising children.

The young age of the employees transferred overseas intrigued me even more when I discovered from the List that 75 percent of them already had five to 10 years of service in Bata. This means that they joined the company in their teens and were young talents rather than experienced managers.

How were they selected? According to several academic papers I have read, the Bata company had a sophisticated system. The lists of suitable candidates were drafted by the personnel officers who were also building 'proven profiles' of the successful employees. The criteria included language skills, state of health, amount of personal savings, impeccable morals and other qualities. The personnel managers also applied psychological tests, paying special attention to intelligence and self-reliance. Formal education was not important to Bata.

Once the management decided on a candidate, there was little leeway to back out; it was not something the employee could refuse. As one can imagine, not everyone was excited about an overseas transfer – some were bitter and disappointed because they had pictured their career at Bata differently, or they had incompatible personal plans or family commitments.

A good example is Josef Kramoliš. He was dreaming of becoming a manager at the main Bata store in the Czech city of Brno and had just started constructing a new house with his father when, suddenly in September 1932, he received an order to travel to Singapore. In his diary, Kramoliš recalls how his supervisor reacted to his hesitation: "You see, Mr Kramoliš, either you go, or you will be gone."

The bosses at Bata did not even consider a planned wedding as sufficient excuse to reject a transfer abroad; only advanced pregnancy or a serious illness in the family could have saved an employee from relocation. So, in most cases, a rejection was followed up by termination.

The statistics in the List also summarise the educational level of the employees: 125 had completed primary school while 516 graduated from secondary school; all had joined Bata at a very young age. A university degree or higher qualification was quite rare. However, 315 (that is, about one-third) were marked as graduates from the Bata School of Work, a special system that Bata created for its young recruits.

Most of the employees sent overseas – 433 of them – worked in the sales department, followed by 176 in shoe fabrication. There were only

30 recorded as managers or directors. The most relevant profession in the story of Silvestr Němec is that of 'pedicurist', the job that he was assigned to in Singapore. The List tells us that in total, 23 employees from Zlín were dispatched to work overseas in this role.

The Bata company, in the List, also registered 67 family members who accompanied their employees abroad. In 1944, they received allowances from the company totalling 51,000 Czechoslovak crowns per month (that is, on average, 760 crowns per person per month – a decent income at that time). This was probably a way in which the company tried to maintain the income of its employees who were transferred abroad. However, it seems that married couples sometimes struggled to maintain the standard of living they enjoyed in Zlín.

The problem was further exacerbated in the British colonies where the Czechoslovaks had to adopt the lifestyle of the white European class. This meant that they were expected to have their own cars with salaried drivers, keep several servants to run their homes, and join a club. Not doing so affected their social status, but these were all additional burdens on their limited finances.

Beyond the introduction and summary statistics in the List, you will find the actual catalogue of employees arranged in alphabetical order. The entry for each individual is presented in a very long row, so long that you have to unfold each sheet to see its full length. The details of the document are impressive, and there is even a miniature photo portrait attached to every name.

I jumped swiftly to the letter 'N' and there he was! It's hard to describe how I felt when I first saw that photograph of Silvestr Němec and, next to it, some key facts about him.

The next thing I noticed was that the Bata clerks had later pencilled two crosses next to Silvestr's name. Upon a quick check on several other names, similar crosses were also drawn next to his close companions – Janeček and Vítek – who had perished during the time of war. So the crosses were to indicate that he had died. This only made the moment more emotional for me.

Taking a deep breath, I returned to Silvestr's record. In addition to the information already sent to me earlier by Marek, I learnt that Silvestr – being a pedicurist – worked for the sales department of Bata, and that the company had arranged his pension insurance in Singapore commencing 1 October 1940.

In addition to the original records in the List, every entry had an extra sheet of paper that was glued in later. These contained handwritten notes, obviously made after World War II, when the List was used to account for everyone who was abroad during wartime.

There are four such notes next to Silvestr's record, and they give us a hint of how the information about his fate gradually reached Zlín:

1. *To an inquiry, we replied that we will inform once we find out ourselves.*
2. *Mr Lachs says that he was in Singapore in 1943.*
3. *Report from Bata Batanagar via Bata Limited London – Mr Němec, who suffered a serious injury when he was fighting in Singapore, was reportedly killed when the Japanese occupied the hospital in which he was a patient.*
4. *Killed in action in Singapore – according to a telegram from Mr Jugas.*

The first of the notes most likely refers to the post-war inquiry letters by the family around mid-1945.

The third note may be dated November 1945 – which is when Vyhnálek reached London after several weeks' journey on a ship from Singapore. I found out that when he arrived in London, he filled out his 'liberation questionnaire' at the British War Office. It is quite likely that he also visited the Bata office in London and shared information about the war in Singapore. It is logical that the company would then pass this on to the headquarters in Zlín, where it was eventually recorded in the List. When I checked the additional notes in the List for Vyhnálek, I indeed found this entry: "Bata Ltd. London reports that he was liberated as a prisoner of war and is on his way to Europe – letter is dated 4 November, delivered to us on 7 November". This pretty much confirms my hypothesis.

The fourth note may be from early 1946, because we know that Jugas sent a personal letter with similar content to his family on 22 January 1946.

The most mysterious is the second note which states that, according to a certain Mr Lachs, Silvestr "was in Singapore in 1943". Lachs does not appear in the List of Bata employees stationed in Singapore in the 1940s – it will be interesting to find out who he was. I found an almost identical note next to the name of Rudolf Janeček – another Bata employee who, like Silvestr, signed up for the volunteer defence forces and did not survive the war, having died – as a prisoner of war – of malaria and beriberi in February 1945.

But is it possible that Silvestr and Janeček were still alive in Singapore in 1943? Could Lachs, or the Bata clerk writing down his information, have mistakenly reported 1943 instead of 1942? This piece of information conflicts with many other reports and documents that suggest he had gone missing on 15 February 1942, possibly having been murdered in Alexandra Hospital on 14 or 15 February. Again, as with the earlier mention of Silvestr being a prisoner of war, this raises the possibility of an alternative story of Silvestr's fate. In any case, I added tracing Lachs to the to-do list of my ongoing research.

Insights into Bata's Operations

Through talking to people and reading many documents at Zlín, I was able to learn about how the Bata company functioned when my granduncle Silvestr was working there, and how the employees felt about certain practices, which could be perceived as amazing or downright shocking. All these details helped me piece together Silvestr's life and experiences as a successful Bata employee.

I gathered that one of the reasons for Bata's phenomenal success was its relentless drive to improve efficiency, save materials and lower production costs. We already know about Tomáš Bata's master move in 1921, when he cut his production costs in order to halve shoe prices during the post-war economic crisis, while managing to protect the purchasing power and standard of living of his employees.

In a similar fashion, he reacted promptly to the Great Depression a decade later. Following his credo that "the art of buying is worth more than the art of selling", he gradually moved to control the whole supply chain of raw materials and services, allowing his company to become independent of suppliers.

Tomáš Bata took the same approach even in banking services: he simply created his own bank in Zlín and established 'Leader A.G.' in Switzerland which he covertly controlled. It later became a principal source of capital investment for his expansion overseas.

A bigger problem was the impact of the Great Depression on Bata's ability to export its shoes. In the late 1920s, the European markets accounted for nearly 80 percent of Bata's exports, but by 1932, the export volumes had dropped by half. This was a result of the import barriers through which the governments sought to protect their domestic industries and markets.

Tomáš Baťa reacted to this challenge by relocating production directly to the countries where his shoes were sold, as well as by exploring new markets around the world. This was the goal of his famous journey by plane from Zlín through North Africa, the Middle East, British India, British Malaya and Batavia (then the capital of the Dutch East Indies, present-day Jakarta in Indonesia), which we will explore in detail later.

During his visit to British Malaya, Baťa proclaimed that his mission was to provide shoes to five million barefoot people who lived in the region – and it became the job of Baťa's branch in Singapore to make that happen.

Another principal driver of Tomáš Baťa's success was his ability to adopt modern management and production methods. He was excited by what he had observed during his second trip to the United States, when he visited the factories of Henry Ford in Detroit. These factories had pioneered belt manufacturing as a means for serial, cheap, mass production. From the 1920s, Baťa was introducing similar mechanisation into the shoe industry – this enabled him to produce in larger volumes at lower cost, while many of his central European competitors still produced shoes in the old-fashioned way.

But for such an innovative way of manufacturing, his company needed workers with a different approach and better discipline. One of the many practical publications that Tomáš Baťa produced is cleverly titled *The Selection and Education of an Industrial Man*. He understood that it was much more effective to drive innovation by shaping boys from a young age than trying to change the old routines of adult craftsmen.

That is why Baťa focused on recruiting young men not only from Zlín, but also from the poor villages all over Czechoslovakia. Because he was dissatisfied with the level and quality of their formal education in the state schools, he established his own Bata School of Work in 1925. Initially, the school admitted only boys – whom Baťa referred to as 'Young Men' – but it started admitting girls four years later. Intended for graduates of elementary schools, it offered three years of additional studies alongside factory work.

The students worked during the daytime and attended classes in the evenings and on weekends. Even lunch breaks were not 'wasted' – the apprentices were shown educational films. For these young students, there was no room for idleness or individual pursuits. Their daily regimen was guided by a principle that "the best education is to keep a young man fully occupied from early in the morning so that he is tired and has no time for loafing."

Josef Štach, who was born in the poor, mountain village of Pozděchov, was admitted to the Bata School of Work in 1930. He recalls:

> My childhood was like most other children in our village, but a serious problem occurred after I finished my elementary school: my family had no means to support me in further education, and it was difficult to find a job as an apprentice. It would therefore be a huge win for me if I got accepted by Bata in Zlín. I decided to apply, and I succeeded. I was recruited in 1930 and admitted to the boarding school as a 'Young Man'. It was both joy and sorrow. Life at the boarding school was not easy.
>
> Wake-up call was at 5 am, followed by warm-up exercise, cleaning up of room, then running for breakfast before reporting to the factory by 6.45 am. We worked till noon, had lunch at 12.10 pm, and then it's back to the factory by 1.45 pm. More work from 2 pm to 5 pm, then rush to the boarding school, grab dinner, run to evening classes, and quickly back to the dormitory. Curfew was at 10 pm.

The Bata School of Work provided the children of poor country folk with accommodation, good food, educational supervision and other forms of care. In exchange, it demanded that they observe strict discipline, are devoted to the company, and constantly strive for personal growth and self-education.

This may seem like a harsh regime, but it must be realised that – especially at that time – an opportunity to work for Bata was the only chance for thousands of children to escape the crushing poverty of their rural families, receive a good education and gain material security.

The competition to be recruited was very stiff. Out of tens of thousands of applications every year, Bata selected only a few hundred. The admission criteria were strict, and the company used detailed questionnaires to examine the applicant's family background, personal attitudes and habits, including the ability to responsibly manage money.

Their ideal profile was a recent graduate of a state elementary school coming from a poor peasant or artisan family with a good background. It's interesting to note that Bata automatically rejected children who grew up without a father.

Strict discipline was not only expected of pupils and apprentices, but also all Bata employees. The company took pains to plan hourly schedules for each day and detailed schemes for the movement of workers at production belts, as well as to provide manuals describing every task in detail. The binding nature of these documents was emphasised by use of religious terminology such as 'Catechism of the Working Procedure' and 'The Ten Commandments of the Salesman'. I discovered in the Zlín archives a catalogue of all decisions taken by the company's director, and its title was telling: "The Bible of our Boss' Decisions".

Every single worker in the Bata factory had a carefully calculated norm for outputs. If this norm was not met, the worker's wages were automatically reduced. Another method that Baťa introduced to motivate his workers was the direct participation in the profit-and-loss of their organisational units. There were also ongoing competitions to publicly recognise the 'Best Worker of the Week' and the 'Best Unit of the Week' in both the factories and retail shops.

Strict supervision and control were imposed even on the private lives of Bata employees. This included an austere management of their personal income, which the company partially controlled by transferring a portion of their earnings to a savings account in its own bank. If employees chose to withdraw larger amounts, they had to declare the purpose.

The company had zero tolerance for its employees being late or getting drunk, and this even extended to outside working hours. Repeated offences were grounds for immediate dismissal. Even the households of workers in Zlín were subject to random checks by a delegation from the company's personnel department – they were expected to be clean and tidy, and harmonious relations were to be observed between husband and wife. This was based on the conviction that any problems in the family would negatively affect the employee's performance.

From a present-day perspective, these rules and expectations seem extremely hard to follow, but they arose from Tomáš Baťa's mission to ennoble humanity. In some of his writings and speeches, we come across references to an 'ideal man'. Such a person had to be honest, moral, hardworking and fully responsible for his life as well as for the company he worked for. He should strive not only for his own well-being, but also for the well-being of the whole company. I use the masculine pronoun consciously here, as we have already seen that Bata rarely employed women, especially after they got married.

This 'ideal man' would then live in an ideal environment: a modern city providing everything he needs, such as state-of-the-art healthcare, quality housing, schools of all kinds, cultural and sports facilities, and other services designed to support the residents in their never-ending effort to improve and cultivate themselves.

In line with this vision, Bat'a worked for decades to transform what was once a small, poor city of Zlín into such a 'city of the future' – and he largely succeeded. The revolutionary architecture and urban plan, which gives Zlín its unique character, can still be seen today.

The Bata company was applying the same concept overseas, wherever it was building its factories. Besides the already mentioned Batanagar in India, there are many other examples of modern settlements built around Bata's factories, many carrying the 'Bata' reference in their name: Batapur in Pakistan, Bataville in France, Batawa in Canada, Möhlin in Switzerland, Belcamp in USA, East Tilbury in the United Kingdom, Batadorp in the Netherlands, Gwel (today's Gwer) in Zimbabwe, Bat'ovany (today's Partizánske) in Slovakia, and Mornington in Australia. During the 1930s, a similar plan for a mini Bata settlement was developed for Singapore, but it was disrupted by war.

Bat'a's vision of an 'ideal man' and of a better world for humanity clearly contained strong elements of social engineering. In fact, I can identify many parallels with the Communist ideology. Paradoxically, the Communists in Czechoslovakia fiercely hated Bat'a because he managed to implement much more successfully what they were trying to achieve. The hostility, however, was mutual. Bat'a's management, in their effort to eliminate the pre-war Communist cells agitating in Zlín, did not shy away from brutal beatings to suppress the local Communists.

My parents' generation would often juxtapose Bat'a's style of business management with that of the Communists, but I think many of these similarities only become apparent with the benefit of hindsight. The common ground includes detailed planning of production and sales in annual and five-year plans, ostentatious emphasis on modern scientific methods of management, collectivism enforced through a combination of strong social control, competitions with public praise of the 'best workers' and repression when needed and egalitarianism (Tomáš Bat'a insisted that his employees be referred to as 'co-workers' in order to emphasise that rules and career opportunities applied to everyone). It's hard to overlook the cult of the iconic leader or director – who, within the Bata company, was almost religiously referred to as 'Mr Chief'.

Both the Baťa and Communist visions aspired to a 'betterment of mankind' through liberation from a crushing material poverty and enhancement. Each aspired to be an example for the world. These parallels were undoubtedly recognised by Jan Antonín Baťa, who declared with great confidence that "Zlín is more than Moscow. Zlín will remain a model for Moscow to follow".

I was very surprised to learn that Tomáš Baťa had a leading role in the celebration of Labour Day or May Day as it is known in Communist countries. My curiosity was first triggered when I came across a photograph of him holding a small Czechoslovak flag while taking part in a Labour Day parade. How strange that the most powerful capitalist in Czechoslovakia at that time would do something like that! But when I looked up more information, I learnt that Tomáš Baťa actually organised a Labour Day festival in Zlín every year from 1924. He also sent invitations to all his employees to attend the celebration:

> Friends! Our working family is so big that we all don't even know each other. That's why we will gather on Labour Day, 1 May, to celebrate together after a full year of work. Bring your wife and children! They will all be welcomed. Yours sincerely, Tomáš Baťa.

As everything else in the Bata company, these celebrations were carefully orchestrated and planned to the last detail, including the preparation of allegorical chariots, banners and attractions for the children. Tomáš Baťa and other company directors led the parade, and then watched the *defilé* of employees from the grandstand. Those who failed to participate were penalised (exactly as I remember during the socialist regime in Czechoslovakia).

The speeches emphasised mutual solidarity and loyalty of the employees to the company. This feeling of belonging was intentional and served to prevent social conflict. It took the oxygen away from the Communist agitation by virtually replacing it with a controlled version of something similar.

To be fair, it was not just propaganda. In many respects, the company was indeed socially progressive. Besides the exemplary care for its workers and their wellbeing, it shortened the work week to 40 hours in 1932, and established work-free Saturdays 36 years earlier than the Communists in Czechoslovakia.

After gaining all these fascinating insights, I kept thinking about how Silvestr was able to learn, adapt and grow within such a system. I must admit that I would probably not be able to stomach some of these heavily controlling practices that infringe on my personal space. Yet, Silvestr who joined Bata at the age of 16, was not only able to survive in that unique and challenging system, but also to rise up the ranks and eventually be included in a pool of exceptionally talented young people selected for transfers abroad.

To better understand Silvestr's journey to Bata, I was eager to reconstruct his childhood. The next step in my search would, therefore, take me back to the town where Silvestr was born and where he grew up prior to joining the Bata company – Vémyslice.

- IV -
Tracing Roots in Vémyslice

VÉMYSLICE, in the southeast of the Czech Republic, had a population of 700 citizens in 2019. It was where, as a child, I spent almost every weekend and most of my summer holidays, staying in my grandparents' house. It was also where I had the best adventures imaginable: climbing trees, fighting imaginary battles in fortresses made of bales of straw, baking potatoes over campfires in autumn, fishing in the river with a homemade rod (then running away when an official spotted us), jumping into huge piles of grain at the cooperative farm, reading old magazines found in a huge wooden crate in a dusty attic, picking grapes in our small vineyard, and doing chores around the farm which, to the surprise of many, I genuinely enjoyed.

In my grandparents' house, hanging in the entrance hall, was a portrait of a young man in a fashionable hat. I often walked (or mostly ran) past it without paying much attention to it. It was only years later, when I was a high school student, that I became aware that it was a photograph of Silvestr, my grandmother's youngest brother who never returned home after World War II.

However, this is not the Němec family house. My grandfather, who was from a poor family in the nearby village of Dukovany, had moved to Vémyslice. And after my grandparents got married, they built their house at the uphill end of the town.

The original Němec house is downhill, in the centre of the small town. It was here, in house number 23, that Silvestr was born in October 1919 to his father Sylvestr Němec and mother Františka (née Netoušková).

Silvestr was the youngest of their four children: he came after the oldest son František (1908), daughter Julie (1911, who in 1920 died of chronic infection as the result of falling into a toxic pond in her baby carriage when she was about 2 years old) and my grandmother Františka (1914).

Unfortunately, I have not met Silvestr's parents – my great-grandfather and great-grandmother – as they passed away in 1968 and 1970 respectively, just before I was born. My mother, however, shared with me that her grandparents lived and slept in the front room of the right wing of the house, and that her grandfather used to smoke a pipe. She also recalled seeing a thick book about the Bata company, filled with pictures, on a shelf in their room.

When I was a boy, we used to visit this house occasionally. Every Easter, I would knock on its door and recite special rhymes before collecting treats. In researching Silvestr's life and death, I went back to this house again. Even though it was a surprise visit, my aunt offered me the special homemade cookies that I used to love – it was nostalgic to taste them again after more than a quarter of a century!

We, of course, had a chat about Silvestr. It turned out that my aunt also collected a few documents, one of which was a print-out of the historical essay by Ivan Procházka about Czechoslovaks in the Far East during World War II. Remarkably, I learnt that the story told to my family in Vémyslice is that Silvestr was killed in a Singapore hospital when it was bombed by the Japanese. I was surprised by this. When I consulted with several historians, they confirmed that Alexandra Hospital was never bombed. So, I concluded that this was either information that had been inaccurately passed down or perhaps, a merciful lie told to the family after the war. I can imagine that his parents were already suffering enough – there was no need to hear about a brutal massacre by bayonets in the hospital.

The most valuable material I retrieved in Vémyslice was a set of historical photographs: four portraits of Silvestr and two photographs of the family taken before he was born. What caught my eye was an impressive picture of Silvestr's father posing in the garden, wearing a fashionable hat and with a cigar clasped between his fingers. He stands tall, like a hero in some Western movie.

While in Vémyslice, I also made a special trip to the local memorial erected for the victims of both world wars. It is located near the central square, a slight distance uphill, and facing the Catholic church. My grandmother used to go there from time to time, always bringing fresh flowers, watering the patch and tidying it up.

I remember when I was a child, I was fascinated by the portraits of the fallen ones, framed in small ovals next to their names. After years, though, those photos have been entirely bleached by sun and rain. I was therefore very pleased when I learnt that one of the local history enthusiasts, Arnošt Hrdina, was gathering original photos from the families for his restoration work. Of course, I gladly provided him with the photo of Silvestr, which I had in my possession.

On a more recent visit to Vémyslice, I had the pleasure of seeing these restored portraits and it warmed my heart to see how well they were done.

How War Touched Vémyslice

I was lucky with the timing of my first investigative trip to Vémyslice because, by coincidence, the town's bulletin board was displaying a chronicle of local events during World War II – this provided some background to the 16 World War II victims whose names have been inscribed on the war memorial, as well as insights into what was going on in Silvestr's hometown during the war. Here is a translation of the content:

> The events of late 1938 impacted Vémyslice very badly. The Munich Agreement resulted in state borders [between Czechoslovakia and Nazi Germany] being redrawn and moving very close to our town. It also resulted in a loss of access to our regional capital, Moravský Krumlov. Although Krumlov had a majority population of Czechs, it was annexed to Nazi Germany. Vémyslice therefore had to be administratively attached to Moravské Budějovice, which was very far away. Another complication was that our citizens were no longer able to use the railway as the nearest train station in Rakšice was suddenly in German territory; only those with special permits were able to access it.
>
> Our Vémyslice parish had to take care of the church in the neighbouring village of Rybníky, which was left in limbo after the Moravský Krumlov parish was cut off.
>
> Like all other cities, persecution came upon Vémyslice. It started when the storm troops of SS Sturm Polizei from Německé Jablonné, led by SS Sturmfuhrer Herold, arrived in early June of 1941. They ransacked the garage number 254 and took a freight car from there.
>
> Two local families, the Vybírals and the Nerudas – both recent

arrivals – declared themselves German, while 12 of our citizens were arrested for political reasons, including eight members of the family of Kubiš who were unlucky just because of their surname [Kubiš was the surname of one of the soldiers and parachutists who led the famous assassination of Reinhard Heydrich in Prague, May 1942].

During the Nazi retaliation that followed Heydrich's assassination, the Cyrils and Františka Vafek, as well as their son František, were executed on 1 July 1942 at the Kounitz Dorms in Brno. Dr Jaroslav Kotbauer, Karel Bašta, the Cyrils, Jana Vafek and teacher Josef Sedláček died in the concentration camps. A Jew, Jakub Neumann, also perished in Auschwitz.

On 10 December 1942, 10 German families – so called Bessarabians – arrived from Constanz in Romania. [Bessarabia is a historical region between Ukraine and Romania, largely corresponding to today's Moldova] They took over the farms and houses that were confiscated from those who were either childless or who committed offences against the Germans. Local citizens did not welcome these newcomers and largely ignored them.

On 23 January 1943, a German primary school and a kindergarten were established to serve the children of the Bessarabian families. Other German pupils also came from villages nearby. Those German schools operated until the very end of German rule when the Bessarabians fled to the west to escape the approaching Red Army.

The local municipality was abolished on 9 June 1943 and the mayor, Josef Bašta, was deposed. The government appointed a local fascist, František Podhradský from Rybníky village, as an official commissar; however, the actual power was in the hands of the renegade, Štefan Vybíral.

Czech national associations such as Sokol, Orel and National Unity, were also dissolved and their property confiscated. On 18 March 1943, the villagers had to say goodbye to their church bells as they were taken away for the purpose of war.

As the Red Army advanced through Hungary, several young men from Vémyslice were mobilised and forced to dig defence trenches near the Nezider Lake. Several machine gun posts were later set up around our village, and an anti-tank barrier placed near the church.

A resistance was formed under the umbrella of the Obrana národa (National Defence); however, its activities were stopped during the persecution. Two citizens from Vémyslice joined Allied Armies as sergeants: Ota Hrdina from house number 168 went to England, and František Sobotka from house number 165 joined the partisans in Italy. When the front passed by, the locals cut the German telephone lines twice to interrupt their communications.

On 18 April 1945, while the Czech citizens eagerly awaited the arrival of the Red Army, the German civilians fled the village. Vémyslice, however, found itself on a sideline of the main military operations as the Russians made a surprise advance through the city of Ivančice, north of Vémyslice. In any case, the locals prepared their shelters against air raids.

On 7 May 1945, from 7 am, the Russian air force began to drop light fragmentation and incendiary bombs on Vémyslice. During this air raid, two civilians – Antonín Bašta and Josef Plachý – were killed, and 15 houses caught fire.

Throughout the night, from 7 to 8 May, the German troops retreated towards the village of Tulešice. They mounted a brief resistance only on the hills near Rybníky, in Ledvice, and on the southern and western edges of Vémyslice.

On 8 May, shortly after 8 am, the Red Army took over Vémyslice. The Russians had no casualties while the Germans lost four soldiers. During the fighting, Jan Vybíral was also killed. The Russians established a field hospital in our local school, where two Russian officers eventually succumbed to their earlier wounds.

On 9 May 1945, the first local national council was established under the chairmanship of Josef Bradáč.

Knowing these details about how Silvestr's hometown was impacted by Nazi occupation and persecution gave me a sense of the everyday life of his family during the war and what Silvestr might have been concerned about halfway across the world.

What also triggered my interest was the direct link between Vémyslice and a renowned heroic act of the Czechoslovak resistance – the already mentioned assassination of Reinhard Heydrich. Heydrich was one of the highest-ranking Nazis, very close to Hitler and a principal architect of the Holocaust. This action, called 'Operation Anthropoid', was the most remarkable success of the wartime Czechoslovak resistance and several movies have been made on it.

The Vémyslice link to this event is hidden under one of the 16 names engraved on the Vémyslice war memorial – that of Viktor Jarolím.

Jarolím owned a mill on the Rokytná River, halfway between Vémyslice and the neighbouring village of Tulešice. He was the biological father of Adolf Opálka, another parachutist from the Out Distance commandos who participated in Operation Anthropoid. That was why the Germans executed Jarolím during their brutal retribution.

The story of Jarolím and Opálka is actually a very sad one. Opálka, born in 1915, was Jarolím's illegitimate son; his mother was chased away from the mill. Thus, he grew up without a father and mother as she died when he was only eight years old. Subsequently, his mother's sister Marie took care of him. Marie, too, was executed by the Germans in 1942, for being a close family member of Opálka.

The Vémyslice of Silvestr's Childhood

My research of Silvestr's family is primarily based on historical documents about Vémyslice found in the Czech State Archives in Znojmo, a former capital of the region. The archive maintains an impressive collection of documents about Vémyslice – if stacked in a pile, they would exceed eight metres in height! One of the custodians of these records, Ms Pekárková, was extremely helpful in guiding me through the rich material.

The collection includes several rare medieval parchments that relate to the extraordinary history of the town. There are also several chronicles written by the municipality and its various schools. These school diaries, where key contemporary events in the village were recorded, complement the official municipal chronicles. From these sources, I gathered much of the following information.

As we know, Silvestr was born on 20 October 1919, the fourth and youngest child in the family of Sylvestr Němec. I managed to trace his direct ancestors seven generations back, to Václav Němec who was born around 1655 in Horní Kounice, a small town several kilometres from Vémyslice. Silvestr's grandmother Marie Sklenský was a descendant of another old local family. Her oldest known direct ancestor was Pavel Ripl (born around 1580), who served as a mayor of Vémyslice.

The school chronicle mentions that in 1919, the year Silvestr was born, seven legionaries returned home to Vémyslice from Vladivostok in the Russian Far East. It's interesting to see a reference like this, reminding us of one of the most heroic achievements of the Czechoslovak army in World War I. Records also show that some of these men, on their long way home, sailed through Singapore. I will expand on this in the following chapter on the history of Czechoslovaks in Singapore.

Just a week after Silvestr was born, the village celebrated the first anniversary of Czechoslovakia's independence. The country was established in October 1918 as a result of the partitioning of the Austrian-Hungarian Empire that lost World War I which it initiated four years earlier. Czechoslovakia was built on the vision of its founder, Tomáš Garrique Masaryk, as a modern, democratic, multinational state. Its citizens were predominantly Czechs and Slovaks with several million Germans, Hungarians, Rusyns and Poles. The headmaster of a school in Vémyslice – Mr Orlíček – who apparently had a very progressive, idealistic vision of society, wrote a proud entry about it.

An important event that significantly reshaped modern Vémyslice – and with it, Silvestr's childhood – was the state land reform of 1924. In February that year, Earl Kinský received a court order to be evicted from Vémyslice Manor. The manor, established by the Tišnov monastery in 1740, was sold to the Lichtenstein family who, in turn, sold it to Earl Kinský. As a result of the land reform, the manor land was divided into allotments and distributed to new owners. The Vémyslice chronicles document that 90 families applied for a share of the land. The municipality, too, claimed part of it and eventually obtained the meadow and a park attached to the manor. In the following years, three modern buildings were built on this newly acquired public land: a new school, a local gym hall, and a Protestant church. Together, they established a new centre of public life in the town, and we can be fairly certain that Silvestr would have spent quite a bit of time in all these three buildings during his childhood.

The land reforms also involved another allotment, a large meadow called Závist (Envy). It was, by an old deed of the Tišnov monastery, reserved for the families of men from Vémyslice who served as guards in the monastery complex. Thus, new settlers in Vémyslice had no access to it. The chronicle further states that the meadow was used according to a 10-year roster: eight families could use it for each of nine years, then the municipality used it in the tenth year. When the state land reform was instituted, the chronicle read:

> This year, in 1924, the old families utilised their privilege for the last time. In the future, the meadow will be accessible to anyone, and so the new settlers won't have to envy the old families anymore for using 'Envy'.

The chronicle listed the 80 old families of Vémyslice who had the ancient privilege, and the Němec family was among them.

There is another mention of the Němec family in the context of land ownership in Vémyslice – an entry about a public auction of the vicarage land in 1923. The school diary states that one of the three auctioned allotments – a 4,600 square-metre garden – was purchased on 23 March 1923 by Sylvestr Němec for 18,000 Czechoslovak crowns.

After the municipality became the owner of the Manor's meadow, there was a proposal to build a modern school on it. The town council discussed this in August 1924 and agreed, by a narrow majority of eight votes to seven, to take further steps. This decision was quickly challenged by a petition signed by 42 citizens. Headmaster Orlíček, who listed the names in the school diary, added a comment: "It is only through work and education that we can reach salvation!"

The dispute over the new school continued. A member of the local educational board, who opposed the proposal, was quoted by Orlíček as saying: "What we need are people who will clear out the dung in our stables – not people with academic education. All the educated people will just run away from the farming work!"

The narrow majority, however, managed to push the project through despite all the obstacles, and the new school building was completed in August 1926, allowing the next academic year to begin there. This was much to the delight of the chronicler who commented:

> School – the monument of progressive efforts of the Vemyslice citizens – has been finished, radiating the unbreakable will of the majority who are in favour of education, a fundamental factor of prosperity.

The old school building was later converted into a police station.

Everyday Life in Vémyslice

By the time Silvestr enrolled at the school, the Czechoslovak educational system had been modernised into a compulsory eight-year programme: five years in primary school, and three years in the secondary level. Some pupils could then advance to the so-called continuation schools, which provided specialised education.

From Silvestr's date of birth (October 1919) and his starting date at

Bata (September 1936), one can deduce that he attended primary school from September 1925 to June 1930, and secondary from September 1930 to June 1933. According to his record in *Bata's List of Employees Overseas*, he attended a business academy before joining Bata.

The primary school in Vémyslice had two classes, one for six- to eight-year-olds, and the other for those aged nine to 11. In the academic year of 1925/1926, when Silvestr began his formal education, his class had 43 pupils. The teacher was Mrs Vlasta Musilová. At that time, the new school building was under construction and – according to the school diary – due to the lack of rooms in the old school building, classes took place in what was a teacher's apartment.

Like children everywhere, some of Silvestr's schoolmates were mischievous. When I read the records of naughty behaviour in the old school chronicles, I had to laugh. Four boys (Hlávka, Růžička, Sklenský and Kopeček) got the lowest grade for their conduct because they "destroyed bird nests and made fun of beggars". A record of a teachers' conference on 3 March 1926 read, "Miss Musilová suggests that Leopold Hejmala from the first class be sent to a reform school because of his regular thieving, lying and disobedience."

Two events in the village during Silvestr's first year at school must have excited the young boy. The church in Vémyslice was equipped with three newly manufactured bells, the original ones having been requisitioned by the Austrian army during World War I. (Sadly, these new bells would suffer the same fate in World War II).

Then in July 1926, during Silvestr's first summer break, a brick road was laid in the centre of Vémyslice – until then, the town had only a dirt road. A historical photograph even captures the steam roller parked in front of Silvestr family's house – and standing on it, with a happy smile, is Silvestr himself.

The new school building opened in August 1926, so Silvestr's second year of education must have already taken place there. Bad behaviour of students continued to be an issue. In September, one of the boys was "caught in a pub during the local festival, despite an explicit ban by the school principal". In December, two girls stole some money from the cloakroom. A few pupils were also reported to have used swear words, thrown stones and broken the planks of fences. At the end of Silvestr's second academic year, the principal made a speech about upholding proper behaviour during the summer holidays. In the light of existing records, his words were ineffective.

ABOVE: Silvestr's parents, Sylvestr and Františka Němec, around the time they got married in 1907. Interestingly, Sylvestr senior wears an Austrian army uniform.

LEFT: A family photo of Silvestr's parents and siblings probably taken shortly before he was born. The boy on the left is the oldest son František, the girl standing is Julie who tragically died at the age of 10, and the little girl held by her mother is Františka – my grandmother.

LEFT: *Silvestr in his early teens.*

BELOW: *The steam roller used to modernise the main road of Vémyslice. The house on the left is Silvestr's home, and the man on the far right is Silvestr's father. Silvestr is very likely the boy in the hat on the extreme right.*

RIGHT: *Silvestr's class. He is in the front row, to the right of the boy holding the sign.*

BELOW RIGHT: *Silvestr's home in Vémyslice as it looks today.*

LEFT: *Three new public buildings in Vémyslice, Silvestr's hometown, in his childhood. On the left is a gymnasium. In the centre is the school which opened when Silvestr was in the second year of primary school. And finally, the Protestant church.*

BELOW LEFT: *A photo from the Vémyslice school chronicle showing a gardening lesson in progress.*

ABOVE: *A Bata shop in Vémyslice between 1938 and 1945. It is possible that a few years earlier, Silvestr had started his career at Bata here.*

BELOW: *Bata May Day lunch for all employees and their families. Zlín, 1927.*

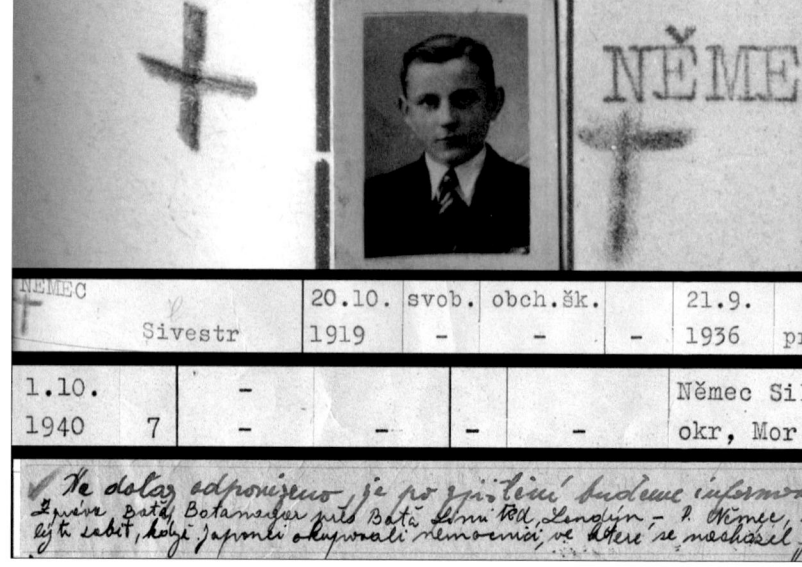

ABOVE: *Silvestr's entry in Bata's "List of Employees" compiled in Zlín in 1944. It includes several handwritten notes added after the war.*

RIGHT: *A portrait of Silvestr dated 1937, when he was 17 years old.*

FAR RIGHT: *Silvestr, in February 1938 – less than a year before he departed for Singapore.*

Sivestr

| 31.12. 1938 | Singapore Str.Settlem. | pedikér | Zlín |

slice 23
otec — —

ls sdělují že v r. 1943 byl v Singapuru.
vážné známění, když bojoval v Singapuru, měl prý
/Zabit při akci v Singapore - dle telegramu od
Jugose/

RIGHT: *Batamen, travelling from Czechoslovakia to Singapore in 1937 on board* Conte Biancamano, *a modern liner of Lloyd Triestino. It is most likely that Silvestr sailed on this same ship in January 1939.*

BELOW: *A group of Bata employees in Batanagar, India, circa 1940. The third man from the right resembles Silvestr. It is possible that he paid a visit to Batanagar during his tenure in Singapore.*

That summer holiday was an extraordinary one for Silvestr as he would have witnessed the 10-day artillery exercise of the Czechoslovak army near his town. A training firing range was also set up. The chronicles captured this vividly:

> *Military training at Vémyslice. The field command is based on the first floor of our school, the ground floor accommodates 25 soldiers. Horses and the rest of the men are accommodated in the buildings of the former Manor. A telephone centre was established in our pub. Live firing training carried out in the vicinity of Vémyslice and surrounding villages. An observation point is based on top of our hill. The behaviour of the army was perfect; officers were friendly and addressed any concerns of our citizens.*

As Silvestr advanced to his third academic year, there was no shortage of excitement for him. In September 1927, electricity was connected to the village and the first electric light was switched on. A month later, an earthquake shook the town slightly:

> *Earthquake, a natural phenomenon very rare in our country, was felt on Saturday 8 October at 8.45 pm. Glasses, plates and other dishes clinked, the furniture trembled, and the tremors were felt the strongest when lying in bed.*

In April 1928, the school organised a donation drive to help victims of a major earthquake in Bulgaria. In total, 362 Czechoslovak crowns were collected from the pupils. The first doctor's office was opened in town. But perhaps the most memorable event of that academic year happened in June, when the Czechoslovak president, T.G. Masaryk, paid a visit to the region. All the students from Vémyslice went to the city of Moravský Krumlov to welcome him.

The next school year saw a harsh winter that brought massive snowdrifts and temperatures as low as -30 degrees Celsius. A new principal arrived at the school, and Orlíček embarked on a different mission in another town. One can feel his frustration from his final entry in the school diary. Quoting Jesus from Luke 4:24, Orlíček wrote, "Amen, I tell you, nobody is a prophet in his own land."

In July 1929, a new Protestant church building was erected and held its inaugural service on 1 September 1929. This was very relevant for

Silvestr's family. The local Protestant community was first recognised in the census of February 1921, when 170 out of 934 Vémyslice citizens declared that they belonged to the Czechoslovak Hussite Church.

The church had very harsh beginnings, as documented by the town chronicler:

> On 8 May 1921, the local branch of Church of Hussites was established in Vémyslice. It is chaired by Mr Jiří Šeiner from house number 56. As a result of continuous harassment (banned from using the bell during funerals, not allowed to use crosses or have their own church building), the Protestant movement weakened a little, yet as of today [15 August 1921], 136 members of the Catholic church dared to convert to Protestantism.

From the February 1921 census, I found documents indicating that Silvestr's family declared themselves as Catholic. But a note in Silvestr's record in the town's registry states that he converted to Protestantism – as did his whole family, in July 1921 – just six months later. I remember my grandmother (Silvestr's older sister) attending Sunday services at the local Protestant church that has a Hussite symbol – a red chalice – above its entrance, along with the slogan "The Truth Will Prevail".

The 1921 census papers also gave me additional insights into the life of the Němec family. They reveal that the Němec household comprised of Silvestr, his two siblings, his parents, his grandmother and grandfather (of Netoušek family), grandmother Němcová, and finally, Uncle Jan. It must have been a fairly crowded house, but that was quite common back then.

With the departure of Orlíček, the town chronicle was taken over by Mr Dubšík, a teacher in the secondary school. He was the one who recorded the completion of the Protestant church – the last of the three new municipality buildings at the uphill end of Vémylice. Next to the school and the Protestant church, a gym had also been built. Dubšík refers to these as the "three centres of progress, endorsing health (gym), wisdom (school) and devotion (church) – in line with the three noble ideas of humanity: beauty, goodness and truth".

The academic year of 1929/1930 was Silvestr's last year in primary school. In October 1929, local elections took place in Vémyslice. I found it interesting to read that 92 percent of the townsfolk voted – a figure that is hard to imagine today as the electoral turnout has halved.

Then in March 1930, the municipality prepared spectacular celebrations for the 80th birthday of the Czechoslovak founder and president, T. G. Masaryk. According to the chronicles I read, most of the houses and buildings in Vémyslice were decorated with national flags, and on 7 March, a day-long celebration was held. At sunset, a parade took place. It was headed by the pupils of the school (I immediately imagined Silvestr marching there!), followed by a band, members of the town council, policemen, fire brigade and national gymnastics associations Sokol and Orel. Records show that 1,400 people marched in the parade. Given that Vémyslice only had 980 citizens at that time, it is quite likely that almost half of the participants came from the neighbouring villages.

In academic year 1930/1931, when Silvestr was 11 years old, he entered secondary school. The classrooms were on the second floor of the new school building, and the chronicles says that there were 28 pupils in Silvestr's class.

The next school year of 1931/1932 brought several tragedies to Silvestr's life. The chronicle has a big headline "Murder" with a detailed report following:

> On 25 November 1931, a local woman – Marie Němcová from house number 28 in Vémyslice – was murdered as she walked from Moravský Krumlov back home. The crime happened at the top of Perk Hill. She was carrying 2,000 Czechoslovak crowns in cash for the sugar beet delivered to the Krumlov sugar factory. She was supposed to have 13,000 crowns on her, but the factory gave her only a first payment. It is speculated that the killer assumed she would carry the full amount, otherwise he would not have killed for only 2,000 crowns. The investigation has been complicated by the fact that initially, based on an autopsy by Dr Janíček, the death was said to be caused by a car accident. It took some time before they found a shot in the back of her head. The murderer has not yet been found.

The chronicler got the victim's name wrong. The woman was in fact Františka Němcová who was a relative of Silvestr, though not from the immediate family. Yet, this tragedy must have shaken everyone in the Němec household.

A small monument of this violent death, which says the murderer was never identified, still stands on Perk Hill. As a boy, I often walked by it on my way to catch a bus home from Moravský Krumlov.

Another death that undoubtedly shocked Silvestr and his friends took place in February 1932 when their teacher Marie Vašková died in childbirth.

In August 1932, Vémyslice was finally permitted to establish its own post office – the result of much effort, as its first application was submitted in 1892. The success came after the municipality appealed yet another rejection of the general directorate of the State Post in 1931. It seems that the neighbouring villages were against the idea of establishing a post office in Vémyslice as they were all under the jurisdiction of the post office in Moravský Krumlov. Now, to their dismay, their postal services were transferred to Vémyslice. I have also learnt from the chronicles that the post office was opened on 1 October with three employees: a chief officer and two postmen.

In November, another tragedy occurred in the community that must have been a big story for the school kids:

> *On the evening of 15 November 1932, a passenger car driven by Mr Šustáček from Moravský Krumlov was arriving from Džbánice when it turned in front of Mr Pelaj's house, skidded, and the left wheel was stuck in a ditch next to the road. As a result of this impact, a worker Mr Hrubeš was ejected out of the car directly into a plum tree. The frontal hit killed him. Both the tree and its surroundings were covered in blood. Mr Šustáček, who works as an innkeeper and tax collector in Krumlov, managed to survive with only minor injuries.*

March 1933 saw a new telephone and telegraph connection to Vémyslice. We also learn that the municipality council collapsed as a result of severe political disputes, and new elections were held in March 1933. Its outcome was again tight, with a majority of eight votes to seven, so the disputes continued. Apparently, the political life in Vémyslice was quite lively in those years!

What I found really interesting was a chapter in the municipal chronicles by Dubšík that describes winter sports in Vémyslice, since I can vividly imagine Silvestr taking part in these:

> *Many modern winter sports have recently become popular among the local youth. People are ice-skating above the Steinmetz weir and on the section of the river towards Rybníky. The boys are passionate about*

hockey, which substitutes football during the winter season. Much of the influence comes from radio reports of various sports events, including the Winter Olympic Games. Sledges are widely used on the slopes of Kopec and Šibeničník. Adults are joining the children, mostly during the weekends and holidays. In the evenings, things are very lively even downtown, where boys and girls ride their sledges on the main road from the fire squad's warehouse down to the pub – if the police do not prevent them.

Most recently, a new phenomenon called 'skiing' arrived in our village. Previously, this beautiful winter sport was unknown to us. I started promoting it myself back in 1928, especially amongst the students and members of the local gymnastics associations. The number of young skiers has been growing since. I taught them elementary techniques on skis made at home with wooden planks or bought for a small sum of money at the local warehouse. This winter, skiing became very popular here, and many children and teenagers dare to ski down from the steeper slopes of the hill at the brick factory, trying to perform acrobatic turns.

The following summer surely entertained Silvestr with another artillery training in his town, as the chronicle reports:

An observation point was set at the hill above Vémyslice. From there, the soldiers as well as our citizens had an opportunity to watch the explosions of the shells fired from cannons. The shells that failed to explode were recovered immediately and destroyed with small charges. Yet, many farmers were afraid to plough the fields in the autumn, for fear that they may run into a forgotten shell.

Silvestr attended a business academy after graduating from elementary school. I have not managed to identify the academy, but quite likely, it would have been in Moravský Krumlov, the nearest city. If this were the case, he was probably still living at home and commuted daily.

At that point in time, neither Silvestr nor his family could ever imagine that one day, he would end up working far away in Singapore.

- V -
Czechoslovaks in Singapore

BEFORE WE DELVE into the era of Bata company's presence in Singapore, it would be useful to share some impressions of early travellers from the Czechoslovak region to Southeast Asian countries like Thailand, Malaysia and Singapore, as recorded by the Singapore press.

When Olek Plesek, author of the dossier about Batamen in Singapore, shared with me some of the references he used, among them was a truly amazing tool: the online archives of the Singapore press on the website of the National Library Board.

The Singapore Government must have invested significant resources into its development because it contains more than 20 periodicals published in English, Malay and Chinese which go well back in time. The oldest is the 4 January 1827 issue of *Singapore Chronicle*, published eight years after the British colonised Singapore.

What's more, the newspaper archives are fully digitised and allow a full-text search for keywords – across epochs, themes and publications. As such, one can easily search for articles covering Bata company, reports about Czechoslovakia or Czech citizens, and even about Silvestr Němec himself.

Early Czech Presence

There were at least a dozen Czechs and Slovaks who travelled to Siam, British Malaya and Singapore before World War I to document or photograph the cities, landscapes and peoples. They included Josef Kořenský – a teacher, palaeontologist and entomologist who visited Malaya and Singapore between 1893 and 1901 – travel photographer and writer Enrique Stanko Vráz, scientists Karel Domin and Jiří Viktor Daneš, as well as writer and diplomat Jan Havlasa who created a great set of photographs of Malaya in 1913.

It was not until late 1918 that these travellers could be referred to as 'Czechoslovaks' – citizens of a sovereign, democratic country that emerged from the breakdown of the Austrian-Hungarian Empire at the end of World War I. I found several articles which reported the recognition of Czechoslovakia by the British government and other Allies. The creation of Czechoslovakia was quite a unique political development when colonialism still defined post-WWI geopolitics.

Shortly after, Singapore encountered – for the first time – Czechoslovaks not as individual explorers but as organised groups of patriotic citizens of an independent republic. This was when soldiers of the Czechoslovak Legions, who were fighting the Bolshevik Red Army along the Trans-Siberian Railway between 1917 and 1920 returned home from Vladivostok, a harbour city on the Pacific coast, via Singapore. The arrival of many of the transport ships was well documented by the Singapore press.

The first mention of these legionaries that I found is from March 1920, when the *Malaya Tribune* announced the arrival of 2,071 Czechoslovak soldiers onboard *SS Madawaska*. Similar announcements followed later in 1920.

While these men were in transit, they took a welcome one- or two-day break on their long journey to explore the vibrant city and perhaps to even enjoy its nightlife. They sometimes actively contributed to the social life of Singapore, for example, *The Straits Times* published in May 1920 a long piece about the Czech Symphony Orchestra that performed a concert in Victoria Theatre. The programme included pieces by Czech composers Antonín Dvořák and Bedřich Smetana. The article also mentions that the proceeds of these concerts were donated "to the comfort fund of Czechs invalided in the war". Two months later, the press reported another musical performance by a different Czech band at the Boustead Institute.

Sports was another type of social interaction. I discovered that the Czechoslovak legionaries formed a team and played football matches against the local British officers: in May 1920, the team of the 5th Czechoslovak Regiment managed a 1-1 draw, while the team of the 4th Regiment lost 2-4.

The presence of a previously unheard-of nationality did make people curious. *The Singapore Free Press and Mercantile Advertiser* published an article in July 1921 making fun of cultural misunderstandings resulting from various connotations of the terms 'Czech' and 'Bohemian' [Bohemia is one of the regions of Czechoslovakia]. The same newspaper, when reporting on the YMCA's global survey of youth of different nations, dedicated nearly half of the story to what was perceived to be the key characteristics of a Czech teenage boy. *The Straits Times* also published a long and detailed article headlined "A Dream Come True" about the creation of modern Czechoslovakia, which included the role of the Czechoslovak Legions in Siberia.

It took another decade or two before the number of Czechoslovak long-term residents in Singapore significantly increased. During my research I have established that by the end of the 1930s, there were over a hundred Czechoslovaks living and working in Singapore – a very diverse group comprising artists, missionaries, businesspeople and adventurers. About two-thirds of them were employed by the Bata Shoe Company, with some accompanied by wives and children. Those 'Batamen', as they referred to themselves, were a tightly organised community with very strong and specific traits that shaped their views and habits. Nothing testifies to the successful localisation of the Bata company – including its unique methods of production, sales and management – better than the fact that many people in the region today consider Bata to be a Singaporean, Malaysian or Indian brand.

Bata's First Decade in Singapore

From a keyword search of 'Bata' from the digitised newspaper archives, I found that the earliest mention of the company was in August 1926. It was a small advertisement in *The Straits Times* announcing a "New Shipment of Bata Shoes" to a shop called Yap Hen on Queen Street.

A major milestone of Bata's presence was the opening of the company's own store at Capitol Theatre on North Bridge Road. It was launched in the middle of February 1931, and Bata had placed large advertisements in *The Straits Times* a week earlier, inviting all customers to visit the shop. In the same week, *Malaya Tribune* printed a longer piece, entitled "Cutting the Cost of Living", which described the strategy of the Bata company and its plans in Singapore. The article is accompanied by a portrait of Tomáš Baťa, the founder and owner of the brand.

Bata Shoe Company Inc was registered in Singapore in August 1931. It had 12 local employees by the end of that year. In 1932, another two Bata shops were opened. By the end of the decade, Bata was running 150 stores, distribution centres and service points across British Malaya and Singapore.

Bata had much publicity in January 1932 when Tomáš Baťa embarked on his famous airplane journey to the Far East. Although his main destination was British India, he extended his itinerary to cover Singapore and Batavia.

When Tomáš Baťa arrived on 9 January 1932, the Singapore press published a series of celebratory articles, including "Shoe King in Singapore" in *The Straits Times*. The newspapers reported detailed information about the plans he unveiled: an intention to open a new shoe factory using modern machines, and to purchase a rubber plantation to secure direct supplies of raw materials needed in the shoe production.

It took a few years for these plans to materialise under the leadership of Jan Antonín Baťa, in the wake of Tomáš' tragic death in July 1932. The Bata rubber plantation was purchased at Bukit Tiga in Kulai, Johore, in 1934, and a big Bata factory producing cheap rubber and canvas shoes (the so-called 'plimsolls') opened in Klang, British Malaya, in 1937. Eventually, a smaller factory producing leather shoes commenced operations in Singapore in 1939.

A year later, Bata in Singapore celebrated another milestone that elevated its profile and visibility: the company opened its own 'Bata Building' on North Bridge Road, just a stone's throw away from Capitol Theatre. It was a modern, four-storey building that housed both the new store and the company's offices. After World War II, business returned to the premises, but it was demolished decades later to make way for a modern, high-rise building – today's Peninsula Plaza.

According to a document I found in the Zlín archives, the Singapore hub of Bata oversaw its broader regional operations in the late 1930s. These included Bata branches in Hong Kong, Shanghai, Manchuria, Australia and the Philippines. Interestingly, the Bata branch in Thailand remained independent with its own registration in Bangkok. The other two exceptions in the region were branches in Saigon and Hanoi, which were under the management of Bata in Strasbourg – probably because they were operating in French Indochina.

A commemorative book that Bata Shoe Company published on the

20th anniversary of its presence in the region – *Bata 1931-1951: 20 Years of Progress in Malaya* – captures these details and many other important moments in dozens of rare photographs. It also provides some statistics that testify to its successful expansion in its first decade. For example, the annual output of the factory in Klang increased from 220,000 pairs of shoes in 1937 (when it first started) to 2.4 million pairs in 1941, more than tenfold growth in just five years.

I also found a report from 1941 by the Czechoslovak consul in Bombay (present-day Mumbai). It said that the Bata Klang factory employed about 1,200 local workers and eight Czechoslovaks at that time, while the Singapore Bata factory had some 800 workers.

In addition, several pre-World War II articles from the Bata periodicals in Zlín provided more details about Bata in Southeast Asia – of particular interest to me is the company's rubber plantation in Kulai. The estate in Johore, Malaya, had about 120,000 trees taken care of by 200 local workers. Its manager was a Czechoslovak, Mr Rája. He wrote a long article "I Was Growing Rubber Trees". As it was published in December 1938 – shortly before Silvestr's departure to Singapore – it is quite possible that he read it to learn about the exotic country he was about to travel to. Rája, who was managing the Bata branch in Malacca in 1935, wrote:

> "The mail arrived, tuan!" said my boy Wang Min when I returned to Malacca, covered with sweat and dust after touring through kampongs to purchase several tonnes of rubber. I quickly washed myself and sat at the desk to read the letters. Correspondence from Zlín always has the highest priority.
>
> I had been expecting this for a while, but now it's official. I will have to hand over the rubber purchasing business and move to Kulai to the rubber plantation that we bought last year from some Chinese.
>
> As decisions are always implemented quickly in Bata, things moved fast. I wrapped up my business in Malacca, passed it to a new colleague who had just arrived, packed my things and travelled to the plantation. It is about 29 miles from Johore Bahru.
>
> What does it look like? It's a forest of trees; some are planted in a regular pattern, some grow randomly. A basic unit of the plantation, called a 'task', consists of 350-360 trees. Two such 'tasks' are managed by one tapper who collects the rubber milk from each 'task' every other day, letting the other 'task' rest. Ten to twelve 'tasks' form a 'block'. And

multiple 'blocks' then form the whole plantation.

Ours was located on a bit of a hilly landscape, which I liked at first sight. I moved to a wooden house which was empty except for an iron bed and a few chairs. I therefore made a short trip to Johore Bahru on my first day to buy the essentials that would allow me to start working there.

He also summarises his achievements during the four years he spent there as the main manager. What he wrote illustrates the ethos so common in the Bata Company:

> Early in the morning on the second day, we walked around to explore the whole plantation. Things were reasonably in order, except the huts for our Chinese, Indian and Malay tappers. They were in horrible shape – broken wooden planks in their walls and leaking attap roofs. I made my first decision: these will have to go. The universal rule is that when people's well-being is taken care of, when they have good housing and live healthier lives, they also work with much more enthusiasm. So, I had to build new, clean and decent housing.
>
> To be honest, the work was hard and exhausting every day, but it was also rewarding because we were making good progress. Although many of the locals thought that "the tuan has gone mad", I reformed everything at the plantation, from the bottom to the top, step by step.
>
> I taught my people to start work at dawn, because the rule that "the early bird catches the worm" also applied at the plantation. Besides, if we start late, it gets too hot and not much work would get done. I also introduced management of work by assignment of specific tasks, and I paid our tappers based on the 'milk' they collected. We also cleared 136 hectares of jungle and planted pineapples there first, in order to expand our plantation.

This part of the story is confirmed by Josef Štach who worked for Bata in Malaya between 1936 and 1939. He wrote in a magazine in Zlín:

> In Johore, Malaya, about 700 hectares of forest were purchased in 1935 and a rubber plantation was established in Bukit Tiga. The manager of the plantation was Mr Rája [...] In the first phase, the forest was burnt and the area was planted with pineapple as the first crop. At the time I was there, the pineapple harvest was so huge that

it didn't pay to take all of it to the cannery. In the end, we ended up dumping them in earth pits.

And in the words of Rája:

> The number of employees grew to 140. I put in place a system to identify damaged trees early and to specially treat them. To make sure everyone got proper rest, I also introduced a 9 pm curfew and a ban on card games. The new, clean houses created a miracle.
> And so, I worked in the hot, humid weather and under tropical rains in Kulai for nearly five years. You can bet that after such a long time, a person really starts longing for the fresh, cold breeze that I knew from my hometown in Czechoslovakia. So, I sent a request to Zlín to be substituted.

I was lucky to find a photograph of Rája at the Bukit Tiga plantation. He is standing outside his house with two dogs. The caption reads: "Mr Rája, accompanied by his dogs to protect him from snakes, sets on a tour to oversee the rubber plantation".

I think it would be very interesting to hear from Bata's Chinese and Malay employees in Kulai. Although they were probably used to the command of a white man, I wonder whether they noticed that their new boss did not have the arrogance of a 'superior' race but by genuine effort, improved the conditions in which they worked and lived. Were the changes, which Rája was so proud of, as effective as he reported? Sadly, we'll probably never know.

Contributing to War Funds

Bata was mentioned in the Singapore press throughout the 1930s. Apart from advertisements, the reports were most frequently related to contributions to various charities, including donations to war funds after Britain engaged in World War II in Europe.

The Straits Times in 1940 and 1941 regularly recorded Bata donations, in large sums of several thousand dollars, to the War Fund. Similarly, the *Morning Tribune* in 1939 informed its readers about a gift of 1,000 dollars that Bata contributed – on top of another 400 dollars collected from its employees – to the Patriotic Fund. It appears to have been quite common that various collections were organised by staff, to which the management added a donation on behalf of the company.

I was most excited when I found Silvestr Němec on a donors list, published in *The Straits Times* on 8 June 1940. The newspaper printed, in three columns, the names of those who donated to the War Fund, and we learn that Silvestr gave 50 dollars – not a small amount in those times – as did a number of his colleagues, including Rudolf Janeček and Karel Vítek. In all, the Bata employees donated 2,100 dollars, which the Bata company topped up to 5,000 dollars.

Many Bata Czechoslovaks contributed to the Christmas Appeal organised by the *Malaya Tribune* in 1939: Karel Vytopil donated 50 pairs of rubber shoes to the value of 19 dollars, and several dollars each were given by Kožušníček, Ambrož, Janeček, Vítek, among other colleagues and friends of Silvestr.

Other funds Bata or its Czechoslovak employees in Singapore contributed to include the Cent-A-Plane collection, the Polish Relief Fund and those organised by the YMCA or Salvation Army. A rather unusual donation, reported in July 1941, was that of Viktor Koš – a chief financial manager of Bata in Singapore – who donated 50 dollars to the War Fund "in lieu of a flower wreath for the late Mr V. Rojt, Director of Bata Shoe Co. Ltd. in Singapore".

Bata company also launched its own charity drives that were covered by the Singapore press. In April 1941, Bata announced a special project to collect shoes for air-raid victims. The company called on people to bring in old shoes which it promised to repair and donate to victims of the war. According to a follow-up report published later in the year, several hundred pairs of repaired shoes were given to those in need.

The last charity activity organised by Bata before the Japanese Occupation was in January 1942. The newspapers announced that the company would donate 20 cents from the sale of each pair of its new 'Victory' shoes sold to the War Fund.

The wives of Batamen in Singapore also engaged in various charity efforts. When the *Singapore Tribune* published an "Appeal to Malayan Women" in October 1939, the Czechoslovak women actively responded and joined the Interallied Women's Association of Malaya. *The Straits Times* reported that they – along with French, British and Polish women – collected money to buy wool and gathered every Wednesday to knit warm clothes for the Allied soldiers in Europe.

In one of the more creative events, the Allied women prepared various traditional national costumes and paraded them at the Cyrano's

War Fund Night in July 1940. A Czech woman in national dress is among a group of nine costumed women who appear in a photograph published by *The Straits Times*.

A year later, the Czechoslovak women formed their own charity organisation named The Czechoslovak Ladies Club of Singapore. It had 25 members and collected 120 dollars in two months to buy wool to make clothes for distribution through the Czechoslovak Red Cross in London. The embassy in Mumbai reported that in November and December of 1941, the association produced and shipped 85 pullovers, 20 scarfs, 16 pairs of socks and a blanket, all made of warm wool.

The Bata company in Singapore was a firm supporter of the Czechoslovak government in exile. According to a report by a consular representative in Singapore, in just two years, the combined donations from Bata and its employees amounted to about half a million Czechoslovak crowns – a comparable amount to what Bata contributed to various British charities.

In appreciation, the Czechoslovak Minister of Finance in exile, Mr Outrata, sent a special 'thank you' message to the employees of Bata in Singapore in January 1941. In his letter, he wrote:

> *Dear gentlemen, please accept my sincere gratitude for the donation of 330 sterling to support our international efforts. Your dedication provides great encouragement for our work towards liberation of our country.*

The Batamen responded in poetic language and pathos:

> *We, the Czechoslovaks in Malaya, trust that it is all worth it. The storm of the war will vanish one day, and we unwaveringly believe that the truth and justice will prevail with the victory of the British and Allied armies. And then, the Czechoslovak flag will be raised again above Prague on a fresh, sunny morning and the Czechoslovak people will tear off the Nazi leech from its body. Then we, the Czechoslovaks in the Orient and around the whole world, will increase our efforts to rebuild and organise Czechoslovak industry and businesses both at home and abroad.*

The press reported news on the company at various times, with increased coverage in late 1939, due to the opening of the new shoe factory in Singapore. It was a complete production line, shipped from Zlín, as part of the strategic pre-war transfers.

In October 1939, an article entitled "New Bata Factory Will Start Large Scale Production Soon – Ingenious Machinery for Making Socks", published in the *Malaya Tribune*, provides a very informative overview of the company's plans:

> What will be Malaya's most up-to-date shoe and sock factory is rapidly taking shape in Prince Edward Road, Singapore, where employment will be available for about 200 when the factory runs to full capacity in approximately a month's time.
>
> Production has, in fact, already started, but only manual labour is now employed. Ingenious machinery for stitching and sock manufacturing is being installed, and when these are ready, the factory will commence large-scale production.
>
> This is the second factory to be erected in Malaya by the Bata Shoe Co., Ltd. The first was constructed in Klang where more than 30,000 pairs of rubber shoes are being churned out every week. Present production rate of the Singapore factory is about 500 pairs of leather shoes a week, and these are now largely handsewn. When the machines come into use, this rate is expected to be more than doubled.
>
> Local men are taken and trained by two experts sent out here from Europe. Normally, it takes about a fortnight to train an employee to make him or her useful in some capacity or other. Their skill, of course, increases with experience.
>
> In the manufacture of the shoes, the factory uses only British materials, so that the finished product, turned out by local labour, is 100 percent British.
>
> The factory is well planned, and adjoining it is the company's store, where all dispatches and deliveries by road, sea and rail are attended to with the greatest expediency.

As the Singapore factory commenced full production, there is more coverage in the press. A reporter from *The Singapore Free Press and Mercantile Advertiser* even recalled his conversation with Tomáš Baťa back in 1932 and used his slogan in the title: "Bata's Ambition Expressed in a New Shoe Factory: To Serve Malaya's Five Million Pairs of Feet".

The Straits Times published another piece, packed with more interesting information:

> Shoes are now being manufactured in Singapore by the mass production methods developed by Thomas Bata in the great Czechoslovak factories of Zlin. Bata yearly sells 1,500,000 pairs of shoes in Malaya.
>
> Singapore journalists yesterday visited the new factory of the Bata Shoe Company in Prince Edward Road and saw Chinese trained by Czechoslovak technicians at work on an endless belt unit comprising 35 machines and capable of producing at least 1,000 pairs of shoes a day.
>
> Work that takes an hour by hand is done in a few minutes by the machines, the most modern of their kind. The splendid factory organisation, which includes a special printing department, is a small replica of the system that has made the name Bata world famous.
>
> The company has nearly 990 employees in Malaya, working in sales depots, the rubber shoe factory at Klang, the new Singapore factory, a rubber estate at Kulai, and the head office.
>
> At Klang, girl workers are housed in comfortable dormitories and the food and living conditions are under the care of a woman supervisor. There are facilities for badminton, volleyball and tennis. In Singapore, plans are at hand for a 'Bata colony' where special quarters will be provided for the staff and playing fields, and a swimming pool will eventually be available.

Sadly, the war disrupted these plans, and we can only imagine how this 'Bata colony' might have looked, and to what extent the concept of Zlín would have been replicated in British Malaya.

The war created headache for the management of Bata in Singapore long before the Japanese invaded Malaya and Singapore. Just a few months after the opening of their new factory and a wave of positive publicity, clouds of suspicion and doubt hovered over the firm. The local newspapers reported that the Bata company and its 140 worldwide subsidiaries ended up on the blacklist of the Board of Trade, with the only exceptions being six subsidiaries located in Britain and Allied countries not overrun by Hitler's Germany.

The Malaya Tribune explained in June 1940 that, as a consequence, the British authorities decided to bring the Bata Shoe Co. in Singapore under direct supervision of the Custodian of Enemy Property. The main reason was to avoid 'trading with the enemy' during a time of war. From that moment, all Bata operations in Singapore and British Malaya were officially cut off from the headquarters in Zlín. It was also reported that the supervisors had no intention of interfering with the business of the company, which was explained as a "fine gesture" from the authorities.

This obviously created not just operational challenges, but also a negative publicity that the Bata management in Singapore tried to mitigate. They followed up with media communication and three days later, the *Malaya Tribune* reported that "Bata Shoe Co. Carries On":

> *The information published in the issue of Friday stating that the local Government has appointed a supervisor to control the business of the local Bata Co. does not mean that it is now entirely taken over and controlled by the Government. The local company is not included in the blacklist published recently and the measure taken by the Government is only a precautionary one to see that no dealings are being carried on with business concerns in territories over-run by the enemies, such as Holland, Poland, Czechoslovakia etc.*
>
> *The Bata Shoe Co. in Malaya is carrying on its business as usual. Ever since the commencement of hostilities in September last year, the local company has intensified its programme of local production of footwear. Their factories at Klang and Singapore are producing the rubber and leather shoes that they need for Malaya, this being supplemented by supplies received from British India. The raw materials for the shoes come from Australia, British India and some are obtained from local products.*

The Straits Times also printed a "Position of the Bata Company" which tried to clarify that:

> *The Government has not taken control. Mr Philip Kinsey explained the appointment by the Government of Mr A. J. Kane, formerly the company's auditor, as its supervisor. He wished to correct the impression that the Government had taken control of the company. The appointment of Mr Kane, he said, in no way interfered with the ordinary routine of business and was merely to watch the company's exports from Malaya. He emphasised the loyalty of the European employees to the British Crown.*
>
> *Mr A. Jugas, manager of the sales department of Bata Shoe Company, outlined the extent to which the company had expanded in Malaya, stating that a fortnight ago, its rubber shoe factory in*

> Klang had moved into new premises to enable it to meet the increasing demands for products. He also offered to place the facilities of the company and its expert knowledge at the disposal of the Government should the time come when it was necessary for the Allies to require manufactured goods from their overseas possessions.

This was all very unfortunate, as it also coincided with the opening of the new Bata Building at North Bridge Road. The newspapers advertised that the company would move there by the end of June 1940, and would rent out its old space on Robinson Road, where it occupied three floors with 200 square-metres of space for its offices.

An interesting announcement of a different kind was published at the beginning of August 1940 in *The Straits Times*:

> The Bata Shoe Company is one of the few undertakings in Malaya that shut the doors of its offices, godowns and factories completely for one week each year. From yesterday until 12 August, over 800 of its employees will be on holiday with pay.

The Bata company's holidays however did not necessarily mean complete free time for its employees. As we already know, the workers at Bata were expected – even outside of work – to participate in joint educational, sports or cultural activities. And indeed, we can find small pieces of information about that August – for example, a badminton match between a team of Bata Klang and Malaya Teachers, in which Bata won 5-2. Judging from the names, most of the Bata representatives were the local Chinese, with the exception of Jan Boďa – a Slovak working in Klang.

I also found other press coverage of Bata in relation to sports – dozens of references to a football team that the company established and sponsored in Singapore. It first appeared in the newspapers as 'Bata Shoe F.C.' in 1936, but a year later, changed its name to 'Moravians', with a direct patriotic reference to the Morava region of Czechoslovakia where Zlín is located.

Occasionally, an article would include the list of players and the team setup. It is not surprising that the team comprised both Czechoslovaks and local employees. In the first year, the Czechoslovaks in the line-up included Karel Vytopil, Slavomír Blažek, Josef Bleha, Karel Obruča, Rudolf Kožušníček and Antonín Jugas.

In the late 1930s, when Silvestr was already in town, there was only one Czech name among the Moravians players: the goalkeeper Josef Zuna. I can only speculate that there weren't as many Czechoslovak Batamen involved because such intense physical activity in the tropical weather, to which they were not accustomed to, felt too hard on them.

Glimpses of Everyday Life

In the late 1930s, the Czechoslovak community in Singapore numbered over a hundred people. This is based on my research, after compiling and cross-checking a list from various sources: 45 employees of Bata, 36 of their family members (19 wives and 17 children), and another 43 Czechoslovaks of other backgrounds, who left their own footprint in the local press, beyond Bata-related publicity.

By combining findings from the Singapore newspapers and other documents like personal letters, diary entries and articles written by them, I will attempt to reconstruct – in their own words – the experiences of the Czechoslovaks in Singapore and Malaya.

As we already know, most of the Bata employees who came here from Czechoslovakia were young boys from poor village families; it is therefore not hard to imagine that Singapore was a completely different world for them.

Silvestr was only 19 years old when he arrived in Singapore in March 1939. Shortly after his arrival, he wrote a letter to his parents. In this excerpt, which is the only known document we have of his direct voice, we get a sense of his first impression of Singapore:

> *The city of Singapore lies on an island that is separated by a narrow strait from the rest of the country called Malaya. The inhabitants are mostly Chinese and Indians, but there are also 8,000 British people and 30,000 soldiers here. The main occupation is salesman – these are mostly the Indians; the Chinese are mostly carpenters, blacksmiths, tailors etc. The shops here are organised in such a manner that one street is full of shops selling fabric, another street with stationery, and another street filled with kitchens. Let me tell you more about these kitchens. There are a number of Chinese workers here who do not cook at home, therefore they go to eat out in these kitchens. But it is different from at home, it's not the women but the males who are cooking here [...]*
> *Every European family has its own cook, a boy-servant, a gardener,*

and if it has a car, then also a chauffeur. The houses are built either in a Chinese style or a European style, but almost all of them have flat roofs. They have a nice airport here, a zoological garden, animals of all kinds and a beautiful museum. Singapore is heavily fortified and there are many guns around, but they are hidden, so even the locals do not know where they are located. They also have a great harbour for big ships here. You can see English churches, as well as Chinese temples, even Indian ones – those are the dirtiest of all because every Indian is spitting on the ground, outdoors as well as indoors. A European person can enter only as an exception and has to be barefoot [...] The English as well as the Chinese men dress up in a European style, but their women wear a kind of pyjamas, with trousers and a longer jacket on top. The Indians wrap themselves in clothes similar to a bedsheet and have a towel around their head to wipe the sweat. They also wear clogs that make a terrible noise.

What I find interesting is that young Silvestr, understandably, was referencing what he saw in this foreign land to what was familiar to him back home, thus describing the Chinese women's attire as "pyjamas" and the Sikh turbans as "towels". Other Czechoslovaks have also done the same thing. Here is an excerpt from Josef Vyhnálek's memoir:

Singapore looks like a huge orchard. Nature is green all year round, while some trees drop leaves, their other leaves are just opening. The coconut and oil palms are towering towards the sky and bear fruits all the time. The island is so beautiful.

Vyhnálek continues:

There are nearly a million people living on [the island]. Three-quarters are Chinese who moved here for business. Many Malays then retreated to Java and Sumatra, but some remained in Singapore and live here in the so-called 'campongs'. These are villages in which the natives mostly live by fishing. It is enough for a typical Malay to get a good catch of fish two times a week. This allows him to buy rice for his family, and he can rest for the remaining time. Some Malays here work as taxi drivers, but they are rarely seen in business. Then there are Indians who also moved here for business and work. Singapore is divided into quarters based on nationality. Thus, before the war, it was possible to go on Sundays and visit a Chinese town one week, an Indian town the next week, and then even to a Japanese part of the city.

For the Czechoslovaks who were accustomed to the temperate climate of Central Europe, a major adjustment was the tropical weather: the high temperatures, humidity, thunderstorms and monsoon rains. Many of them complained about how difficult it was to operate in such an environment. The difference in climate did grate on their nerves.

The excerpt below is interesting because it illustrates exactly this. It is a recollection by Josef Kramoliš, who left Singapore after less than a year, following an outburst with his superior. As Kramoliš himself contemplates, this was probably triggered by the fact that his patience had been worn thin by the unbearable tropical weather.

> *The unbearably humid air was increasingly annoying me. In Singapore, your clothes are constantly wet, sticking to your skin. There are daily rains followed by bright sun. Only in the evenings, the weather becomes tolerable.*
>
> *My other troubles are the various animals. I try to repel the insects by smoking but to little effect. The blood-thirsty mosquitoes are all around. When I sleep, I use a protective net, but at least one will somehow find its way in. Also, the house is full of vermin such as lizards, snakes and scorpions. Strangely, my servants are catching and eating them with delight.*

When Silvestr arrived in Singapore at the beginning of 1939, dozens of his Czechoslovak colleagues were already there. The work at the Bata company was no doubt demanding, but there were always weekends spent with friends to look forward to.

From several sources, I gathered that they went to the beaches on nearby small islands, enjoyed the city and sometimes even travelled to Malaya. Silvestr describes this in his letter:

> *We go to the remote islands to swim every Sunday afternoon, taking a small boat to get there. There are very nice sand beaches there, as well as swimming pools going out to the open water. The sea is fenced off by a wire anchored in the seabed and the nets reach out about 100 metres from the shore. The water is six to seven metres deep. We wear blue shorts, white shirts with red silk scarfs around our necks.*

The last remark is interesting as it suggests that the Bata staff had a common 'dress code' even outside of work. The combination of colours – red, blue and white – is also notable as they reflect the colours of the Czechoslovak flag.

Those trips to the beaches were idyllic but also sometimes scary. Josef Vyhnálek shared the following account in his memoir:

> The beauty of the sea is impossible to capture. Imagine coral islands covered with greenery and flowers of all colours. The sea is crystal clear, and along the coastline, you can see through to the clean bottom and colourful coral reefs. A variety of fish, jellyfish and other sea creatures are swimming through. We often go to these islands for a swim. One day, a colleague took along his dog who was excited as we were all swimming in the sea. He swam a bit further and then we heard a loud bark. The dog had submerged, then blood appeared on the surface. He was swallowed by a shark! Imagine how quickly we were running out of the water.

Since Josef Vyhnálek was not only a colleague but also a close friend of Silvestr's, it is very likely that he too experienced this dramatic event.

Apart from the sea and sand, the young Czechoslovaks also enjoyed exploring downtown Singapore after work. This is how Josef Kramoliš remembered it:

> In my spare time, I like to walk to the harbour where the big ocean liners are landing, as well as other ships coming from all corners of the globe. It's very easy to make acquaintance with the passengers who arrive. We had most fun with the Americans. While their ladies are eager to see the sights of Singapore, such as the magnificent botanical gardens, the gentlemen's tastes are somewhat different. They have a hunger for sensation and an unusual interest in local entertainment venues; and they usually have fat wallets [...]
>
> Once, Bleha [Josef Bleha worked for Bata in Singapore during the 1930s as a salesman and later as a deputy store manager] and I got an idea to pretend to be tourists who had just arrived in Singapore and didn't know a word of Malay. We were immediately taken care of by a lively native who offered to show us around and then he was luring us to make a 'very profitable purchase'. In the shop, he told the Malay shopkeeper that he brought two fat cats that deserve to be scammed. I

was having a great time, but Bleha's patience didn't last long – he kicked our Malay guide in his ass and started cursing in Malay. The poor guy blushed and then he quickly disappeared.

Naturally, the young men also enjoyed Singapore's nightlife. Josef Kramoliš recounts:

Singapore also has a lot of garden restaurants where life goes on late into the night and closing time is 2 am. In addition to high-end restaurants and cafés, the city also has a lot of opium-smoking dens and other dubious establishments. Opium can be smoked even in the more luxurious places since it is not officially forbidden. Because I have heard and read a lot about opium, I was curious to experience the intoxicating smell of opium smoke myself.

For this purpose, I chose a remote café and after a hearty dinner, I asked for an opium cigarette, which was promptly brought to me. I paid 200 Singapore dollars for it, but the experience was well worth it. I smoked the entire cigarette slowly, savouring every inhale. While smoking, I felt wonderful. But it got much worse a few hours later when the opium haze started to wane. Soon I was in terrible pain and was not able to move for a long time. The following day, I arrived at work very late. My subordinates probably speculated about the reason, but fortunately, no one ever learnt [the truth]. Of course, I didn't tell anyone about my adventure, and no one accompanied me to witness it. I took away a lesson from this incident and rejected opium smoking from then on.

While there is virtually no documentation of their intimate lives, it is almost certain that many of the Czechoslovaks in Singapore established such relations with the local women. As most of the Bata staff who came from Czechoslovakia were young males, and there were only two or three Czechoslovak single women in the group, it seems almost unavoidable. Interestingly, one of these women – Vlasta Šebová – got married, while in Singapore, to an Englishman named George Tarry in April 1941. The wedding celebration took place at the Seaview Hotel. We know of this because it was mentioned in *The Singapore Free Press and Mercantile Advertiser*, along with the names of some of the guests. It was how I learnt that Silvestr Němec attended the wedding too.

Although records of intimate relationship are sparse, there is indication that Josef Kramoliš was in a serious relationship with a girl – named Mercedes – from a Eurasian family. I also found out that two other Bata employees married locally: one (Oldřich Lebloch) to a Filipino woman and another (František Wakerman) to a Singaporean Chinese partner. Being in inter-racial relationships was probably quite common for the young Czechoslovak men.

Several personal accounts mentioned occasional trips "up country". I have learnt that groups of Bata Czechoslovaks travelled from Singapore to several destinations in Johore, which is the southmost state of Malaya.

Josef Vyhnálek recorded that some of their favourite Sunday trips were to the Kota Tinggi waterfalls. Here, he details a peculiar way they gained access to it:

> *Some 60 kilometres north of Singapore, a landscape of hills and jungles begins. This is also where you can find gorgeous Kota Tinggi waterfalls. We sometimes choose this place for our Sunday trips. The waterfalls are part of a private reserve of the Johore Sultan, and it is only possible to enter with his personal permit. We have therefore been using the opportunities, when he comes to our shoe shop, to ask him for his permission. He has always, very kindly, agreed.*

It seems that Sultan Ibrahim not only frequented the Bata store at North Bridge Road as a customer, but also maintained warm relations with the Bata management. I found a photograph of him in a friendly conversation with the company directors in Singapore.

Another fun activity in Malaya – at least for Bata pioneers such as Josef Kramoliš and Emil Marischler – was the private car races across the peninsula. This was not only mentioned in the memoirs but also surfaced in several photographs from the archive of the Kramoliš family.

Yet another leisure activity enjoyed by Bata's Czechoslovak employees in Malaya were visits to the Kulai plantation when pineapples were being harvested. The archive in Zlín has a group photograph of them standing at the edge of a jungle, holding several fresh pineapples in their arms. The caption reads: "Batamen from Singapore came for a visit to collect pineapples".

These experiences – being in nature and the tropical countryside – must have been magnificent, but Singapore and Malaya were far from being a paradise. In those years, it was a British colony where the white Europeans represented a small but highly privileged segment of society, while the majority of the population was still living in poverty.

At that time, the colonial regime imposed a rigid form of racial segregation, a practice that did not go unnoticed by Vyhnálek:

> There were only about 7,000 English in Singapore before the war, including several thousand military officers. The governmental bureaus were usually run by Englishman, with the rest of the staff being Chinese or mulattoes. The swimming pool was for white Europeans only, all other races were banned from it. The Chinese, however, in retaliation to the British, built their own beautiful swimming pool.

I found similar remarks by other Czechoslovaks in Singapore, as they observed the arrogance and condescending attitude of the British in both civilian life and within the volunteer corps. Some of these quotes will be shared later.

These mentions of attitudes make me wonder about the similarities and differences between the Bata system that they represented and the British colonial rule in Malaya and Singapore. Of course, there were some obvious parallels between the two, like the declared mission to "civilise" poor people and turn them into "better humans".

On the other hand, the vision of Bata originated in a country with no colonial history – if anything, it had itself been colonised by the Austrian Empire for centuries. So, while the pioneers from Bata started to organise shoe production in the British colonies with a setup of a 'white boss' directing and supervising local workers, it seemed more a matter of practicality and convenience than an act of racial segregation. This speculation is supported by the fact that in various sports and cultural activities, the Czechoslovaks mixed freely with the local workers of different nationalities. In some ways, the Czechoslovaks in Singapore must have felt caught in-between two worlds.

Shadows of War

Looming over these accounts of work and social life for the Czechoslovaks in Singapore were the dark, ominous clouds of a war that was fast approaching.

Although World War II did not start in Europe until September 1939, Czechoslovakia was a target of Hitler's aggression much earlier. Claiming that the German minority living mostly in the border areas of Czechoslovakia (known as 'Sudets' or 'Sudeten' in German) were being oppressed, Hitler demanded that the Czechoslovak government cede these territories to Germany. His plan was eventually forced upon Czechoslovakia by the infamous Munich Treaty, in which Hitler agreed on 30 September 1938 with Italian, British and French negotiators – in the absence of Czechoslovak representation – that Germany would indeed annex these lands.

There were several articles published in the Singapore newspapers about these developments. The *Morning Tribune*, at the end of September, also published a direct quote from Winston Churchill: "The partition of Czechoslovakia amounts to a complete surrender by the Western democracies to a Nazi show of force".

This was a major blow for the sovereignty of Czechoslovakia, which must have felt betrayed by its Western allies who, shortsightedly, brokered such a deal in the hope that it would appease Hitler and avert a military conflict with Germany. Churchill, who was at that time in opposition to the British government, said famously to then-Prime Minister Neville Chamberlain: "You were given the choice between war and dishonour. You chose dishonour, and you will have war."

As already mentioned, with the example of Silvestr's hometown of Vémyslice in the previous chapter, the seizing of a significant part of its territories paralysed key infrastructure such as railways and road networks in the country, thus causing future defence of Czechoslovakia against Germany futile, since the massive defence line around its borders was now in German hands. This situation, which brought Czechoslovakia a huge step closer to a full occupation by Germany, naturally made the population very angry and concerned about the future. It was in the light of these developments that Bata decided to accelerate the already mentioned 'transfers' of entire production lines and 'units' of best talents from Zlín abroad. And that's how Silvestr ended up being sent to Singapore.

In Singapore, the Czechoslovaks must have been increasingly worried about the developments in their country and the situation of their families and friends there. I would imagine their mood got even darker when it was announced in November 1938 that the Czechoslovak consulate in Singapore would be closed because "such a decision has been necessitated by the recent events in Europe", as *The Straits Times* put it. The newspapers further reported that the needs of "about 65 Czechoslovaks currently living in Malaya" would henceforth be taken care of by the Czechoslovak consul in Batavia.

At the beginning of February 1939, the newspapers published an update on the situation: the Czechoslovak consulate in Singapore would close at the end of the month and its last day of service would be 15 February. Contrary to the earlier report, the consulate role would be taken over by the Czechoslovak embassy in Calcutta. Such developments must have been very upsetting for Silvestr and his colleagues.

The Straits Times later provided an important detail: the consul Vladimír Polodna, who helmed the consulate from July 1937, was departing Singapore on 2 March aboard the *Conte Biancamano* liner operated by Lloyd Triestino. Given the frequency of passenger ship connections between Singapore and Europe, and the fact that Bata regularly used the liners of Lloyd Triestino to send its employees to Asia, I am almost certain that Silvestr Němec, who left Zlín on 31 December 1938 and boarded one of the Lloyd Triestino ships in Genoa at the beginning of January 1939, travelled on *Conte Biancamano* to Asia while Polodna boarded her as she was returning to Europe.

Shortly after Mr Polodna left, more bad news reached Singapore. On 15 March 1939, Czechoslovakia ceased to exist. Slovakia declared its own independent fascist state, and Hitler's army invaded what was left to accomplish a full occupation of Prague.

When Polodna – who was still on his way to Europe – got the news, he decided to go to France instead of returning to occupied Czechoslovakia. From there, he travelled on to the United States and in October 1942, became a head of diplomatic mission of the exiled Czechoslovak government in Lima, Peru.

Silvestr, who had just arrived in Singapore, could have followed in the local press the news about Hitler's ultimatum and the eventual German invasion and occupation of Czechoslovakia. Imagine, then, how he must have felt when just a day later, the *Malaya Tribune* published a piece quoting the Japanese foreign minister Arita congratulating Ribbentrop, his German counterpart, for the successful occupation of Czechoslovakia.

In March 1939, the newspapers in Singapore also reported the dramatic turn of events in India, where the Czechoslovak consulate in Calcutta was handed over to Germany. However, the consul in Bombay, Ladislav Urban, refused to obey the German occupational authorities and declared his loyalty to the exiled Czechoslovak government in London. Thanks to him, the diplomatic representation of Czechoslovakia in Bombay continued throughout the war, and since it was put in charge of Singapore, its archived documents became another great source of information for my research.

In May 1939, *The Straits Times* reported that 550 Jewish refugees from Europe had arrived in Singapore en route to Shanghai, and about a dozen of them were from Czechoslovakia. In August, readers were informed of a new regulation implemented in Prague, where Jews were forced to wear the yellow star, which forbade them from entering 'Aryan' restaurants, markets and gardens; they could now only use entrances marked with a big sign 'Jewish Company'. The article also stated laconically that pogroms against Jewish shops and their destruction continued in Bratislava, capital of the newly formed Slovak fascist state.

In December 1939, if Silvestr had been reading the *Morning Tribune*, he would have come across an article entitled "Hitler's Threat to Bomb Prague" which reported on the escalation of Nazi terror towards the Czechoslovak resistance against German occupation. Then in April 1940, the same newspaper published this disturbing piece, "Czech Girls at Soldiers' Mercy":

> *Reports have reached the Czech provisional government authorities in Paris regarding several "hundred Czech girls from Moravia" who were "conscripted" by the Nazi authorities. They were first sent to Storm Troop and army barracks to perform menial tasks, and then were thrown over to the mercies of the soldiery and Gestapo agents. Some of the girls have now been sent back to their homes, ill or dying. A number will never return. They were killed by S.S. men.*

It's not hard to imagine how such news was impacting the small Czechoslovak community in Singapore and Malaya. Understandably, some of them decided to do something and not just watch. They were probably encouraged by an article published in *The Straits Times* in January 1940, announcing that "Czechs Plan to Raise New Army in Britain". As a result, several of the young Czechoslovak men decided to return to Europe to fight Hitler. In May 1940, the *Morning Tribune* reported:

> *Mr J. Zuna, who left Singapore shortly after the outbreak of war, is now serving with the Czechoslovak Legion in France. He was formerly*

with the Bata Shoe Co.'s branch as a chiropodist, and was a member of the Moravia Sports Club, being custodian of their goal in the local soccer league matches.

I found out that there were at least two others who did the same. Artur Goldmann, who worked in Bata Shoe Co. in Singapore as a controller of samples, also rushed to France and later served as a commander of an Allied military unit on the European battlefront. After the war, like many other people of Jewish origin, he changed his name to a more neutral one and became 'Artur Gonda'. František Řehoř, a seller-chiropodist colleague of Silvestr Němec, joined the legion in France and after retreating to England, became a RAF pilot in the Czechoslovak squadron 310. Řehoř went missing during a mission at the end of August 1944, quite likely shot down over the Channel.

As for the rest of the Batamen who remained in Singapore, they chose to sign up as volunteers with the local British forces. Most Czechoslovaks registered with the Straits Settlements Volunteer Force (SSVF) or the Local Defence Corps (LDC) in 1940, although a number of them had already joined the volunteers earlier. We read in the November 1940 issue of *The Straits Times* that the "Czechs give fullest support to LDC – no fewer than 31 out of the 50-odd Czechs in Singapore have applied". We will explore this further in the chapter on Singapore Volunteers.

Besides getting ready to fight, the Czechoslovaks in Singapore also organised educational and charity efforts to support their cause. For example, in March 1941, one of them was presenting the story of Czechoslovakia's oppression by German Nazis on the local radio. The segment was entitled "Rape of Czechoslovakia – Last Night's Broadcast from Singapore" and was covered by *The Singapore Free Press and Mercantile Advertiser*:

> The rape of Czecho-Slovakia by the Nazis and the untold torture which thousands of students, young girls and their parents underwent in October 1939, were recalled in vivid detail by a Czech citizen of Singapore in a broadcast talk from the local station last night.
>
> The speaker described how almost two years ago, on 15 March 1939, Hitler trampled down on what had been left of Czecho-Slovakia after Munich and how Nazi soldiers goose-stepped their way through the peaceful streets of Czech and Moravian towns.

> He stressed with special emphasis the riot which took place after the funeral of a Czech student who was killed as a result of the treatment of the Gestapo during the anniversary celebrations of the Czech National Independence Day on 28 October. 1939, and how the Germans, provoking the citizens and students, caused discontent and agitation which was reflected some days later when thousands of Czechs were either killed or arrested and tortured inhumanely by the Nazi beasts.

There had been an earlier broadcast on the situation in Czechoslovakia in December 1939. This was also covered by *The Singapore Free Press and Mercantile Advertiser* in "Singapore Czech Talks to Malayan Listeners":

> With the challenging title 'Czecho-Slovakia Lives!' Mr P. Robitschek, a member of the local Czech community, last evening broadcast a talk from the B.M.B.C.
> "Anyone passing along the Esplanade in Singapore on the morning of 28 October," said Mr Robitschek, "might have noticed a small group of people at the Cenotaph. That group was the Czech community of Singapore, and they were celebrating their national day, the anniversary of the foundation of the Republic of Czecho-Slovakia. Although Czecho-Slovakia is now living under Nazi tyranny, the national spirit of the Czechs is strong and unbroken, and they are only waiting their chance to rise against the German invaders and get back their independence."

Pavel Robitschek was referring to the gatherings of Czechoslovaks which, according to the Singapore press, took place at the Cenotaph in 1939 and in 1940. Detailed information appeared in the newspapers as these celebrations happened. Several articles were accompanied by photographs, showing the small group gathered around the memorial (it's impossible to recognise the individuals, but it's very likely Silvestr was among them), as well as details of the wreath laid by Bata director Václav Rojt, with the assistance of Kvapil and Vodak. Attached was a message in several languages: "Dedicated to Czechoslovakia".

The *Malaya Tribune*, whose reporter counted 40 participants at the event, even quoted a declaration of the local Bata employees:

> On this National Day of the Czech nation, we, the Asiatic staff, extend to you our heartfelt wish that the successful conclusion of the

present war against the Nazi regime may bring with it the speedy restoration of your country to you. May peace and prosperity be yours always. Long live the Czech nation!

This is another example of how I imagine the Czechoslovaks in Singapore being caught between different worlds. It must have had surrealistic dynamics: a community of Czechoslovaks celebrating their relatively new independence from the Habsburg Empire, just as it was being taken away from them by Nazi Germany, while other nations around them were still struggling to gain their own independence from British colonial rule. We don't know what the position of the British authorities was towards such gatherings; they must have at least tolerated them.

The Czechoslovak community also organised a special charity event to raise funds for 'Czechoslovak Forces in Great Britain'. In April 1941, *The Straits Times* mentioned "A Czechoslovak Badge" – initiated by Vilém Zamara, head of Bata's sampling department in Singapore – that could easily be fitted to a car. It could be purchased for 10 dollars at the Bata store or Automobile Association of Malaya. A thousand dollars had already been collected.

The struggle for liberation of Czechoslovakia in the Singapore community was also reflected in an article that appeared on the front page of *The Straits Times* in November 1941. The article included a reproduction of a Czechoslovak underground pamphlet by the resistance movement, which bore the title "*V boj!*" (Into Battle!). Also included was a brief explanation of the Czech resistance movement's slogan: "I will not betray! Death for betrayal".

All these newspaper articles illustrate the young Czechoslovaks' refusal to play a passive role in the war. Even in Singapore, thousands of miles away from home, they found various ways to fight for their country.

But in the shadows of war, fractures within the small Czechoslovak community in Singapore had begun to widen and divide. In trying to reconstruct Silvestr's movements in those last days and the various scenarios of his death, it is important for me to also confront those dark areas.

- VI -
Troubles Within the Community

SINCE I LAUNCHED my blog where I share my journey of reconstructing my granduncle Silvestr's fate, I have been receiving comments and messages from readers. I'd describe these responses as falling into three broad categories. First, those expressing interest, support and sympathy. Second, cynical comments and speculations as to what my true intentions are for embarking on this research and insinuating that I must have some hidden profit-seeking motives. Third, those expressing doubt as to whether digging into the past is worth the effort; perhaps it's better to leave it alone, lest I regret what I find.

If my motivation was to idealise the past, to produce yet another publication full of admiration for Bata or to uncritically celebrate the heroism of the dead, then this would be the point I'd have to think carefully about proceeding as, in the process of mapping the Czechoslovak community and Bata's operation in Singapore, I also came across some disturbing information.

But as I have embarked on this journey with a desire to discover and document the past events as accurately as possible, I cannot omit the following facts, as disappointing – and, for some, as hurtful – as they may be.

This should not come as a huge surprise as we are all human. As such, within the small community of Czechoslovaks in Singapore, there would also have been rivalry, jealousy and mutual denunciation. Involvement in petty crimes also surfaced in my archival search: for example, in December 1938, *The Straits Times* reported a certain Czechoslovak citizen was prosecuted for a theft of 30 dollars from Lim Cheng Liong.

But more importantly, the archives of the Czechoslovak government exiled to London contain a number of documents showing that the Czechoslovak community in Singapore was painfully divided into two fiercely antagonising groups.

The first and larger faction consisted mostly of the Bata employees and was led by the company's local director Václav Rojt. The second faction was composed of Czechoslovaks who came to Singapore for other reasons – they were independent merchants or representatives of other companies, such as Skoda or *Československá Zbrojovka* (Czechoslovak Arms Production Factory). This second group was led by Richard Reiser, a former co-owner of the *První Pražská Sladovna* (The First Prague Malt Factory) who was sent to Singapore in 1935 by the Czechoslovak Export Institute, but later worked independently as an agent of other companies. Reiser also worked closely with the British security agents and, at the beginning of the war, agreed upon request of the British authorities to work for them as a censor.

The tension between the factions escalated after the Czechoslovak consulate in Singapore was closed in February 1939. It seems that Rojt from Bata then started to liaise with the Singapore government on behalf of the whole Czechoslovak community. This was disliked by those close to Reiser, who then sent several complaints against Rojt to Mr Urban at the Czechoslovak consul in Bombay. In response, Urban informed the London-based government in November 1940 that:

> Mr Reiser, together with some other Czechoslovaks, submitted a grievance petition addressing the Czechoslovak government via the British secretary in Singapore. They request that an official representative of our government carry out a formal investigation of their complaints against Mr Rojt.

The archive of the exiled Czechoslovak Ministry of Foreign Affairs holds several documents related to the disputes within the Czechoslovak community in Singapore. One of them, dated early 1941, reads:

> The consulate holds an opinion that it cannot step into the affairs that fall formally under the British jurisdiction – a position we fully support. The Bata company is employing Czechoslovak citizens who, according to the consulate, joined or support the resistance, all enrolled [in the military service] and make financial contributions to our war efforts. There is therefore no reason to act against them.

Subsequently, in February 1941, the Ministry sent instructions to the consulate in Bombay saying:

> *The Czechoslovak government has no intention to deal with the affairs of the Bata company because we have no authorisation to deal with matters under the British jurisdiction. As for the personal conflicts within the Czechoslovak community, it is up to the consulate to use its influence to reconcile those.*

The consulate in India subsequently decided to dispatch one of its employees, Josef Luley, to Singapore to act as its official agent. Mr Luley reached Singapore in March 1941 and remained there till early February 1942. In a report, he stated that:

> *By the time the Japanese army started to attack only 11 miles away, south of the Johore Strait, I had already lost my hopes to be able to evacuate. However, I was lucky and managed to get onboard a military transport ship in the night from 6 to 7 February.*

One of the issues that Luley faced was the case of 12 Czechoslovak volunteers who arrived in Singapore from Shanghai. They were initially accommodated with Australian soldiers at Bidadari, but shortly after, the British authorities interned them on St John's Island, which was used as an internment camp for subjects of the German Nazi Empire. This is because Czechoslovakia – which, at that point, had been broken to pieces and occupied by the Nazi army – was a German dominion. As such, its citizens were likely regarded as enemies of the British.

An interesting and related fact: this was also how Helmut Newton, who later became a famous photographer, ended up there. He reached Singapore in 1938 as a Jewish refugee from Germany, but was interned when Britain declared war on Germany, since he carried a German passport. In September 1940, Newton was deported to an internment camp in Australia.

Of the 12 Czechoslovak volunteers, some continued to the Middle East, while several others were stuck in the internment camp. Luley, through his intervention with British officials, succeeded in having these Czechoslovaks released. They were allowed to move freely in Singapore before joining their companions at the Middle East front.

While Luley was successful in that negotiation, he failed entirely in his mission to reconcile the Czechoslovaks in Singapore. Perhaps one of the reasons was that he did not arrive as a genuine independent mediator but was perceived to be partial to the Bata company and its interests. Records suggest that it was Bata's director in India, Jan Bartoš, who initially requested that the Bombay consulate dispatch Luley to Singapore. The company had paid for all his expenses from the very start. As consul, Urban reported back to London:

> For the start, I have used the 5,000 Indian rupees that were confidentially provided by Jan Bartos, the director of Bata Shoe Company in Batanagar [...] The whole amount was given to our consular agent, Luley, as cash advance. He already used part of it to pay for the travel of himself and his family.

Consul Urban was aware that such an arrangement was inappropriate, and came up with a proposal to the government to cover it up:

> In order to diminish the controversy of the financial dependency of Luley on the Bata company, I propose that Luley will continue to be paid through the general consulate in Bombay, while we agree with Bata company that it will be sending contributions to a war fund that will be at least equal to the cost of Luley and his operation.

A copy of this proposal is kept in the archives with an additional note: "Passed on to the Minister who agreed".

Today, this would be a textbook example of corruption by a state institution accepting corporate money. It's however quite likely that the exiled government did not have enough resources to afford Luley's mission. In my opinion, the circumstances of war provide a different perspective on this act. It was still better, for all Czechoslovaks, to have some biased representation in Singapore than none at all.

And so, the conflicts continued. The Czechoslovak community made several attempts to establish an association but failed as a result of disagreements over its bylaws and the candidates for its Chair. At some point, Reiser went ahead and established a Czechoslovak Association with just his own followers. According to the reports collected by the Ministry, it had about 33 members. The creation of Reiser's Czechoslovak Association was even covered in the Singapore press in April 1941.

Bata director Rojt then ordered his employees to stay away from that association, which he dismissed as "a bunch of Jews" [When I came across several names of its members in the documents, it indeed appears that many of them were of Jewish origin]. Reiser responded by relentlessly recruiting members from Bata employees. He was targeting, in particular, those who had conflicts with the Bata management or were fired from their jobs at Bata.

According to the files, several employees of Bata became 'secret members' of the association: there are mentions of Rudolf Janeček and Karel Vítek being among them. I am sharing their names here because it opens a possibility that Silvestr, too, joined Reiser's association. I have two reasons for this assumption: first, he was probably a very close friend of the two, as they jointly signed up for the Straits Settlements Volunteer Forces as a trio: Vítek was registered as Private No. 13777, Janeček as 13778 and Němec as 13779. Second, Silvestr was among those employees who repeatedly got into conflict with director Rojt.

Two independent witnesses, whose statements were collected by the exiled Ministry, said that the Bata management in Singapore was withholding part of the salaries of their staff. Here is one of these statements that not only describes the practice but also explicitly names Silvestr Němec as one of the employees who protested:

> The employees of Bata arrived in Singapore before the occupation of Czechoslovakia [by Nazi Germany] and based on their contracts made in Zlín, but the local Singapore management refused to acknowledge these and forced them to sign local contracts instead, with lower salaries. In order to force them to agree, they were being threatened by statements like "we will send you back to Hitler". The new arrivals, mostly single young men, then filed a complaint with the British Immigration Office. The British government put in place a regulation that required Bata to pay a minimal wage of 60 dollars weekly. However, Bata management was bypassing it via a sophisticated scheme that left its employees with 30-35 dollars only. They did it by transferring the salaries to their private accounts, and when the balance reached 1,000 dollars, the employees had to either return 500 dollars back to the company or donate it to the Czechoslovak War Fund. The management was justifying this practice by arguing that the staff "do not have a right to this money" and that the company had to pay it to

them "only because of the stupid British regulation". Several employees refused to give their money back and were subsequently fired (Zuna, Řehoř, Wakerman, Ambrož, Janeček, Němec, Sedláčková and others).

Does this mean that Silvestr really left Bata while he was in Singapore? It would be unwise to rush to conclusions based on just one testimony; however, I did collect more evidence to suggest that he indeed lived on his own for several months at the end of 1941. We will come to that soon enough.

Another well-documented conflict between some of the Bata employees and the company's management in Singapore was triggered by their involvement with the Volunteer Forces. It was likely that the Bata company encouraged its employees to apply, perhaps not so much for patriotic reasons but for improving its profile in the eyes of British authorities.

As such, the Bata directors would have been caught by surprise when they were informed that all volunteers had to undergo a two-month training camp in the spring of 1941, and that the company was expected to pay them their salaries in full. Again, the management refused. And again, the frustrated Bata volunteers complained to the Colonial Secretary. One of them, Vilém Zamara, reportedly took legal action and filed a lawsuit against them. It's safe to assume that Silvestr was also involved in this dispute, and that was probably when he lost his job.

After these 'troublemakers' were fired by the Bata management, they sought support from Reiser's association (this is another indication that Silvestr might have been affiliated with it, possibly as a 'secret member'). Around September or October 1941, Bata director Bartoš arrived from India and offered them new positions at the Batanagar branch, on condition that they withdraw their complaint. According to a statement by Erich Lachs, "the volunteers refused to revoke the truth".

You may recall that Erich Lachs was referenced as a source for claiming that "Silvestr was in Singapore in 1943" – as captured in the *List of Employees Overseas* in Zlín. Now we finally learn more about who he was: Lachs was sent by Bata to Singapore in December 1938 as head of production and sales of stockings. Once in Singapore, he left the company and started to work for Thomas Cook. He was evacuated to Durban on 10 February 1942, which confirms that his "1943" statement was probably a mistake and that Silvestr's record should have said 1942.

I also found another confirmation of the fact that several young men were fired by Bata Shoe Co. in Singapore around the middle of 1941. Viktor Koš, who was the financial director there, wrote in his detailed diary the following entry:

> [The immigration officer] knew director Bartoš from his last visit to Singapore in October 1941. Back then, Mr Bartoš visited him to ask for visas for several young men who were to be transferred from Singapore to Batanagar and were causing some troubles; they did not want to accept the Batanagar positions."

Highly relevant is another note in the diary of Koš:

> Several days before 8 December 1941, the volunteers were mobilised. Among them were seven of our employees and four former employees.

Given that Koš was a meticulous accountant and that he wrote down his memories in detail after escaping to Medan in 1943 (while his memories were still fresh), we can treat this as a reliable piece of information. In his diary, several pages later, he lists all 11 names: R. Kožušníček, L. Mráz, E. Matuš, H. Bohman, S. Jedovnický, J. Vyhnálek, A. Čepka, S. Němec, P. Ambrož, R. Janeček and V. Zamara. It is very likely, in the light of the other testimonies, that Silvestr was among those "four former employees", along with Rudolf Janeček and Karel Vítek. We can guess who the fourth was: possibly Pavel Ambrož, another close friend of Silvestr's.

Another document suggesting that Silvestr Němec was not a Bata employee came in the form of a telegram that Antonín Jugas sent to Zlín on 16 October 1945. When updating the Bata headquarters about the state of affairs in Singapore, he listed all who survived, were dead or went missing "from our staff", and five names were left out: Ambrož, Janeček, Němec, Vítek and Vyhnálek. This suggests that he no longer considered them "his staff" and that they had indeed left the company before the Japanese Occupation.

I therefore take it as certain that Silvestr left Bata Shoe Co. around the third quarter of 1941, meaning that he spent the last couple of months before the mobilisation on his own. This would fit perfectly with another discovery I made, which is that his last-known address was in the newly built social apartments at Tiong Bahru. It is very unlikely that Bata employees would live there – I learnt from Vyhnálek's memoirs that he was accommodated in bungalows at Chancery Lane upon arrival in 1939. The same apartment at Tiong Bahru where Silvestr lived was shared by another 'rebel', Rudolf Janeček, and (speculating from a clue in one of his letters) quite possibly Pavel Ambrož.

One thing we know for sure is that Silvestr Němec was among those employees of Bata Shoe Co. who found themselves repeatedly in conflict with its director Václav Rojt.

Based on all the information that I collected, it seems that Rojt was indeed a very difficult person to deal with. According to several other memoirs of Bata managers – including that of already familiar Josef Kramoliš – he was a choleric man, whose trademark was rudeness towards his subordinates and a tendency to fire people on the spot for showing any disagreement. I came across other books by Inocenc Krutil and Josef Vaňhara that all portray Rojt as a rough manager who shouted and swore a lot at others.

Together with Jan Novosad, Václav Rojt is repeatedly mentioned as the least favourite boss at Bata. However, due to his loyal service from the early years of the Bata company, he belonged to the innermost circle of Tomáš Baťa. Rojt joined Bata before World War I and contributed to some major achievements in shoe production in the early years. In his personal files at the Zlín archives, I even found a letter of appreciation from Tomáš Baťa, dated 14 September 1929, where he expressed his gratitude to Rojt for the "extraordinary zeal shown during the protection of our factory against a devastating fire". Judging from their strong bond, we should therefore not be surprised that Rojt's problematic side was tolerated by the leadership of the company.

Rojt's explosive and uncivilised behaviour could probably be attributed to his lack of education: although he climbed the corporate ladder to the top – due to his dedication and hard work – he was still only a graduate of an elementary school. When he was 50 years old, he left the position of Director of the shoe production department in Zlín and moved to Kotva, one of the subsidiary companies of Bata that was organising its exports. The occupation of Czechoslovakia happened while he was on an inspection trip to the Far East, and subsequently he decided to stay there and not return to Zlín. Around the middle of 1939, he was promoted to the position of Director of Bata Shoe Co. in Singapore.

Now we can understand even better that with his personality and temper, Rojt could have easily ended up firing a number of otherwise loyal Bata employees in Singapore. I imagine Silvestr, being highly adaptable, was capable of coping with the many challenges of working for Bata – after all, only a select few were sent to Singapore. But even Silvestr's ability to tolerate injustice from the management had its limits. At some point, the proverbial straw that broke the camel's back happened and Silvestr decided to fight back.

It is quite possible that this final trigger came with a severe misconduct that Rojt committed in Singapore. This is a case that is very well substantiated by documents from the Zlín archives.

Václav Rojt, a widower, was a sexual predator who harassed several wives of his Bata employees in Singapore. There is a well-documented incident where he assaulted Mrs Ondruššková in April 1939 when her husband had returned to Singapore from Manila (after working for the local branch of Bata there) and the couple was provided temporary accommodation at the Bata Building in Singapore. It did not take long before a conflict ensued between Mr Ondruššek and director Rojt, following which Rojt fired him. When Mr Ondruššek broke the bad news to his wife, she confessed to him that a few days earlier, Rojt had come to their apartment above his office and made her an indecent proposal, promising her that he would in turn provide her husband a good future at Bata. However, she slapped him and made him leave. Learning this, Mr Ondruššek created a big internal scandal, sending a telegram to Zlín followed by a long letter, in which he threatened to take legal action and demanded that the company arrange for their return to Zlín immediately.

What's worse is that this case was not an isolated one. Similar complaints about Rojt's behaviour were sent to Zlín by Josef Bartoš and František Řehoř. As such, the management in Zlín became very concerned and noted:

> *There are more people who left us because of Rojt [...] His branch is falling apart since he tried to indulge in intimacy with Mrs Ondruššková. The Ondruššek couple is now back in Zlín and seem to be alright. However, there are more consequences of Rojt's blindness that will continue to undermine his position.*

I even found a record of a direct instruction by Jan Antonín Baťa on how to deal with Rojt's unacceptable behaviour:

> *We will need to do something to help Rojt in Singapore. From what we know from the letter of Řehoř, and earlier from Ondruššek, it is likely that the affair will grow wider [...] The best would be if Rojt finds a new wife. I am really tired of his endless lechery towards the wives of our people. I don't know how much longer I can bear it, despite his excellent sales results. I can't let him go wild and conflict with our principles. I can't allow him, one of the highest positioned directors, to be seen as an exception to the rule. Women are sacrosanct in our company. And so, we must prepare for a scenario where Rojt may be forced to step down from his position; something I would regret as he has performed very well. Mr Chief.*

In the end, no further action was needed as Václav Rojt died in July 1941, at the age of 56, probably from a heart attack. This news was covered in all English newspapers in Singapore. From more detailed reports of his funeral, we know that the ceremony took place at the Cathedral of the Good Shepherd and that he was buried at Bidadari cemetery. What's more, *The Straits Times* included a list of attendees of his funeral, and from that list, we found out that Silvestr Němec was present. This was the third and last mention of his name in the Singapore press (the other two we have already mentioned: Silvestr being a donor to the War Fund, and him attending the wedding celebration of Vlasta Šebová at the Seaview Hotel).

There is just one more incident of Bata's management in Singapore that I'd like to mention, and this eventually led to a formal prosecution and court verdict. Director Rojt apparently bribed one of the colonial censors who was checking the incoming and outgoing mail for the British colonial authorities. The censor, named Kwasigroch, was of Polish origin and was in-charge of correspondences in Slavic languages. He unlawfully read all the letters of the Bata employees and reported their contents to Rojt. This was exposed one day, when the censor and the Bata management withheld official documents related to a legal complaint filed by Mr Vaníček, one of Bata's ex-employees from Hong Kong. At the court hearing, director Rojt pleaded guilty, and the censor was sentenced to three months' jail.

In Rojt's defence, it should also be noted that, in this last case, spying on employees was probably not his personal initiative. When I was going through details of Bata's operations, it became clear to me that maintaining a network of informers, and monitoring employees and their activities, was common in Zlín. In 1938, Bata installed gramophone-based devices to record important meetings, as well as a system to tap into phones and listen to conversations of employees. Such practices were not uncommon in other companies too.

My final reflection on these troubles within the Czechoslovak community is that we need to see them in a wider historical context.

It was very sad and embarrassing for me to learn that my compatriots resorted to squabbling and playing dirty tricks on each other. As the Czechoslovak community was small – just over a hundred people – the scale of the problem was magnified. Even the exiled Czechoslovak government had to deal with it, and they were undoubtedly facing very different priorities and challenges in a time of war. But to my surprise, I found other documents in the archives of the Czech Ministry of Foreign Affairs, which revealed that other Czechoslovak communities – such as those in Shanghai and South Africa – were ridden with similar tensions and troubles. So, it appears that the discords in Singapore were not an exception.

Having said that, we must consider the psychology of a situation where a handful of mostly young, inexperienced people suddenly found themselves in a totally unknown and strange environment. They must have been challenged by the language barrier, cultural differences, humid weather and anxieties about what was going on in Europe: escalation of hatred against the Jews, rise of Nazi Germany, collapse of Czechoslovakia and just the overall uncertainty of the times, which raised concerns for their families back in the occupied motherland. Taken together, these events must have triggered anger, frustrations, tensions and divisions within the community of Czechoslovaks. After Hitler's occupation of their motherland, several members of the Czechoslovak community in Singapore even declared their loyalty to Nazi Germany and requested German passports!

I have a conflicting view on the Bata company and the actions of its management. On the one hand, I fully appreciate how the company provided unique opportunities to thousands of children from poor countryside families (particularly during the economic depression), offering them not just good jobs but also a decent education, decent salaries, care and career possibilities. It was in the business of providing good quality shoes at affordable prices to the masses and had proven its ability to innovate and compete across continents.

On the other hand, it demanded hard work and unconditional

loyalty. It perpetuated a highly competitive system where those who could not keep up were promptly replaced. Its management put Bata's success and interest above all, even willing to compromise integrity by spying on its employees or resorting to corruption. The management however was not, in most cases, driven by selfish personal interests but by Bata's vision and ideology of a greater good. Their wrongdoings cannot be excused – especially not personal misbehaviour like that of Rojt – but at least we can understand their company culture better.

Lastly, I also found some reconciliation in the fact that once the war arrived in Malaya and Singapore, and especially during the horrors of internment in the Japanese camps, the Czechoslovaks came together again and demonstrated solidarity and mutual support. That is another chapter of the bigger story of Czechoslovaks in Singapore, yet to be explored.

But first, before we delve into the impending war, we will segue into the reason for Silvestr's presence in Singapore in the first place – his assigned role as a pedicurist for Bata.

- VII -
Silvestr's Vocation

WHAT WE KNOW for sure is that from September 1936 to December 1938, Silvestr worked for Bata as a seller – a position he assumed when he was just about to turn 16. When he was sent to Singapore, it was as a pedicurist. Naturally, I had a lot of questions about what a seller or pedicurist did in a structured and well-organised company like Bata.

Learning the Art of Shoe-Selling

The growth of Bata in Czechoslovakia was staggering. In 1918, when World War I ended, Bata had just 18 stores. By the time Silvestr was recruited, the distribution network in the country had grown to more than 2,000 shops. Tomáš Baťa formulated his ambition with these words: "Every town and village that has a church and police station must also have a Bata shop".

Since Vémyslice – Silvestr's hometown – met the criteria, it is possible that Silvestr started his career at Bata right there, or in the nearby city of Moravský Krumlov. I managed to find an old photograph of a Bata shop in Vémyslice, likely taken during the German occupation as the signboard was in both Czech and German; but whether Silvestr actually worked there remains unknown. He could have started working in or near his hometown, and someone took notice of his talent, or perhaps he applied for the job directly in Zlín.

We get a sense of Silvestr's journey through the story of Václav Sklenář documented by Judita Matyášová in her diploma thesis:

> This is how Marie Zemanová described her father's beginnings at Bata: "My dad grew up in the family of a farmer, in the smallest

cottage of Rovné pod Řípem. His mother was at home taking care of the household while his father worked in the fields as well as in a factory to make a living. We had an elementary school in our village. After my dad finished school, he joined Bata at the age of 13. He started working at a shop in Roudnice and worked there for three-and-a-half years, after which he was invited to come to Zlín."

Marie's sister, Hana Gregorová, added: "He learnt everything related to selling shoes in the Roudnice shop. Very often he was tasked with accounting because he was very good with numbers. One day, an inspector from Zlín arrived and when he saw our dad and how well he works, he offered him to come to Zlín."

A typical Bata store employed four people. The smaller shops were usually run by a single manager assisted by his wife. Shop managers were part of the company's scheme – to have them co-share profit and loss. As with other parts of the Bata organisation, each shop had its own detailed plans of projected sales – these were called 'assumptions'. They were calculated on a weekly basis, which was also the stipulated period for cash income from sales and inventories of goods to be collected. If the manager exceeded his 'assumptions', he would receive a proportional bonus. However, if his sales were below the target, he had to pay a fine.

The pressure to perform was therefore substantial. I managed to get my hands on a Bata manual for shop managers from that era; it even explicitly says:

> What do you do when sales are weak during the low season? There is no such thing as a 'low season' or a 'weak day' for a good seller. A good manager will always find a way to turn a weak day into a strong day, and a low season into a high season.

The key to success was, however, not quantity of sales but quality of service. This entailed giving full attention to the customer, providing expert advice, keeping the shop clean and tidy, ensuring well-arranged shop windows and making smart investments in advertising. These were stipulated requirements for every Bata store. Such standards were closely monitored by special district inspectors who came by regularly to also inspect their accounting books and inventories. Usually, each Bata inspector was assigned about 30 stores, so they probably turned up about once a month.

To get a better sense of Silvestr's job, we can look at this description of an 'ideal seller' from Bata's educational poster:

> *This is what an exemplary seller looks like:*
> 1. *Carries all accessories – such as measure, shoe spoon and others – in his right pocket.*
> 2. *Maintains a small notebook to take daily notes and to help him make sure that every issue is quickly addressed and dealt with.*
> 3. *Takes any excess items out of his pockets.*
> 4. *Keeps the storage filled with up-to-date sortiment [range], shoe boxes clean from dust, and every pair of shoes wrapped in paper.*
> 5. *Always wears clean clothes and perfect shoes, has cropped hair, is shaved and smiling, making it clear to the customers that they are being served by an expert.*
>
> *A seller that is not only focusing on quantity, but has the service to customers as a priority, will end up selling more.*

One of the instructions to sellers was to ask customers for their address and other personal information, and to keep these records systematically in a filing cabinet. Good shop managers would then use the data to send them special offers, as well as card-notes for their birthdays. In this way, Bata managed to collect over a million of its customers' personal records by 1932.

I have also learnt that newly hired sellers underwent a two-week standard course, during which they learnt all the necessary procedures and instructions of the job. We can picture the routine of a Bata seller through this account by Inocenc Krutil in *Unusual Experiences of Bata Exporter*:

> *I improved as a seller and became a winner of our competition. One busy Saturday, when I was assigned three chairs in our shop and all customers who sat on them became my responsibility, I made 102 sales in an hour, which was my life record. We were using the system of a 'comprehensive offer' – meaning that when a pair of shoes was being sold, we also offered our customers the shoe cream and other accessories, as well as repair of old shoes, and finally, a pedicure treatment. It was a complex procedure, not to mention the drawing of the customer's foot contour on a special paper to be added to his personal file in our filing cabinet.*

One of the interesting documents I found in the Zlín archives was a contemporary brochure, "Seller's Manual", which is 70 pages long and accompanied by a manual titled *The Roadmap to 100% Success – Tips for Sellers*.

I found it quite amusing probably because I was reading it with today's eyes. The introductory section provides a theoretical framework for selling shoes. There are statements like: "Who is the seller? A person who finds his existential legitimacy and the basis of his living in the fact that people need to wear shoes and have their feet healthy."

The theory is illustrated with examples from real life. For example, the principle that "the customer is always right" is followed by this short story:

> *A female seller was arguing with a customer because of some misunderstanding. She was trying to convince him that she was right, and she would have succeeded if it weren't for the intervention of the shop manager. Thanks to him, the shop retained a customer who otherwise would be lost due to the unwise seller.*

The famous Bata slogan "Our Customer – Our Master" was found on the walls of many Bata shops, including the one at Capitol in Singapore. It's visible in old historical photographs of the store's interior from the 1930s.

Another expectation of the sellers was that their external appearance had to be perfect. This emphasis is illustrated in yet another story:

> *In one of our shops, the manager had to sell the customer the very shoes that the manager was wearing because the customer thought that they were better than the same pair being brought to him from the storage. This is proof of how important it is that the seller always has shiny shoes that are in perfect condition.*

Besides being packed with these slightly bizarre stories, the brochure also includes specific guidelines on how to approach different customer archetypes: 'indecisive', 'inflammatory', 'talkative', 'accompanied by friends', 'factory worker', 'village woman', 'demanding city woman' or 'child'.

Of interest is the accompanying manual which is divided into 10 chapters. At the end of each chapter is a table used for scoring one's level of knowledge on a particular subject. It is quite likely that this was used during the initial training course of new sellers – and I couldn't help but imagine Silvestr using that very textbook when he started his work at Bata. Judging from the components, it seems that every seller had to master a broad range of knowledge: from sales operation and expert terminology to management of repairs, pedicure, shop window dressing, advertisement, and preparation of the weekly plans.

Learning the Art of Chiropody

For the story of Silvestr Němec, it is important to pay attention to a milestone in Bata's operation: the introduction of pedicurist (or chiropodist) care in 1929. Bata began to develop this service with the help of doctors and health specialists who had started working at the Bata Hospital in Zlín two years earlier.

Searching on the Internet, I came across a dissertation paper written by Barbora Mikošková in 2009 at the Tomáš Baťa University in Zlín. She included some information about the history of foot care in the Bata company and this is how she described its beginnings:

> *With growing experience in the area of anatomically designed shoes, the company was facing the need to better educate its workers. A special training was prepared for designers, shoemakers, salesmen and everyone who had something to do with orthopaedic aspects. Initially this was being organised by Dr Albert, however later, Dr Račanský took over. He was regularly publishing educational articles in the weekly magazine for Bata employees.*

Mikošková's paper also captured this key milestone:

> *An important step in setting up the educational activities was taken by Dr Račanský when he established a cooperation with the Orthopaedic Clinic of the Charles University in Prague, namely its chief, Dr Tobiášek. Dr Tobiášek conducted a course from 21 to 30 March 1929, and Dr Račanský attended, along with 10 other Bata employees.*

To raise the qualification of their sellers and specialists in chiropody, Bata not only offered them training but also published a special textbook written by Dr Račanský. Given that Silvestr became a pedicurist by

LEFT: *A photo of a rubber plantation in British Malaya as it was presented to the Bata directors in Zlín in 1935.*

BOTTOM LEFT: *In 1936, Bata purchased and started to manage its own rubber plantation at Bukit Tiga in southern Johore. It had 1,800 acres and 120,000 rubber trees.*

LEFT: *Bata employees from Singapore visiting the Bukit Tiga rubber plantation harvesting pineapples that were grown as a transitional crop after the jungle was cleared and before rubber trees were planted.*

BELOW: *A Bata advertisement in Jawi included in the comprehensive business report from British Malaya dated 1935.*

BOTTOM LEFT: *The Bata store at Capitol Theatre, 1943.*

Příklad uspořádání kabiny:

ABOVE: *The prescribed layout of the pedicure cabins at Bata shoe stores from the company's textbook by František Kocourek. It is safe to assume that Silvestr used this book during his pedicure training.*

RIGHT: *A Bata advertisement promoting pedicure care provided to customers of its shoe stores in Singapore.*

FAR RIGHT: *A photograph of Antonín Baťa receiving a pedicure treatment to advertise the pedicure services offered at Bata stores in Czechoslovakia and overseas.*

Pedikura má býti instalována podle možnosti tak, aby měla dostatek denního světla. Je-li z technických důvodů vyloučeno, pak je nutným osvětlení umělé o dostatečné síle.

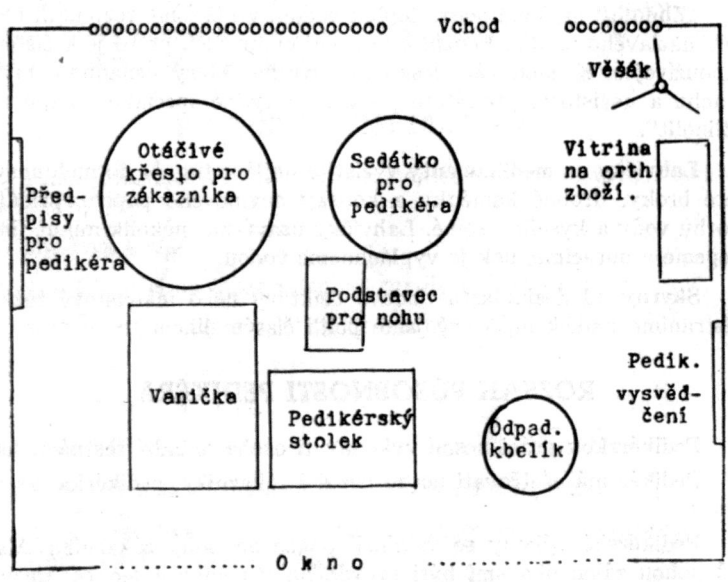

Uspořádání zařízení v kabině.

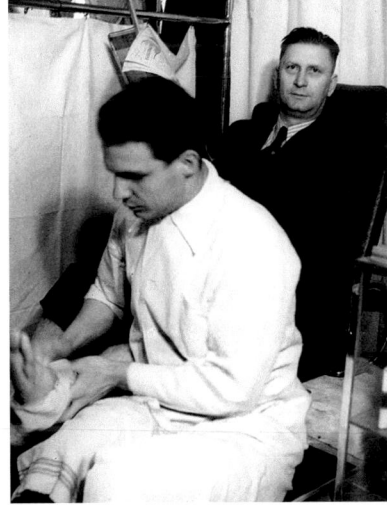

A sample of Bata shoe shops in British Malaya. This collection was part of a business intelligence report about British Malaya written in 1935 for the Bata headquarters in Zlín. The slogan "Our Customer - Our Master" is one of the most famous credos that people in the Czech Republic recall even today in relation to Bata.

Bata

KATONG STORE

LEFT: *Bata Shoe Co. opened its new office building on North Bridge Road, near Capitol Theatre, in June 1940. Peninsula Plaza now stands on the spot.*

BELOW: *Czechoslovak Bata managers kept good relations with important figures of Malayan political and societal life. Here, Antonín Jugas hosts Sultan Ibrahim of Johore, a regular customer of Bata's flagship store on North Bridge Road.*

profession, we can assume that he had a copy of it.

As such, let's take a closer look at what Mikošková said about the textbook in her dissertation:

> *The handbook contained facts about anatomy and healthcare of human feet, along with recommendations of procedures and suggestions to salesmen on how to use it to attract regular clients who would then keep buying Bata products. The shoe stores thus began to offer a broad range of services. The salesmen were trained to offer assistance and if necessary, facilitate a health check of customers' feet by a proper doctor who was also available at the store. A chiropodist provided consultation and treatment. If necessary, he or she also advised on orthopaedic shoe adjustments and aids. One of the services available was a foot massage – an enjoyable and relaxing experience for the customer.*
>
> *A common standard at every larger Bata shop was a pedicure treatment. The salesmen were encouraged to convince their customers of the benefits of regular and preventive foot care. The first step was not easy; however, once the clients overcame the initial embarrassment, they often became regular visitors.*

The training sessions were initially led by Dr Račanský in a classroom at the Bata Hospital. If we take his textbook as a reference, then the standard pedicure procedure offered at Bata shops looked like this:

1. Wash clean and dry customer's feet.
2. Painlessly, without causing bleeding, remove the hardened skin, calluses and corns. Prior to the intervention, ensure that a proper disinfection is applied.
3. Disinfect the nails all around.
4. Irradiate the feet with a blue-filter lamp for 5 to 10 minutes.
5. Provide a thorough massage of the feet using a foaming soap, perhaps add a bit of physio-therapeutic movements, and refresh with a massage rub.

Should the chiropodist accidentally cause an injury to the client, the shop manager was obliged to arrange a doctor's check and write down a protocol about the incident.

In the first year – that is, 1929 – Bata trained 81 pedicurists. Just four years later, in 1933, it already had more than 2,000 trained specialists. Because the training required a full-time instructor, František Kocourek took over from Dr Račanský. I was lucky enough to meet Mr Kocourek's grandson, Jakub Neradílek, who keeps a big suitcase of hundreds of photographs and other documents related to his grandfather's chiropody work at Bata. Some of these materials became very useful for my research.

Mr Kocourek wrote a practical guide for feet care: it was 80 pages long and probably a key reference used in his courses. It explains in detail the setup and equipment of a chiropodist's workplace and uses many pictures to illustrate the step-by-step procedure. I was browsing through an original print of it when I was at the Zlín archives and felt a special connection with my granduncle Silvestr, whom I imagine was holding the same book in his hands too.

It is possible that Silvestr underwent chiropodist training while he was working as a seller for Bata somewhere in Czechoslovakia, although the *List of Employees Overseas* only mentions pedicurist job in relation to his new mission in Singapore. It is, however, also true that a number of sellers at Bata were simultaneously trained to offer chiropody care.

The timing of Silvestr's transfer to Singapore in December 1938 seemed to coincide with the period when Bata was introducing this new customer service in India. The November 1938 issue of *Batanagar News* had a frontpage article under the headline, "Creation of a New Profession – An Opportunity for Hundreds of Surgeons and Experts". The article appealed to and invited Bata employees in India to sign up for training in this new qualification:

> Every pedicurist, being our best salesman, will be a specialist and expert in the profession. Therefore, he will also receive wages suited to his responsibilities. Even though we are now just developing the line of chiropody, we can already see their high wages and the possibility of earning and bettering their positions. For instance, in the Bata Shop in Chowringhee, Calcutta, the chiropodist is getting an average weekly salary of Rs. 22 to 28. To reach this and even higher income is not a problem for any pedicurist in any place, when he sees in his work the best fillip to his life and when his work will have the spirit of 'service to public'.

On page six of the same edition of the weekly *Batanagar News*, I found an English translation of a speech on chiropody that Jan Antonín

Baťa delivered to the employees. Part of the original speech, which was delivered in Czech language in the early 1930s, was even recorded on film and is available on YouTube. Here is an excerpt:

> *This new service will prove to be the most profitable business for yourselves. The proceeds from the practice of pedicure are left, for the most part, to yourselves. In addition, it helps you to increase the sale of shoes, stockings and small necessities. Start this work with courage and enthusiasm! Do not be afraid of treating people whose feet are in very neglected conditions. Your service must be somewhat similar to that of a true physician, who treats with sacrifice patients who are seriously ill, even when contact with them is very often disagreeable and possibly dangerous. The customer will be thankful to you for this service and leave the store as your most sincere friend and enthusiastic client. You will learn this service of foot care by carrying it out every day. Like a priest starting his daily work with service to God, you must personally perform daily foot care as a service to the customer. You will become masters only by regular work, done methodically every day.*

One of the doctors working in the Bata Hospital in Zlín was Dr Eugen Straussler. He was recruited by Bata in 1932 and seven years later, sent to work for the company in Singapore. While there is unfortunately not much to be found about Silvestr in the Zlín archives, there are more interesting documents and details about Dr Straussler. This includes a record of his preparations prior to leaving for Singapore:

> *Induction of Dr E. Straussler before departure to Singapore:*
> *One week in the shoe-making school*
> *One week in the rubber processing school*
> *One week in the sales department (half-week in the main Zlín shop, half-week in the chiropody section of the shop)*
> *One week assisting the personnel manager in the social department.*
> *Altogether four weeks of training. Finished on 1 March 1939.*

In Zlín, I also found one group photograph of the trainees of the Bata pedicurist course, two dozen saleswomen and salesmen who graduated from this 10-day training in January 1940.

I'm almost certain that Silvestr attended a similar 'crash course' as opposed to the broader induction of Dr Straussler, who held a more senior position and was therefore probably expected to learn about various other departments to gain insights into the Bata operation.

After their inductions, Silvestr, Dr Straussler and others would have prepared to leave for their new overseas appointments – how they travelled from Zlín to Singapore is a subject we will explore in greater detail in the next chapter.

- VIII -
From Zlín to Singapore

SILVESTR, like all other Bata employees transferred abroad, had to undergo a prescribed set of departure procedures. As a pedicurist, he had to not only pass the chiropody training but also a crash course in the English language and a detailed health check that included vaccination against tropical diseases; he was also likely equipped with a personal medical kit.

As there wasn't much time between the decision to send someone abroad and the actual departure, everything had to be done quickly. Josef Vaňhara, who contributed to many Bata publications and documented the development of the company in photography, also published several memoirs. In one, he noted:

> Candidates needed to pass the preparatory geography, language and also chiropody or shoe-selling courses within a few weeks [...] And so our colleagues were departing suddenly, disappearing from the workplaces, playgrounds and cafeterias [...] At one point, one such group, eagerly awaited in India, was listening to the last instructions of their instructor ahead of Monday's departure, when one of them felt the need to flag that "as far as I'm concerned, I've graduated from the course and have all my travel documents in my pocket; but let me be open that I can't speak any English." The tired instructor [...] just waved his hand, "Well, you still have the whole Sunday ahead of you, don't you!"

Similarly, Jiří Kramoliš – the son of Josef Kramoliš, whom I managed to meet personally in his hometown of Hodslavice – remembers how his father took English classes while already en route to Singapore. It was common that the employees heading abroad had to build up their foreign language skills on the go, and they had no option but to manage. Josef Kramoliš himself wrote in his memoirs:

> *Two weeks before my departure, I was taking intensive English courses in the afternoon [...] And then suddenly, I was a second-class passenger on a luxurious ocean liner. Alone among strangers, I had to rely on myself. Although I had a very high opinion of my knowledge of English, I soon realised that I still had a lot to learn to be able to function in Singapore. So, I was using the opportunity to practise my English every day on the ship, since most of the passengers were travelling from Britain.*
>
> *It took about three months in Singapore before I was able to use English without problems. There, no one really cares how you speak English because the population of this crown colony is really a mix of various Asian and European nations. Even native Britons speak different varieties of English. I could distinguish three kinds of this language here: street English, written English and diplomatic English. I knew a bit of each, and so the native speakers quickly recognised that I was a so-called 'continental European'. But nobody cared, and my foreign accent didn't seem to attract any attention.*

Finally, I also read how Stanislav Jedovnický, who travelled to Singapore in late 1939 as an accountant, recollected his experience of picking up English while already in Singapore. Interestingly, he is one of the few who remembers director Rojt positively:

> *There were about 12 of us, the young and single Czechoslovak employees of Bata in Singapore. In order to master the English language quickly, we were accommodated separately in a kind of 'boarding house'. The cuisine, which was British – mostly boiled food, a lot of mutton – was not very enjoyable. I was therefore looking forward to Sunday lunches at our director Rojt's place. He invited us over, and these lunches were a welcome reminiscence of our homes: some meat on peppers or even roasted pork on cabbage with dumplings.*

During my search in the Zlín archives, I also found a template of a document titled "To be arranged before departure abroad". It contains a list of 19 items that had to be taken care of, and these include arranging for a passport, deregistering at a police station and cleaning up the apartment of the departing employee.

A special item to be provided to shop managers and chiropodists (and therefore to Silvestr) were "letters with a set of photograph portraits". Everyone, including Silvestr, also had to sign a special declaration, prepared by Bata in 1938:

> *I am aware that it is my duty abroad not to violate, by my action or behaviour, the good name of our company. I know well the values of our company, which are good shoes and good service to customers regardless of their nationality or religion.*
>
> *I fully recognise that my conduct must be perfect under all circumstances, that I have to respect local nations and avoid anything that might offend them – even more so, as my behaviour as a foreigner will be observed closely.*
>
> *I hereby declare that observing all these principles is part of my commitment and duties towards the company. I acknowledge that their violation can become grounds for my immediate dismissal and termination of my contract without any rights for compensation.*

A template on which this declaration was printed was accompanied by this explanatory note:

> *There have recently been incidents in which employees from the Protectorate of Bohemia and Moravia, who work abroad, violated in a scandalous way the laws and regulations of hosting countries, or significantly crossed the lines dictated by decency and proper behaviour.*
>
> *An example is an employee from Zlín, working in a factory in Poland, who was trying to bring along a number of personal items, arguably of insignificant value, and failed to declare them to the customs office. When this was investigated, the way he behaved towards authorities was an unprecedented violation of the good reputation of the Bata company.*
>
> *You must avoid passing criticism of local circumstances, and stay away from debates and conversations about national, political, religious or racial matters.*
>
> *Please read and sign the attached paper to confirm, for the record, that you are fully aware of your duties and the expectations we have in relation to your conduct abroad, and that you accept the steps we may take as a consequence of your violation of these rules.*

Voyage to the Far East

We already know from the *List of Employees Overseas* that Silvestr departed on 31 December 1938. I used that list to extract all Bata employees leaving for Singapore and ended up with more than 70 names. When I organised them by their known departure dates, it became clear that while some of them travelled individually, many of them probably travelled together in smaller groups.

There are four other Bata employees who left for Singapore on the same date as Silvestr: František Řehoř, František Wakerman, Jaroslav Zapalač and Josef Zuna. Remarkably, all were assigned to work as chiropodists, except Zapalač who left as a supply organiser. There is a good chance that two more men travelled to Singapore in the same group: Artur Goldman, controller of the samples, and Vladimír Zelníček, a buyer. Their departure dates differ by just one day, and so it is very likely that they gathered in Genoa, where all seven of them boarded an ocean liner.

In Silvestr's only known letter, he wrote to his parents about his first impression of Singapore, but there is no information about his voyage there. I therefore had to extrapolate from other sources how it might have looked like. A very good source for this approximation is the memoirs of Josef Vyhnálek, who followed Silvestr to Singapore half a year later.

Vyhnálek travelled from Zlín to Vienna (probably by train), and from there, took another train to Venice. After a short stop, he continued via Milan and Turin to Genoa. He noted, "Genoa – the city spreads along the waterfront of a beautiful bay. How magnificent was the view from my hotel across the harbour and to the open sea!"

Shortly after, he boarded a liner operated by Lloyd Triestino. The ship's name was *Victoria*, and it made quite an impression on Vyhnálek:

> There she was – all white, waiting in the harbour for passengers travelling to all parts of the world. They were mostly Italians, along with some English and French, as well as a larger number of Arabs and Germans. After a loud sounding of its sirens, the ship started moving. For the first time in my life, I was in the middle of a sea.

Very much like Silvestr, Josef Vyhnálek came from a poor family in a small Czechoslovak village. Born in May 1917 in Jamné nad Orlicí, he was two years older than Silvestr. His father was a shoemaker who had five children. Josef however could not remember his father because he was killed in World War I near Trieste in Italy. When Josef was five, his mother was remarried to a seasonal construction worker. The family struggled with poverty. Josef Vyhnálek remembers that he, along with his siblings, had to work hard to earn just a little money. In the summer, they gathered wood and wild fruits in the forests to sell. In the winter, they manufactured brushes as well as buttons.

Like other poor village children, Josef was lucky to get a job at Bata. He was hired when he was 14, worked in the shoe factory during the day, and in the evenings, attended the Bata School of Work to get a better education and to learn foreign languages. Three years later, he was sent to work in Bata shops in the Czech cities of Mělník, Brno and Mladá Boleslav. He eventually left for Singapore in May 1939 to work there as a seller-pedicurist – the same job as Silvestr.

What was it like for these young village boys to set off on a long journey to a distant, exotic destination? Surely it must have been a thrilling adventure, to have an opportunity – very likely their first – to enjoy a bit of luxurious life even though they travelled in second-class, which seems to be Bata's standard for its staff. According to Vyhnálek:

> *The Italian dishes are delicious. Pasta and salads are made in various ways, mostly with olive oil. Wine is available daily. We can swim in the pool on the deck, dance in the evenings, go to a cinema – all that is available to us onboard during the cruise.*

The Lloyd Triestino's liner *Victoria* was very modern, and in its time, the fastest liner in service. It often sailed to the Far East, and due to its speed and elegance, was nicknamed the "White Arrow" or "The Dove of the Orient". The maiden voyage of *Victoria* took place in 1931. It was powered by four large diesel motors, allowing it to cruise at 20 knots (about 36 kilometres per hour). Its modern and luxurious interiors also contributed to its international fame.

However, the destructive swirl of World War II eventually brought an end to *Victoria*. She was converted to a military transport ship in November 1939, with its first mission being to join a convoy heading from Italy to Libya. In January 1942, it was sunk by two British torpedoes in the gulf of Sidra close to the Libyan coast.

But back in 1939, when *Victoria* was still a proud passenger ship, it would depart from Genoa to its next port-of-call which was Naples, where Vyhnálek enjoyed the view of Vesuvius with its typical column of smoke. He also recalls that "a number of Italian colonisers and soldiers boarded here, including General Balbo. They were all heading to Italian Somalia in Africa."

General Italo Balbo was a legendary figure of fascist Italy and one of the closest friends of Italian fascist dictator, Benito Mussolini. He was a governor of the Italian colonies in North Africa (today's Libya, Ethiopia, Somalia and Eritrea) during the 1930s. Balbo died in 1940 when his plane was downed by friendly fire above the airport of Tobruk.

After Naples, the next stop mentioned by Vyhnálek is Port Said in Egypt, where "many Egyptians in boats surrounded our ship while we were still a few kilometres from the harbour. They were offering us all sorts of things to buy."

What followed was a passage through the Suez Canal:

> *On the left side is an endless Arab desert, with sand everywhere. On the right is Egypt with a railway and a road running along the Canal. Occasionally we spot clusters of palm trees. It took us the whole night to pass through the Canal, only arriving in the city of Suez in the morning.*

After a one-day stop, the ship continued to the Red Sea:

> *Due to the unbearable heat, this was the hardest stage of our voyage. We stopped in Massawa, where the Italians disembarked. The fascist army was welcoming them with music, but we were not allowed to enter the harbour and had to stay on the ship.*

The next port was Yemen's Aden, after which *Victoria* sailed for five days before reaching Mumbai:

> *It was announced that the ship will stay in the harbour for the whole day, resupplying fuel and food for the passengers, and we were encouraged to visit the city. We visited a poor Indian neighbourhood, saw the shambled shelters of these miserable people. It was also here that I had my first encounter with a real rickshaw [puller]: barefoot, legs full of muscles. [He] keeps running to make a living for his family.*

By nightfall, *Victoria* was steaming out to sea again.

This time, the ocean was not calm, and a big storm was approaching. The ship was rocking from side to side, waves bigger than the ship itself. She however managed to slowly push her way forward and, in the morning when we woke up, the sky was clear again.

Several days later, it reached Colombo in Ceylon (today, Sri Lanka).

Ceylon is a rich island, famous for its quality tea. Now they also have rubber plantations, which are a source of great wealth. Ceylon is also an island of elephants – you can see them everywhere you go.

Another couple of days of sailing, and *Victoria* was finally reaching Singapore. This is how Vyhnálek described his arrival:

As we were approaching, it was hard to spot any buildings, the coast was all green, resembling a huge orchard or park. Only when we got closer could we see the silhouettes of buildings hidden under the trees. Then a city emerged with one of the largest ports in the world – Singapore. There were many boats and ships of all sizes in the harbour.

Regarding the immigration procedure that followed:

Those disembarking in Singapore were handed back their passports and they got off the ship. At the customs office, we were asked if we had any goods to declare, and then we were taken in cars to the immigration office where we had to fill out several forms. When these formalities were done, we were taken to our new home in Chancery Lane. These were European bungalows [...]

This reconstruction of Silvestr's voyage, based on how his colleague and friend Josef Vyhnálek experienced it, is vivid. I have managed to get bits of information described by Vyhnálek confirmed by other sources.
One of these sources is the travel plan of Rudolf Šícha, who left Zlín for Banagar in 1937 as a personnel officer. Šícha travelled from Zlín to Genoa on a train with a third-class ticket that cost 380 Czechoslovak crowns. From there, he sailed onboard the *Conte Biancamano*. Šícha was a second-class passenger, and Bata paid 4,290 crowns for his ticket to Mumbai, plus 340 crowns as a boarding fee. The voyage took two weeks and Šícha completed the last leg of his journey from Mumbai to

Calcutta by train, also in second-class.

You may remember that *Conte Biancamano* was the ship that Czechoslovak consul Polodna used when he was leaving Singapore on 1 March 1939, and (as I explained from my deductions) probably the same ship that Silvestr sailed on to Singapore earlier, in January 1939.

SS Conte Biancamano was built in 1925, and its capacity was 180 first-class, 220 second-class, 390 third-class and 660 fourth-class passengers. It was 200 metres long and had the same cruising speed as her sister ship *Victoria*, which is 20 knots (36 kilometres per hour). In 1939, on one of its last voyages to the Far East, it had onboard a number of Jewish refugees who travelled to Shanghai. At the beginning of World War II, it was captured in the Panama Canal and in December 1941, the US Navy started to use it as a transport ship under a new name *USS Hermitage*. It also helped in Operation Overlord – invasion of the Allied Armies from Britain to the French coast in Normandy – in 1944. After the war, she was returned to Italy. Her last voyage was in 1960, when she sailed from Genoa to New York and back.

When Silvestr was leaving his home in December 1938, the atmosphere must have been quite gloomy: it was just few months after the Munich Treaty which resulted in large Czechoslovak territories, including the immediate vicinity of his hometown of Vémyslice, being seized by Nazi Germany. Czechoslovakia itself was also sliding towards fascism, and the 'Crystal Night' that launched pogroms on Jews in Germany was a very recent event.

Silvestr must have also witnessed the rise of fascism during his voyage to Singapore. Fascist Italy was by then an official ally of Hitler's Germany, and scenes of Italian fascists boarding the ship – as Vyhnálek described them – were probably common when Silvestr sailed too.

Did Silvestr see his departure from Europe as a means to escape the approaching conflicts? Possibly. But we can almost be certain that his parents did think of it that way. Although it must not have been easy for them to let their youngest child go, in their minds, it was perhaps the best option at that moment. None of them would have envisaged then that the brutality of war would soon overwhelm even distant Singapore.

Earlier Adventures to the Far East

When Silvestr and some of his colleagues travelled to Singapore in the late 1930s, they were sailing in comfort aboard modern ocean liners.

This contrasts greatly with how the early Bata pioneers travelled to the Far East at the beginning of that decade. The most legendary of Bata travels from Zlín to the Far East was taken by Tomáš Baťa in 1932 in his airplane.

Tomáš Baťa decided to go on an extensive tour of the Far East by airplane. True to his visionary and progressive nature, he was an enthusiast of aviation, then a modern technology that was just developing after World War I. He bought his first airplane in 1924, a light Czechoslovak biplane *Albatros*. Tomáš Baťa initially used these marvellous machines for advertisement flights and promotion of his company, but five years later, purchased a fully metallic four-passenger airplane – Junkers F.13 – which he started using for business flights across Europe.

The company's weekly *Sdělení* (Communication), published in Zlín, printed an article that summarises Baťa's thinking:

> An airplane is more important to man than a car. An airplane ushers in a new era. With a new ability to fly, humanity is undergoing a revolutionary transformation comparable to when man started to walk on two feet and raised his head from the dust and his mind to God [...]. What impact will aviation have on business? It's hard to say, but one thing I know for sure: one who wants to elevate business, must first elevate man.

Baťa's adventurous journey to India started with a take-off from Zlín in December 1931. He and several others from his team were flying the company's airplane, Fokker F.VIIb/3m. It had a cabin for 10 passengers and was produced in a Czechoslovak factory called Avia. At that time, the only regular airplane connection between Europe and the Far East was operated by the Dutch KLM and the British Imperial Airways – basically the two countries that had large colonies there. The route of Baťa's airplane was therefore charted to follow their key airports.

It consisted of several landings in Italy, after which Baťa crossed the Mediterranean Sea to Tunisia. He then continued across Northern Africa to Egypt, and from there, to Iraq and Iran, and finally to Calcutta in British India, which was the most important destination for Baťa's business mission. However, Baťa continued even further to Batavia, and made a stop in Singapore along the way. This moment has been captured in *The Singapore Free Press* and is also mentioned in Jan Baroš' book about the first decade of Bata in the Far East.

At that time, it was an adventurous undertaking and a unique achievement. By flying more than 32,000 kilometres on his business trip, Baťa set a new Czechoslovak national record. And since aviation was still nascent, there was no shortage of dramatic moments:

> *The journey was indeed a bumpy one. Violent storms and thick fog made it a challenge to fly over the Alps mountains, and thick clouds combined with strong headwinds over Italy even forced an emergency landing there. When approaching Benghazi in Libya, the airplane had an engine failure. An auxiliary plane that Tomáš Baťa called in from Zlín with a replacement engine, failed due to a malfunction over Sicily and another one crashed in the Alps. The contemporary press even ran a false alarm as they had mistaken that airplane with the one that Tomáš Baťa flew and thought that the famous businessman had died.*
>
> *After finally replacing the engine, the unique Baťa's expedition faced new challenges. They had to fly through violent snowstorms, and after landing in Basra, they found themselves in the middle of an epidemic of plague that killed 2,000 people. As they continued to Shiraz, new technical problems arose when they had to fly over the mountains at an altitude of 5,000 metres. The thin air and high revving of the motor caused the spark plugs of the engine to burn […] The radio connection failed entirely. The only solution was a return to Basra and a change of the planned route. Following a different course to avoid the high mountain ridge, they ended up flying through a sandstorm. They made a stop in Jask, and then made it to Karachi.*
>
> *On a return [trip] to Europe, the company's Fokker got stuck in the mud in Istanbul and Tomáš Baťa used a commercial flight from there on the last leg of his trip.*

Despite all these troubles, the two-month-long journey of Tomáš Baťa to the Far East was a great success. It paved the way for the company to establish itself in the huge new markets in British India and British Malaya.

Bata's Intelligence on British Malaya

When I was attending school in the 1970s and 1980s, there was close to nothing about the history of Malaysia and Singapore in the

Czechoslovak socialist curriculum. Now, as I'm trying to piece together Silvestr's world and the sequence of events that led to Japan's invasion of British Malaya, I am compensating for my earlier ignorance by reading extensively. This has made me realise just how much Bata knew back then about the British and Dutch colonies in Southeast Asia, where it had decided to expand its operations in the 1930s.

During one of my visits to the Zlín archives, I came across a remarkable document called "Straits Settlements – A Report from British Malaya, 1935". The report is typewritten on about 50 thin sheets of paper and, together with dozens of attached photographs, was bound in hard cover.

The report was prepared by a certain K. Dittrich. I later learnt that he was a Czechoslovak of German origin, which explains his grammatical mistakes in the report. Dittrich was among those who, once Nazi Germany occupied Czechoslovakia, applied for a German passport and officially became a German citizen. After World War II started in Europe, the British authorities in Singapore interned him, along with other Germans, on St John's Island. However, Bata's director Rojt arranged for his release, and Dittrich then relocated to Thailand to work for Bata there. Erich Lachs wrote a report for the Czechoslovak consulate in Cape Town in 1942, in which he accused Dittrich of joining the Gestapo, the secret police of Nazi Germany, as an agent, who after the Japanese invaded Siam (now Thailand), even became head of its local office.

Back to his 1935 report about British Malaya, we learn from the first chapter entitled "Report on the Results of My Mission" that Dittrich arrived in Singapore at the end of 1933 and took over the Bata shop in Capitol building, which he managed for about a year. He was self-reporting on many achievements: one of them – which is of relevance to our story on Silvestr Němec – was Bata's chiropodist in Singapore.

Dittrich writes:

> [When I started], the pedicure service was just introduced, and we had two to five pedicure customers a week. By the time I handed over the shop to my successor, the number of clients had increased to 25 to 30, weekly.

He also mentioned that he had changed the salary system to the usual Bata model, replacing fixed salaries with performance-based wages. Another interesting fact is that according to Dittrich, Bata Shoe Co. was running about 50 shops in British Malaya then – that is, in 1934.

The rest of his report follows what appears to be a prescribed structure for a comprehensive intelligence report about a given country and shoe market. It includes chapters describing the local government (including individual names of ministers and an analysis of their influence); the composition of parliament, with a breakdown of its members by individual political parties; the usual ranges of local salaries; prices of key food products and other essential articles; the local Czechoslovak diplomatic mission, including individual names of its representatives and an assessment of their relations toward the Bata company; the country's key influential figures, such as its politicians, journalists and leading academics (and their attitudes towards Bata); overview of the main newspaper outlets (and how they report about Bata); the transportation infrastructure in the country, including connections with Czechoslovakia; demand of the local population for shoes and related goods, as well as their usual prices; detailed information about competition – that is, other companies, brands and shops selling shoes – and an overview of local holidays, annual festivals, and how suitable they are for sales promotions. Finally, an annex "with photographs of our shops, shops of our competition, as well as photographs of the native population, both barefoot and wearing shoes".

I found the report very impressive, and even more so because reports like this were prepared not only for British Malaya, but also for other markets that Bata was interested to explore.

Dittrich's report about British Malaya says laconically that "the political situation in the country is good, all nationalities (Malays, Chinese, Indians) follow the rule of the British. There are no political parties. There is no parliament."

Another fact reported by Dittrich that I found interesting was about the huge gap in salaries based on races: "Europeans – shop employees have a starting salary of $350 and highest salary of $700. Asians – shop employees have a starting salary of $40 and highest salary of $150."

The report also provides an interesting clue to Silvestr's voyage when it mentions that there were ocean liners going between Europe and Singapore "once a month". This was what led me to conclude that Silvestr probably travelled to Singapore in January 1939 aboard the SS

Conte Biancamano.

Finally, the annex documents – in rare photographs – various Bata stores in Singapore and Malaya, as well as other shoe shops run by the competition at that time.

My conclusion is that Bata had first-class intelligence about the realities of British Malaya. Reports like Dittrich's certainly helped the Bata management make strategic and sound decisions and thus succeed in places so vastly different from Czechoslovak realities.

As for myself, I also reached out to the Czech honorary consulate in Singapore in the early stages of my research. I was wondering whether it had any information about Czechoslovaks who lived there before World War II. The reply came quickly and was, unfortunately, negative. Mrs Petra Kohn, who wrote to me, suggested however that I approach another compatriot, Pavla Schneuwly who has lived in Singapore for about 10 years and was actively involved with the National Museum of Singapore and the Malay Heritage Centre.

This recommended contact proved to be very helpful, and I have worked closely with Pavla on some aspects of my research, including tracing Silvestr and other Batamen in Singapore. This took place in 2019 when I finally visit the island.

- IX -
Volunteering for the War

WHEN SILVESTR ARRIVED in Singapore at the beginning of 1939, Japan had already been at war in China for nearly two years, and a war in Europe was imminent. The assumption that Japan would be the primary threat to the British Empire in Asia was confirmed when Japan joined the 'Axis' alliance with Germany and Italy in September 1940.

Singapore was, at the time, the principal British stronghold in the Far East – a decision made in London shortly after World War I. The island had a strategic location as it stood in the way of potential Japanese advance to Australia or India – two of the most important parts of the British Empire.

British military strategy for Asia was based on a principle that should there be an enemy attack, Singapore had to be able to defend itself long enough to allow the main British fleet to arrive from Europe. The fleet could then continue to Hong Kong, should it be occupied or besieged, and eventually launch a naval blockade of Japan, forcing it to surrender.

In line with this plan, the British built heavy defences in Singapore, particularly along its eastern and southern coastlines, which face the open sea. This was where they anticipated the enemy attack. An inland invasion from the north was not deemed likely, given that the British controlled the Malay Peninsula. They also assumed that it would be impossible for any large army to pass through its dense jungles.

The coastal defences of Singapore included artillery batteries that operated five massive 18-inch naval guns and a larger number of smaller ones. The combined firing power was impressive and the British touted Singapore as an "impenetrable fortress" and the "Gibraltar of the East".

The second crucial element of the British plan was a major naval base large enough to host the entire British fleet, if necessary. As a matter of fact, even after World War I, the British did not have any large naval base with dry dock capacities east of Malta in the Mediterranean Sea. After considering various options, including Hong Kong and Sydney, their final choice for its location was Singapore – more specifically, its northern coast, along the straits separating the island from Johore (the southernmost state of the Malay Peninsula). To the west of the naval base was a causeway connecting Johore and Singapore by road and railway; it also had a pipeline running through on that brought fresh water to Singapore.

The construction of the naval base, which occupied an area of over 50 square-kilometres, had cost the British treasury a staggering 60 million pounds (about 2.5 billion pounds today). The base was officially opened in February 1938 in the presence of the Governor.

However, when I was browsing through several dossiers of photographs in the British National Archives, it was obvious that large parts of the base were still in early stages of construction as late as 1941. It therefore reminded me of the Czechoslovak defence line (which was inspired by the French Maginot Line) along its borders with Germany. It, too, was being built too slowly and too late. And just like the Czechoslovak defence line, which alone would be useless without an able army to defend it, the British naval base in Singapore turned out to be of little use when – at the most critical moment – there were virtually no military ships to come and use it.

The Singapore naval base was equipped with the largest floating dry dock in the world at the time – tugged there all the way from England – and housed oil depots whose capacity was large enough to cover the needs of the entire British Navy for six months. In addition, the British built a chain of oil depots and supply stations along the anticipated route of their fleet from England to Singapore. One of the reasons was that the warships had to pass through the Suez Canal half empty due to their deep draft.

It was estimated that the time needed for British reinforcements to arrive from Europe – and hence, the buffer time Singapore had to defend itself – was 42 days. In 1938, when the situation in Europe and the Mediterranean became complicated, it was revised to 105 days, and a year later, extended to 180 days. This significantly increased the requirements of Singapore's self-defence capabilities. However, by the time this was recognised, the British were running out of time and resources: it was just two years before the eventual Japanese attack, and they had to concentrate most of their already stretched resources on Europe.

Despite that, the British could not afford to let Singapore fall either. There were a number of reasons for this, including pressure from the Australian government who raised the concern that if they sent troops to fight in Africa and the Middle East, Australia would be left vulnerable. The Australian Prime Minister had thus requested that the British government guarantee protection of Australia, for which the Singapore stronghold was vital.

Therefore, the British government was trying to mobilise whatever was available and could be spared for the defence of Singapore. Thousands of soldiers were thus rushed to Singapore and Malaya at the last minute. In that situation, local volunteers were also in high demand.

Volunteers in Malaya

For the story of Silvestr Němec, the Singapore Volunteer Forces which he and the other Czechoslovaks joined play a crucial role. When I was trying to discover more on the Internet, I landed on the website of the Malayan Volunteers Group, where detailed information about the volunteers in Singapore and Malaya and their role during World War II can be found. I wrote to them via their contact address and soon received a reply from the group's then secretary, Rosemary Fell, as well as from its main historian, Jonathan Moffatt.

They invited me to be a member of their group – a British association with the patronage of Her Grace, the Duchess of Norfolk. Soon after I registered, I received a beautiful welcome package that included a personal handwritten letter, which is something so rare these days. Since then, as member no. 379, I have been receiving quarterly newsletters packed with information and stories of other veteran-volunteers and their families.

Jonathan Moffatt, whom I later met in person when I travelled to London to do research in the National Archives in Kew, is the most knowledgeable person on the subject of Singapore and Malayan volunteers I know. Himself the son of a British officer based in Penang, he went on to study and teach History in the United Kingdom and Singapore. Over the years, he has collected an impressive amount of information about the war in Malaya and Singapore, and more importantly, details of the individual volunteers who fought there.

Jonathan is now retired. This affords him more time to research and to answer inquiries from relatives of the Singapore volunteers, such as the many questions I had. He also writes for the newsletter of the Malayan Volunteers Group and has authored and co-authored several history books. Jonathan gifted me with one – *Moon Over Malaya* – when we met.

My research revealed that armed Volunteer Forces had a long history in the British colonies. The Singapore Volunteer Corps (SVC) was established in 1854, following riots organised by the Chinese secret societies. As the police was not able to handle the riots on their own, the British merchants, government officials and planters – armed with rifles – became a useful organised force.

In 1888, the Singapore Volunteer Corps was reorganised, equipped with Maxim machine guns, and created their own official badge with the motto *In Oriente Primus*, which translated means 'The First Ones in the East'. The volunteers also played a part in suppressing the Sepoy Mutiny in 1915. In 1922, they were restructured and formed two Singaporean battalions of the Straits Settlements Volunteer Forces (SSVF). The SSVF also had a third battalion in Penang and a fourth in Malacca. Their equivalent on the Malay Peninsula was the Federated Malay States Volunteer Force (FMSVF).

As the need to increase the number of volunteers became more urgent towards the end of the 1930s, the SSVF started to recruit non-British citizens, including nationals of other European nations as well as the local Chinese, Malays, Indians and Eurasians.

The government was clearly having difficulties recruiting enough Europeans. This was partly due to their small numbers in Singapore. In December 1940, it was estimated that there were 14,000 Europeans in the total Singapore population of 750,000. Many of them were occupied with what was considered 'strategic' jobs like government officials, traders or managers of rubber plantations.

In addition, the potential volunteers also faced problems with their employers. There were extensive discussions by the press on how the companies in Singapore did not approve of their employees spending time on training and other military-related duties. This was because they were expected to continue paying these employees their salaries and to find temporary replacements for them, which incurred extra cost. After reading several articles exploring this issue, I began to understand better the conflict between Bata and the staff who joined the volunteers – theirs was not an isolated case but part of a widespread problem at the time.

The decision to join the volunteers was probably driven by personal patriotic motivations as well as some amount of social pressure, as there were also many appeals by the authorities for young, able-bodied men to join the volunteer corps.

Shortly after Silvestr arrived in Singapore, there was a radio broadcast by Major-General Dobbie, who was then the General Officer Commanding in British Malaya. At the beginning of February 1939, Dobbie warned that the upcoming year would be a tough one because British Malaya's defences – in the event of a military threat to Singapore – were not yet strong enough and hence, more British young men should step up to help. The *Morning Tribune* quoted Dobbie in an article entitled "Malaya's Defences Now Unsatisfactory":

> I cannot emphasise too strongly, and this I have said on many previous occasions, that even when the regular garrison attains to its full strength, the local forces still will, and must always, form an integral and essential part of our first line of defence. I therefore appeal to all those young British Europeans who have not already joined any of our volunteer organisations, and in particular to those who live in or near towns like Singapore or Kuala Lumpur where facilities for training are, comparatively speaking, easy and good.

In his speech, Dobbie also said that it was a "glorious and splendid task" to help with the defence and preservation of the Empire, even if it came at a cost of "giving up one's freedom and leisure for the sake of the country" – as the volunteers would be rewarded by gaining a new kind of "camaraderie and good fellowship which it is hard to equal in civilian life". The article further explained that 200 more European volunteers were needed in order to reach the desired strength of the volunteer corps of 850 men.

The call for volunteers was also extended to women, who were invited to offer various skills for auxiliary services such as typing, nursing, first aid, car driving, translating foreign languages or cypher and code work. Sadly, it seems that because of bureaucracy and prejudice, the female volunteers did not have it easy. In March 1941, *Sunday Tribune* published a long, critical article entitled "Voluntary Services

Scandal" detailing stories of several women who were discouraged or even turned down by the military officers when they offered help with various forms of 'war work'.

In the end, Dobbie's appeal had only limited success in recruiting more male volunteers. A month later, the local newspapers published several articles expressing disappointment over the low number of new volunteer recruits; an example given was Kuala Lumpur, where only seven out of more than 200 young British men there signed up. The editor wrote that he would refrain from making judgements, as those young men might have intentions of returning to Europe to defend their country or that they were holding back till the situation escalated. In any case, he urged them to reconsider as they could make a huge difference in Malaya should they step forward. He also reminded them that training to become a skilled soldier took time and as such, there was no reason to wait.

Between 1939 and 1941, the topic of volunteering was frequently raised in the Singapore press. Besides repeated appeals and reports on numbers of newly registered volunteers, the papers also carried many polemic pieces. One of the issues widely discussed was that of employment security. This letter, signed by 'Would-be Recruit' and published in *The Straits Times* in March 1939, is a good example:

> *I wish to become a volunteer but before I join, I wish to ask you whether the GOC or Government will guarantee me a job after the war is over. Suppose that I answer a call to fight for this country, and so have to leave my job, and that the war is over in six months or so. When peace time comes, can I get back the job that I was working in before? Will the boss turn round and say that he has already engaged another person to take my place while I was fighting for my country? If I can get back my old job, then I will certainly join up as a volunteer. That's the point I am doubtful about.*

A solution to this widespread and pressing concern was addressed by the Governor, who in June 1940, introduced two new legislations related to mobilisation: one includes a clause making it obligatory for employers to provide returning volunteers their previous jobs; and the other regulation forbade employers from discriminating against those who had intentions to volunteer by terminating their contracts.

These new regulations were in response to certain unfair practices reported against employers at the time. For example, in September 1940, the *Morning Tribune* ran a story on how the owner of Eastern Electric was summoned to the court for allegedly refusing to reemploy Lim Liang Teck, a SSVF volunteer, after his two months' training camp. The court ruled that the company be fined 25 dollars. The judge commented that this was a symbolic fine since it was the first case of its kind, but warned that according to the law, the fine could be up to 1,000 dollars. Eastern Electric was also ordered to compensate their worker with one month's salary.

However, tensions between employers and volunteers persisted, as evidenced by an article published in the *Malaya Tribune* in April 1941, entitled "Employers Must Cooperate". The article mentioned a number of discrimination cases by employers against volunteers, and stressed that "no volunteer, in applying for a job, should be allowed to feel that he is prejudiced in competition with others by the fact that he is about to be embodied."

Although the article did not name specific companies, based on known facts, Bata Shoe Co. was probably among the employers being criticised here. The article's date of publication corresponded with a training camp held in February and March 1941. A number of Czechoslovak employees of Bata were known to have attended that training and later complained to the Governor.

Another polemic common in the newspapers was regarding the outdated weaponry used by the volunteers. A number of readers sent letters to the editors to emphasise the need for investments to update and modernise the equipment used by the Volunteer Forces. For example, in April 1939, *The Straits Times* published an article – "Volunteers' Arms" – that criticised government plans to spend one million pounds in rearmament to improve Malaya's defence while volunteers were still using rifles from World War I. It mentions that back in 1937, "FMSVF possessed about 500 rifles, of which all the barrels and the majority of fore-ends were unserviceable". When Governor Shenton Thomas responded and tried to soften this criticism, he only invited more complaints from the volunteers.

One of these letters, printed in *The Straits Times* in May 1939, reads:

> *The Governor has denied a rumour that the Volunteer Forces are short of equipment. If he referred to SSFV, he is probably correct. I am afraid his denial does not hold good for the FMSVF.*

At a parade in our district this week I noticed that this year's recruits have not yet gotten a single item of uniform – and some have 12 or more parades to their credit since joining – and only a few bits and pieces of web equipment [...] Volunteers who joined two-and-a-half years ago are still parading in their own clothes.

As regards the Bren Gun – well, if we are very good boys, we might get them as per schedule [...] in 1942! Meanwhile, we are gently reminded during the course of our Lewis gun training that this weapon is, of course, now obsolete! But we must hurry up and get to know all about it, except what happens when it is fired. This last item is not considered necessary – and, of course, it is a terrible waste, firing our 1931 ammunition.

The Bren Gun has a Czechoslovak connection. It was a light machine gun invented by Czech engineers in the Brno city's *Zbrojovka* (Arms Producing) Factory and was produced there as 'ZB Mk. 26'. It was later adapted by the British factory in Enfield (the 'Bren' is derived from Brno-Enfield), and with some minor modifications, became one of the most popular weapons during World War II; it was still being used during the Korean War (1950-1953) and even during the Falklands War in 1982.

Another volunteer-related issue frequently discussed in the press was how different races were paid differently. Although the volunteers were not considered regular soldiers, they were entitled to financial compensation for the time spent on training, mobilisation and active service. In contrast to the regular army, this volunteer pay was dependent on race. The differences between Europeans and non-Europeans were two-, three- and even four-fold. What's more, only European volunteers were eligible for extra compensation if they were supporting families.

I found references to this problem even before Silvestr's arrival in 1939, but the controversy intensified shortly before the Japanese invasion of Malaya. In July 1940, the government increased the daily rates of volunteer pay for only Europeans. According to *The Straits Times*, a European volunteer with the rank of Private received 1.06 dollars plus 25 cents for his dependent family per day, while a non-European volunteer of the same rank only received 50 cents with no right to extra compensation; a European volunteer with the rank of Lance Corporal was entitled to receive 1.59 dollars plus family bonus, while his non-European peer only 55 cents; and a European Regimental Sergeant Major was offered 5.39 dollars plus family bonus as opposed to a non-European who only received 1.85 dollars.

David Marshall – a Sephardi Jew attached to the B ('Foreign Legion') Company of 1st SSVF who eventually became Chief Minister of Singapore in 1955 – objected to the content of his pay envelope. He described the situation in a talk he gave in 1994:

> My colleagues all got $1.04 a day and my envelope contained 52 cents a day. So, I said to the Captain Paymaster, "Why do I get less than the others?" The reason is you put yourself down as Asian. $1.04 is for European volunteers; Asian pay is $0.52. I'm afraid I got rudely angry, and I flung my envelope on the table, and I said I refused to accept it. He said, "You're confined to barracks for insolence." [...] I was confined to the barracks all Saturday, all Sunday. Sunday evening at 7 pm, a grumpy Sergeant Major came and said, "You are released from confinement, here is your $1.04."

Indian, Malay, Chinese and Eurasian volunteers did not keep their frustration to themselves as well, as they knew that in the Dutch Indies, volunteers of all races received equal pay.

Several of letters to the editor addressing the discrepancy of pay were published. Here is one from a Eurasian who wrote to *The Straits Times* in July 1941:

> It would, of course, be absurd to suggest that the European volunteer could maintain himself on the rate of pay that are at present granted to the non-European volunteer [...] We non-European volunteers go through the same course of training, exercises, drills, musketry etc. as the European volunteers, yet our pay is not the same as theirs. Why should this be? Is it surprising then that there has not been a rush by Eurasian youths to join SSVF in response to the stirring appeal recently made to them?

The Singapore Governor refused to properly address these grievances, arguing that it is "a terribly complicated issue" for which he did not see a solution. The main challenge, in my understanding, was that if they introduced equal pay to the volunteers, they would also be pressured to grant equal pay to all for civilian jobs – an explosive issue that the Governor was not prepared to deal with.

As a result, only token measures which provided volunteers with small benefits were taken. From July 1940, they could purchase alcohol and cigarettes in their canteens and mess halls at reduced tax-free prices, a privilege regular soldiers had. In February 1941, tax exemption was introduced for food and accommodation allowances during longer periods of training; and in March 1941, pension for veterans who became disabled in battle was extended to volunteers.

These were welcome but insufficient improvements. The racial discrimination that the Indian, Chinese, Malay and Eurasian volunteers clearly felt must have impacted their loyalty and morale – especially as the pay difference was just one of many double standards applied by the British commanders and authorities.

Racial discrimination was one of the reasons the British failed to effectively involve the local Chinese in the defence of Malaya and Singapore, despite the fact that they formed the majority of the population and had the highest motivation to fight the Japanese because of the brutalities committed by the Japanese army in China. The British also did not trust the Chinese. They were apprehensive about providing arms to them as many were active in the Communist movement. One SSVF commander even noted that the most capable and disciplined among the Chinese volunteers were those who were Communists.

Czechoslovaks Among the Volunteers

At the end of 1941, when the Japanese attacked British Malaya, the strength of the SSVF was about 2,800 men, divided into four infantry battalions. They were equipped with Lee Enfield .303 rifles and light machine guns – mostly Lewis and Vickers, with only few Bren and Tommy guns. There were also auxiliary volunteer units: artillery, anti-aircraft, engineers, armoured vehicles and field ambulances.

As we have learnt from the letter of Bata's manager Antonín Jugas to Silvestr's parents, Silvestr was registered as a Private with service number 13779. His two close friends and colleagues, Karel Vítek and Rudolf Janeček, had numbers 13777 and 13778 respectively – indicating that they had signed up with the SSVF together. Tragically, none of these friends survived the war. If you consider that out of the 120 or so Czechoslovaks living in Singapore before the war, only 10 died as a result of the Japanese Occupation, the death of this trio seems particularly unfortunate.

Josef Vyhnálek, whose service number was 13794, thus registered as a Private with the SSVF shortly after Vítek, Němec and Janeček. Five other Batamen entered the Volunteer Corps earlier. With the Singapore Royal Engineer Volunteers (later reorganised to Bomb Disposal Unit) were Alois Čepka (no. 12973) who arrived in Singapore as a seller of tyres in March 1939, František Koblížek (no. 12948) who worked as storekeeper in Singapore since September 1937, Jan Mráz (no. 12949), a stocking seller here since September 1937, and Josef Štásek (no. 12947), a manager at Bata's central warehouse in Singapore since May 1937. Their colleague Vilém Zamara (no. 13019), who arrived in April 1938 as head of Bata's sampling team, was attached to the machine gun unit.

My estimation is that Silvestr joined the SSVF towards the end of 1940. This is based on the service numbers and known entry dates of some other volunteers – information kindly provided by Jonathan Moffatt. Another clue is that Silvestr's friend and colleague Pavel Ambrož joined the SSVF on 15 November 1940, and although I have not managed to find his service number, my guess is that he joined around the same time as Silvestr.

To which SSVF unit did Silvestr belong? Given that almost no official documentation survived the Japanese Occupation, we have to rely on post-war recollections of Silvestr's colleagues.

According to the letter of Pavel Ambrož, Silvestr was attached to the armoured cars while Ambrož himself was with the machine gun unit. This information was corroborated in another letter by Antonín Jugas where he further mentions that Silvestr was with the B Company.

On the other hand, Silvestr's close friend Josef Vyhnálek remembers – in his letter – that three days before the fall of Singapore, he and Silvestr were both part of an infantry counter-attack against the Japanese at the Gap on Pasir Panjang Ridge. And finally, an article from the *Batanagar News*, written by its chief editor Jan Baroš and based on the testimony of Mr Bohman and Mr Jedovnický, says that "Němec was with the rifle corps".

The information that Silvestr was eventually fighting alongside infantry armed with a rifle does not necessarily contradict the other information that he was attached to the armoured cars company. According to the Malayan Volunteers Group website, the armoured cars company "was disbanded 16.12.41 due to age of cars and personnel transferred to SSVF Carrier platoon (Bren carriers)".

It is plausible that as the Japanese advanced and the fighting continued, the number of operational carriers decreased and Silvestr was posted to one of the SSVF rifle units. It was a common practice of the British Army at that time to merge remainders of various units with others.

In addition to the documents and invaluable advice provided to me by Jonathan Moffatt, and several hundred articles about volunteers that I read in the Singapore newspapers, a great source of information about the SSVF is its yearbooks. When a new SSVF yearbook was published, it was sometimes announced in the newspapers. For example, the *Sunday Tribune* in November 1934 praised it as an "excellent magazine just issued", 180 pages long and "profusely illustrated not only with groups and portraits but also with other pictures which, one is inclined to suspect, were taken when the subject was not looking. Printed on art paper throughout and with a four-colour cover, the yearbook is attractively designed." Apparently, they were sold for less than a dollar.

I held three of the SSVF yearbooks, covering 1936 to 1940, when I visited the archives of the Imperial War Museum in London. They are impressive, with full-coloured covers, dozens of pages thick, sections dedicated to various companies, and describing the highlights of the given year – sometimes in a serious, factual way, sometimes with a lot of humour both in the text and accompanying cartoons. I can imagine they were published not only as a kind of reward to the volunteers, but also to help attract new recruits. Sadly, I did not find a copy of the SSVF yearbook for 1940/1941, if it was ever published. It surely would have some details about the Czechoslovak volunteers and possibly even name Silvestr. I am still hopeful that perhaps, one day, I will get hold of it.

The B Company of the first SSVF battalion, to which Silvestr belonged, was formed in the early 1930s for non-British European volunteers. Therefore, all other Czechoslovaks were certainly attached to it too. The SSVF yearbooks mention that due to its composition, this volunteer company was also often referred to as the 'Foreign Legion Company'.

In 1938/1939, this company was divided into four platoons – 5th to 8th. Two of them were composed of experienced and trained volunteers, one consisted of fresh recruits, and the fourth was a reserve, used as a 'home' for the volunteers who were temporarily abroad and not in service. In addition, the yearbook says that the first platoon was further divided into four squads, two of them armed with rifles and another two with the Lewis machine guns. The B company had 76 men in total, 51 of whom were on active duty. Their annual training programme included orientation in maps (a related training took place on Pasir Panjang Ridge), attacks with bayonets, exercises with weapons and watching various instruction movies. The weapons training included not just rifles and bayonets, but also revolvers, Lewis machine guns, hand grenades and other explosives.

A year later, with an influx of additional European volunteers, the B Company expanded to six platoons. The nominal roll in the 1939/1940 yearbook included Vilém Zamara who was listed under the newly established 6th platoon.

My understanding is that before the Czechoslovak volunteers, who signed up in 1940, were eventually attached to their respective squads of the 'Foreign Legion' B Company, they were posted to a special preparatory company that was established in September 1939 for the orientation of new conscripts. It was only after this special intensive course, which lasted six weeks, that the new volunteers were attached to the regular SSVF units. The SSVF yearbook for 1939/1940 mentions that in just three months, 106 new recruits passed through this preparatory company.

To map the contribution of all Czechoslovaks to the defence of Singapore, we should not forget that the government also created the Local Defence Corps (LDC) in October 1940. Its role was similar to a Home Guard and priority was given to those who had some training either in the regular military or as volunteers. It was initially formed by British and European men above 41 years old with the decision to admit a non-British applicant vested with the Governor. In March 1941, the LDC officially opened up to all non-British Europeans without the Governor's consent.

According to the newspapers, 250 applications were received by October 1940, and the *Malaya Tribune* states that at the start of November, these included "French, Dutch and Czechoslovak". We know from the press and a handful of diary entries that several dozen Czechoslovaks from Bata – probably all those who had not earlier joined the ranks of SSVF – joined the LDC.

At the end of November 1940, *The Straits Times* article "Czechs Give Fullest Support to the LDC: 31 Members of Company's Staff Apply to Join" reported:

> *No fewer than 31 out of the 50-odd Czechs in Singapore have applied to join the Local Defence Corps, and* The Straits Times *understands that the entire male members of the Czech colony here may eventually join up. The 31 applications already received are from the staff of the Bata Shoe Company in Singapore.*
>
> *The Singapore LDC is about to be formed. Arrangements have been completed for enrolment parades to commence on 9 December. Applicants will be notified of these parades individually a week beforehand. At the enrolment parades, those who are selected for the first enrolment will be sworn in, and other preliminary details will be settled. The men will attend the parades in batches.*

Interestingly, in the light of the mentioned problem of lack of modern (or perhaps any functional) arms available for the volunteers, the same article also stated that:

> *The LDC is still appealing to the public for double-barrelled hammerless shotguns. There has been a certain measure of response to the original appeal, but the Corps is in need of more of these weapons. It is suggested that in view of the large number of these guns in Singapore, it should not be necessary for the Government to resort to requisitioning, although it has power to do so under the Defence Regulations.*

It was not just weapons that were needed. I also noticed calls in the newspaper for readers to donate binoculars and compasses to the volunteer corps.

Viktor Koš, one of the Czechoslovak Batamen, confirmed the enrolment of his colleagues to the LDC in his diary entry in December 1941: "All [Bata] European employees, except for two or three, became members of the LDC. We entered voluntarily about a year ago." He stated that about a dozen of the Bata 'Young Men' had joined the SSVF, while the older ones and those who had families went to the LDC.

Another interesting article about the LDC that also mentioned Czechoslovaks was printed in *The Straits Times* in February 1941. It praised an "excellent response from the Asiatics" to the calls for enrolment to LDC. It then referred to parades and firing practices taking place on Monday and Friday afternoons, while tactical exercises were organised on Saturday afternoons.

The article also mentioned that the LDC already had about 300 volunteers, and that there was no distinction of races at all in the LDC as "Englishmen, Scots, Hollanders, Frenchmen, Czechs, Chinese, Indians and Malays all mix up freely and train together".

This ideal picture described in the newspapers, however, contrasts with the personal recollections of Viktor Koš:

> *There were many foreigners in the LDC – mostly Dutch, then Czechs, also some French, as well as plenty of Chinese and Eurasians. It was interesting to observe the attitude of the English members of the LDC towards us. For them, we were always just "bloody foreigners". The Australians did not hold such sentiments, but the English were treating them as second-class people too. However, the English were always ready to use us, the "bloody foreigners", for every inconvenient, dangerous or dirty job – in such cases, the foreigners were the first to receive the orders to do it. There was a joke going around: It's often heard that "the English will fight to the last man" but we modified this to say, "the English will fight to the last foreigner".*

Koš was also less than impressed with the quality of the LDC training and its readiness for war:

> *We joined the LDC voluntarily about a year ago. The purpose of these units was to provide an armed guard in the city. Before the war broke out, when we had our drills, it was more like playing soldiers. For example, when we were being taught how to use a bayonet, the instructors couldn't get so-called 'determination' out of us – everyone looked so innocent and confused that it was laughable. It was not surprising as some of us were already of older age and used to a comfortable life for many years. The biggest irony, however, was when we were taught how to shoot at planes. We would kneel on the ground or in a ditch, and with empty rifles, we would point and shoot. But later, when the planes actually flew in and were so high that even the anti-aircraft guns couldn't get a shot at them, we were all terrified and trembling with fear. Sometimes when we went out into the streets to do 'cordons' and had a break to rest somewhere, so many Chinese, especially children, would crowd around us that if something really happened and we, in a few small platoons, were to keep order, they would probably beat us dead just with their hats.*

Silvestr's Volunteer Training

I found a wealth of iinformation on the training of the SSVF volunteers in the newspapers and yearbooks, which enabled me to reconstruct what Silvestr's training in the SSVF looked like.

The new season and annual cycle of volunteers' training started at the end of March, avoiding the monsoon season from December to February in Singapore. The British also assumed that an enemy would not attack at that time of the year, when there were heavy storms. However, this was exactly when the Japanese chose to attack, using the climate as one of their many elements of surprise.

The young men who signed up for the SSVF normally continued with their civilian jobs. The parades and training sessions mostly started at 5.15 pm on working days. Depending on his unit and specialisation, a volunteer would attend training once a week. In 1937, weekend trainings, held once a month, were added.

The training schedules for various SSVF units were regularly published in the newspapers. From these, I learnt that the parades and training were mostly carried out at the SSFV headquarters on Beach Road. The armoured car unit also trained there as the complex included a garage and car maintenance facilities in a basement. It seems that the volunteers occasionally took their armoured cars for rides around Singapore. An ammunition depot and a small arms firing range was near the Beach Road camp. For training in rifles and machine guns, volunteers went to a bigger range at Bukit Timah. I also came across several references that located the weekend volunteer training at Telok Paku in the northeast tip of Singapore. There, the volunteers were accommodated in huts in the Changi barracks.

In June 1939, Silvestr could have read newspaper reports about an annual training of the B Company from the 1st SSVF Battalion – the one that he and other Czechoslovaks later joined – at the Bukit Timah range. The volunteers participated in a shooting competition in a few categories: fast shooting at 300 yards, precise shooting at target at 300 and 600 yards, shooting at a moving target in the range of 100 to 600 yards, and revolver shooting at 20, 15 and 10 yards at stationary and moving targets.

Around that time, the B Company also received two new Lanchester armoured cars. The SSVF yearbook described this event with great excitement, and the celebratory article was accompanied by a caricature.

Silvestr would not have missed the evening parade of the 2nd SSVF Battalion through the centre of the city in July 1939. According to the news, about 650 volunteers participated, marching to the music of Gordon Highlanders pipers and drummers, while "large crowds of people lined the roadside and gathered at several other vantage points to watch."

In September 1939, when the war had started in Europe, the training programme of Singapore volunteers intensified, and the frequency of training and drills increased from one to two or even three per week. The newspapers also reported on the newly introduced "continuous trainings" for volunteers; these were two months long in camps outside the city.

A new law passed in June 1940 specified detailed rules about exemptions: if a volunteer wanted to skip the continuous training camp, he needed to present the SSVF headquarters with a formal application from his employer. In April 1941, *The Singapore Free Press and Mercantile Advertiser* published an article about a Singapore Tribunal hearing on applications for exemptions from an upcoming training camp. Among those granted exemption was Josef Vyhnálek of Bata Shoe Company.

The new regulation also established that the weekend trainings would last from Saturday 2 pm to Monday 8 am. Because of this, the volunteers were sometimes called "Saturday night soldiers" by the regular army.

I found it interesting that the specifics were different for Singapore (SSVF) and Malaya (FMSVF) volunteers. The FMSVF volunteers were obliged to spend two months annually in training camps and another 300 hours in afternoon training, plus a maximum of 20 weekends. The SSVF, however, had to attend 120 hours of trainings during the afternoons and weekends on top of the two months' camp. The reason for the difference was probably economic in nature – a desire to limit the impact on the business activities in Singapore, which was an important global hub of vital materials for the British Empire, in particular rubber and tin.

The first-ever training camp for the SSVF took place in the middle of 1940. The camp was divided into two parts, running from 7 to 28 July and then from 7 to 28 August. Those who had important civilian duties were allowed to leave camp between 1 pm and 5 pm daily. All volunteers could also go home from Saturday lunchtime to Monday morning. The regulation stated that volunteers who chose to stay between the two parts – that is, 29 July to 6 August – could do so and would be paid for those days. The commanders were authorised to select volunteers to arrive several days earlier or stay later to help with preparation and clean-up of the camp. Any volunteer who did not show up without an authorised excuse could be sentenced to prison time by a military court.

The first day of the SSVF training camp on 7 July 1940 was described by *The Straits Times* in detail. The newspaper reported that the intensive training had just started, and the first units of volunteers had already arrived in the camp. From the article, we know that every volunteer had to bring a suitcase or a bag with the following personal belongings: a plate, a cup, cutlery, a comb, a mirror, shaving set, a towel, blanket, socks and rubber boots. The daily training programme ran from 6.30 am to 12.30 pm, and then, after an afternoon break, from 5 pm to 7.30 pm.

In the following days, more detailed descriptions from the camp were provided in the news: the wake-up call was at 6 am, and after a short march in the countryside, breakfast was served at the mess halls where the Chinese and Malays were separated from the Europeans. The morning marches, initially for 3 kilometres, were gradually extended so that by the end of the first month, the volunteers were walking 16 kilometres every day in full gear.

Journalists were invited to watch a machine gun unit during training, and witnessed the volunteers disassembling and cleaning the guns, and firing from behind cover on a slope to learn what was a good or bad firing position.

Some of the SSVF units, including the artillery and engineers, had the opportunity to train with the regular army during the camp.

GOC Major-General L.V. Bond, accompanied by SSVF Commander Lieutenant-Colonial V.G. Stokes, visited the volunteers at a special field inspection. They observed volunteers crawling on wet ground terrain and the volunteer Royal Engineers blowing up a concrete *pagar* [fence] on the beach in front of a government bungalow near Telok Paku. "The explosion made a hole seven feet wide, and wreckage flew a hundred feet into the air, while everybody watched from a safe distance – the wiser for advice given by the GOC, himself a sapper."

In parallel, also during July and August 1940, a training camp was organised for the FMSVF in Malaya. Their regime was a bit different from Singapore's since many of these volunteers were managers of rubber plantations or tin mines. They were allowed to return home daily after the training programme to take care of their business and their families. The planters among volunteers were granted a special week-long break during each of the two months so that they could oversee the rubber collection in their plantations.

Upon the completion of the first SSVF training camp at the end of August, Commander Stokes congratulated everyone for excellent results and announced that the regular afternoon and weekend trainings would commence after a month's break in October.

The good feeling after the intensive training was probably muddied by the news reported in the *Malaya Tribune* in early September that one of the volunteers in Penang, a 24-year-old Loh Kim Thong, had committed suicide in July by taking caustic soda. He had told his mother that "he found volunteering difficult and that he would like to leave the corps." It was probably an extreme case, but there were a number of reports of other volunteers who found the intensive training too hard. Some of them had fallen sick during the camp and one collapsed while on a marching exercise.

General Bond argued that volunteers needed to be properly prepared for a potential war, and that was only possible with tough training. He however acknowledged that some of the volunteers might not have been fit for the drills, and he promised improved health checks before training camps in the future, including the possibility of assigning the less fit volunteers to less demanding supportive roles.

Silvestr and other Czechoslovak SSVF volunteers probably attended the next continuous training camp – announced in December 1940 – which took place in February and March 1941. The announcement said that for those unable to join in February and March, an alternative training would be organised from mid-April to mid-June. This was because the original dates coincided with the high season for rubber collection and, as a result, several important appointment holders were not available.

However, Air Marshal Robert Brooke-Popham, the Commander-in-Chief in the British Far East Command, said that preparation of defence was the priority. The rubber plantation owners were unhappy, and the public questioned whether an exercise "of couple hundred" volunteers was really worth the damage to the plantations due to their absence. The protests, however, could not overturn the decision that was already taken. An official communique was released.

> *The Governor is aware that the first period forms part of the wintering period on rubber estates, during which more supervision of rubber tapping than usual is necessary. He is aware, also, that the calling out of volunteers during this period may mean that the quota for the first quarter of 1941 will not be secured. He understands, also, that for commercial concerns, the first two months of the year are a very busy period, as during it stocks are checked, valuations prepared, and so on.*
>
> *But it is the strong opinion of the Commander-in-Chief, Far East [Air Chief Marshal Sir Robert Brooke-Popham] that these considerations should not be allowed to override the real and urgent necessity for further intensive training of the Volunteer Forces. This is the first need of the moment.*
>
> *The Governor is confident that all those who will be affected by this decision will accept the Commander-in-Chief's opinion as readily as he does. Everyone concerned has now an opportunity to make a real contribution to our war effort, and he feels sure that the planting industry will determine that, at whatever effort, the output of rubber during the training periods shall not be allowed to fall.*

The only compromise was an offer of a short break in the middle of the continuous training period so that the planters could go back to their estates to look after things for a couple of days before they returned to the training camp.

The programme of the early 1941 training camp was modified according to the experiences and lessons learnt from the previous one in 1940. Thus, the first month focused on building individual skills while the second half was for strengthening teamwork. Drills were built around intensive training with modern weapons: rifle, bayonet, hand grenade, light machine gun Lewis, medium machine gun Vickers, anti-tank gun and mortar. This included their maintenance before, during and after battle, which was practised both during the day and in the night. The universal programme further included marches for distances up to 18 kilometres, parades, trench digging, building obstacles from barbed wire, anti-aircraft defence, map reading, signalling, anti-chemical protection, camouflage and night exercises. This was then complemented with a specialised programme for specific units.

The Straits Times wrapped up the reports on the camp with another long article that included this comment:

> *Volunteer soldiers are back in office, men fitter after two months of hard work in camp [...] In the last week of their course in soldiering, rifle companies and machine gunners took part. The stamina called for during these exercises indicated that the training of previous weeks had not been wasted. In one scheme, the entire battalion, equipped for war, marched several miles to an assembly area, fought a three-hour battle among pineapple and rubber-covered hills, and then after feeding in the field, marched back to the camp. Apart from military aspects, this test of endurance was voted a success. The 'Battles of Scarred Hill and Pineapple Ridge', however, will be remembered by volunteers for a long time.*

Volunteer Armoured Car Company

Most of the Singapore Volunteers were armed with rifles and revolvers. Some platoons were also equipped with machine guns or small old howitzers. One Company, however, was quite extraordinary: the Armoured Cars Company of the 1st SSVF Battalion. It was often referred to as SVACC, the Singapore Volunteer Armoured Car Company. This was where Silvestr began his voluntary military service. That meant that, at the age of 21, he was able to drive and maintain an automobile which, at that time, was unusual.

These armoured cars were the six-wheeled Lanchesters, first produced in the late 1920s, and proven to be very effective during the British offensive in East Africa in 1940. Each weighed seven metric tonnes, carried a crew of four, and could reach a speed of 70 kilometres per hour. Thanks to high speed and mobility, they were perfectly suited for scouting. Compared to light tanks and carriers, they had the advantage of operating relatively silently. Mounted with 0.5 and .303 calibre machine guns, they mustered a decent fire power.

The British produced in total 35 of such vehicles in four different modifications, and about half of them were eventually transported to the Far East. From the information I gathered, there were eight of them based in Singapore and seven in Malaya shortly before the Japanese attack.

A SSVF yearbook refers to the armoured cars as "machine guns deluxe", but the volunteers referred to them rather as "ovens" – as they were just that hot.

We can understand how tough this was from a July 1940 article printed in *The Straits Times*:

> *Inside, in practically pitch-dark conditions – only a few specks of light can enter a fully closed armoured car – and in an atmosphere which on a very hot day can register 120 degrees Fahrenheit [nearly 50 degrees Celsius], the car commander and his men have their eyes glued to sights and manipulate some of the five different weapons with which the unit is armed.*
>
> *Even the toughest men in the unit – and almost all are 100 percent physically fit – find that two hours in a closed armoured car, with little space in which to move, firing a hot gun, and shaken from side to side, so that they bless the pads which soften the bumps against the steel sides of the car, is more than enough for one day.*

We also learn that each of the armoured cars had to operate autonomously. Each member of the crew was trained for every required task: to be able to drive it, to use all of its weapons, as well as take care of technical repairs in the field. The crew of each car was supplied with ammunition, tent, food supply as well as cooking tools.

Silvestr's uniform – a standard for SVACC – was a khaki overall topped with "a dark beret at a jaunty angle with the badge of the Royal Tank Regiment for all to see". In 1939, the SVACC unit had 27 men. A year later, when it was expanded to 46 men, it became a Company on its own.

Their weekly training schedule in 1941 – which I reconstructed from newspaper articles – consisted of training every Thursday after 5 pm at the SSVF headquarters, where their cars were parked. In May 1941, Silvestr watched instructional films and joined a ride to Siglap. In July, there were discussions on tactics, mechanics of the cars, and practical exercises for the crew. In August, were trained in firefighting, control of deck guns and car mechanics. In September, survival in the countryside. And in October, back to the deck guns, maintenance and servicing of the light machine guns.

After training, the volunteers gathered in the SSVF canteen where they played games, ordered drinks and had fun together. That snapshot was nicely captured in an interesting book, *Volunteer!* by Paul Gibbs Pancheri, a machine gunner with the Scottish 'S' Company of the 1st SSVF Battalion. Pancheri wrote that the favourite drink was a *stengah* – a "small whiskey with a lot of soda or water" – enjoyed with snacks such as "cracker biscuits with sardine and a dash of Tabasco sauce". The bill was often paid by those who lost a game of dice. According to Pancheri, the dice games (the most popular of which was called 'Bangkok Whoreshops') were a means to get to know other volunteers. There is no doubt that Silvestr had lots of fun spending time with friends and volunteer comrades at the SSVF mess.

In June 1940, the press reported that a big military parade was being organised to celebrate the birthday of King George VI. It would showcase dispatchments of mechanised and infantry units, including a mechanised column with artillery guns, Bren Gun carriers and armoured cars. It was highlighted that the Volunteer Armoured Cars Company was to lead the parade. Over 50,000 citizens were expected to watch the event. Unfortunately, a heavy storm on the morning of the event forced the authorities to cancel the whole parade.

In the middle of December 1941, the Singapore Volunteer Armoured Car Company was disbanded, and its 39 volunteers were transferred to the newly created SSVF platoon of Bren Carriers. Paul Gibbs Pancheri provided interesting and telling details:

> *Our Armoured Car Unit had lost its cars to the Gordons and had been re-equipped with Bren Carriers and guns with only 800 rounds each of a non-standard calibre. These guns had been discarded after brief use, and Lewis Guns, of 1914 vintage, fixed on improvised mounts had replaced them.*

That was already a week into the battle of Malaya.

Looking back, I can't help but think how unprepared our young Silvestr must have felt as the war hurtled him forward to face the brutal, battle-seasoned Japanese army.

- X -
Invasion of Malaya

WHEN BATA sent its employees to Singapore, it probably hoped that these young men and women would be kept safe as war ravaged Europe. Klement Plhoň, who was working in Bata's Singapore factory in 1941, had a 17-year-old son – Zdeněk Plhoň – who managed to evacuate to India with his mother and would pen these words in his post-war memoir:

> The Batamen during 1939 managed to build a new, quality leather shoe factory in Singapore; they also expanded the production of the rubber shoes in Klang. In the years 1940 to 1941, when Europe was already consumed by the war and all supplies from Zlín were stopped, Bata in Singapore prospered; as did their employees and their families who lived in peace, comfort and hope that they will wait out the war here.

By 1941, Japan was already determined to strike south. Its objective was to gain control of the oil reserves in Borneo, Sumatra and Java, and the key to their success would be to capture Singapore, from where the British controlled these islands and the Straits of Malacca.

The British were well aware of the deficiencies in their preparation for war in Asia and the weaknesses in the Singapore defence plans. One of several reports from the late 1930s, which warned of this, found its way into the hands of the Japanese when the German cruiser *Atlantis* raided and sunk a British transport ship – the *Automedon* had carried 15 post bags, including secret military mail on its way to the Chief-in-Command of the British Air Force in the Far East, Sir Robert Brook-Popham. Among the documents were notes of the British war cabinet meeting on 15 August 1940 where the British situation in the Far East was discussed in detail.

From the notes of the meeting, the Japanese learnt that the British Royal Air Force presence in Malaya was much weaker than it claimed, and that in the event of an attack on Singapore, no major fleet would come to its rescue because there was none that the British could spare. These findings both surprised and encouraged the Japanese who, until then, considered the British positions significantly stronger in Malaya and Singapore. From the retrieved British documents, they also found out that its territories in Hongkong and Borneo were considered "indefensible".

British propaganda, however, was painting a different picture. Singapore newspapers supported their stand of military might with extensive coverage, possibly as a conscious attempt to deter the enemy. However, as a result, many British on the 'island fortress' became complacent and believed that the Japanese were not an enemy to be afraid of.

Even the decision makers in London rejected a request to increase the number of military aircraft in Malaya, replying in January 1941 that:

> Both the Defence Conference and the commanders themselves appear to take too pessimistic a view and to overestimate the Japanese. Thus, even in their final estimate, when they propose a first line of 566 aircraft to meet the Japanese total of 600 to 700, some 500 of which are carrier-borne, they allege that they will still be 'heavily outnumbered' and may have to scale up their estimate if Japanese forces increase. This appears to be entirely divorced from reality. The Japanese have never fought against a first-class power in the air, and we have no reason to believe that their operations would be any more effective than those of the Italians.

Viktor Koš, who was based in Singapore, wrote in his memoir:

> As I remember, the risk of war with Japan surfaced about twice in 1940 and 1941. That is, as far as we could have learnt from the newspapers. It however appears that seeing things from outside, the situation looked different. I remember that one of our employees got a letter from his American friend who was asking "whether the Japanese will leave us alone". None of us had ever entertained the possibility that Japan would dare to attack England.

The soldiers began to believe in many bizarre myths, including that the Japanese, with their slanted eyes, don't see well enough to pilot an airplane or fight at night. (Early in the conflict, as the Japanese Air Force was overpowering the RAF, some British believed that the Japanese planes must have been piloted by Germans). The Allies thought that since the Japanese could not beat an inferior Chinese army after four years of war and that they suffered a humiliating defeat to the Mongolian-Soviet forces in Nomonhan, the Japanese would be no match for the Allied Forces. Even Winston Churchill declared that "it is quite certain that Japan cannot possibly compete with the productive energies of either branch of the English-speaking peoples."

This arrogant conviction of their own superiority was one of the key reasons the British Army in Malaya badly overestimated its preparedness. After all, for decades, it had swiftly and easily dealt with the occasional local mutinies.

The soldiers did not bother to explore the terrain they were charged to protect, considering it an 'impenetrable jungle', impossible to pass for any larger army. As a result, much of their tactics were based on defending key sections and road crossings in Malaya.

There were exceptions. The book *Moon Over Malaya*, partly based on recollections of soldiers, told of how a battalion of the Argylls and Scotland Highlanders improved the maps that they were given as they were based on inaccurate civilian roadmaps. They even made new ones based on their own reconnaissance of the area. The Commander of the Second Argylls Battalion, Ian MacAlister Stewart, took the initiative to train troops for fast flanking manoeuvres through the jungle to outwit the enemy (ironically, the same tactic was later successfully applied by the Japanese troops). He even used several armoured cars in these manoeuvres. His battalion was nicknamed "Jungle Beasts", and MacAlister Stewart was retrospectively recognised for developing an efficient method of jungle warfare. But at the time, the High Command did not think this was relevant or important. The British were simply unprepared to defend their own ground.

The Japanese, on the other hand, were preparing meticulously for their attack on Malaya and Singapore. My research in several British archives yielded documents that discuss Japanese espionage activities in Malaya, Singapore and other parts of Southeast Asia. Witnesses and the authorities described how the Japanese pretended to be fishermen, travellers or businessmen. Under the cover of these economic activities,

Japan built an extensive network of informants in the region in the 1930s. The most obvious covert practice was opening photographic studios in locations where it did not make sense.

The British documents mentioned that Japanese residents of Singapore would board arriving Japanese ships, then go to what was most likely an intelligence office in the city. Japanese naval officers were known to have toured the island, including strategic locations such as reservoirs, airport, oil depots, communication centres, military barracks and power plants. The reports also contained warnings of a visible increase of Japanese fishermen who drew maps of bays and marked out places suitable for mooring and landing. The British even noticed that some of the larger Japanese vessels, once further out from shore, were sending radio messages to Tokyo on changing frequencies. I have read a report that some of these boats, under the cover of night, rendezvoused with Japanese submarines to resupply them.

In *Moon Over Malaya*, some soldiers remember how they were often watched and photographed by Japanese 'tourists' as they built defence positions in southern Malaya. These 'tourists' were even observed to have made situation sketches in their notebooks.

Senior officers, however, downplayed the significance of these observations; the prevailing view was that the Japanese methods of espionage were primitive and inefficient. The supervisor of a certain agent Morgan sent this evaluation:

> *Japanese Secret Societies, about which Major Morgan has a 'bee in his bonnet' [...] Major Morgan did not agree when I said that I considered the Japanese methods of espionage elementary [...] he gave the impression that he knew a great deal more about the subject of Japanese espionage than I was ever likely to know.*

In my view, another reason for this nonchalant response was Britain's appeasement approach towards Japan. Unlike his predecessor Chamberlain, Churchill was anything but appeasing towards Hitler, yet he decided that the war in the Pacific was not his to fight. He went as far as temporarily closing the Burma Road after the Japanese voiced their protest. The thousand-kilometre Burma Road which wound its way across the mountains of South China and Burma was built after the Japanese occupied all harbours on the Chinese coast, effectively cutting off the supply of weapons and ammunition to China by the Allies.

Many Chinese patriots in Malaya and Singapore had volunteered to drive trucks through the Burma Road, despite its many dangers, and many lost their lives in accidents on the steep mountain slopes.

Churchill's careful approach is understandable when we consider that Britain was already fighting the Germans in Europe and the Italians in Africa; he did not welcome another front in the Pacific.

What is less easily understood was Britain's counter-productive propaganda war. Consider this long piece in *The Singapore Free Press and Mercantile Advertiser* entitled "No Need to Worry about RAF Strength". It was published in October 1941 – less than two months before the Japanese invasion.

> As the first war correspondent to be allowed to see our secret air bases in the Malayan jungles, I bring you good news – there is no need to worry about the strength of the Air Force that will oppose the Japanese should they send their army and navy southwards.
>
> Flying low through lashing rain of a northeast monsoon and skimming the tops of steaming jungle cloaked by mountains, I have touched down at more than 20 RAF aerodromes torn out of the thickest forest and worst swamp land in the world.
>
> I have been out on reconnaissance flights with British and American bombers that are ceaselessly patrolling the China Sea and the Gulf of Siam at the edge of Japanese-controlled Indochina itself.
>
> Japan has created a new crisis and an ominous threat of war hangs over the Pacific. But if that war comes and the little brown men of Tokio send their army and navy southwards toward Singapore, there is no need to worry about the strength of the Air Force that will oppose them.
>
> The Air Force is on the spot and is waiting for the enemy — swarms of bombers and fighters are hidden in the jungle and are ready to move out onto camouflaged tarmacs of our secret landing fields and roar into action. I flew to a bomber base at Alor Setar, smack on Thailand's western border, from which they will blast the Japanese army with bombs should they attempt to push southwards along the military roads of western Malaya [...]
>
> Then we touched down at Kota Bharu. This is Malaya's most vital airport. It is just south of the Thai border and commands the railway and road along eastern coast [...] so Kota Bharu is magnificently fended, both from the ground and from the air. Its beach defences are manned by British and Indian soldiers and airmen.

In retrospect, we realise just how ridiculous this bragging is as both the key airbases in Alor Setar and Kota Bharu fell to the Japanese in the first few days of the war.

Contrary to the picture British propaganda so successfully created, its Air Force in the Far East was actually very weak. According to their own analysis, a minimum of 336 to 600 aircraft were required for an effective defence of Malaya. However, in December 1941, only 150 were available – most of which, like World War I biplanes, were hopelessly outdated. The best plane available to the RAF was the ponderous Brewster Buffalo.

Requests from the Singapore Command to London in 1940 and 1941 for more and better aircraft were in vain. By that time, the British were in desperate need of their best airplanes for their own defence in Europe. And if anything could have been spared at all, it was sent to the front in Russia as a priority. It was seen as vital by the British government to ensure that the Soviet front against the Germans did not collapse, so about 250 tanks and 200 airplanes were sent every month to support it. In retrospect, it could be said that if just one or two months of such supply were sent to Malaya, it would likely have turned the situation around.

The Japanese, on the other hand, allocated 600 modern aircraft for their attack on Malaya. This included the legendary Zero (Mitsubishi A6M), whose manoeuvrability outperformed any western airplane of the time. As the Japanese only introduced it in 1940, the Allies had little idea about its superb abilities and believed that the Japanese Air Force only flew second-tier machines.

The Command of the British and Allied armies in Malaya was assumed by Lieutenant General (Lt Gen) Arthur Percival in May 1941 – just 205 days before the Japanese attack. He took over from Lt Gen Lionel Bond who stopped the construction of defences – initiated in 1937 by his predecessor Lt Gen Dobbie – in southern Malaya. But Percival himself was sceptical about the need for massive defences, arguing that they would trigger defeatism and undermine morale. Although Percival had some major achievements in World War I, he was not up to this new assignment. While he, unlike many others, did not underestimate the Japanese enemy, he proved to be weak and indecisive at critical moments.

When the Japanese attack happened, Percival failed to respond quickly and effectively to the surprising tactics, as well as to exercise sufficient authority over the Australian troops. They were under the command of an egomaniac, Major General Gordon Bennett, who had frequent clashes with Percival. The mutual animosity and mistrust between the British and Australians escalated when their troops suffered humiliating defeat after defeat against the advancing Japanese army in Malaya. John Curtin, the Australian Prime Minister, seeing the inability of the British to stop the Japanese, lost his faith in the British promise to defend Australia and openly approached America for help. This surely did not help the dynamics between Percival and Bennett either.

The task to invade and occupy British Malaya was assigned to Lt Gen Tomoyuki Yamashita who was acknowledged as one of the most capable military leaders in Japan. However, as he sympathised with the 'Kodoha' faction of the Japanese army that advocated a strike north against Russia, he fell to disgrace in 1936 and was sent to Korea to command a brigade. He thought his career was over, but because he was known as an expert on Germany, he was assigned to a secret mission to Berlin in 1941 to negotiate an exchange of military technologies with Hitler.

Yamashita believed deeply that Russia was the main enemy of Japan. However, in the light of looming U.S. sanctions to pressurise Japan to give up its hard-won gains in China, he accepted the need to attack the Allies as an act of self-defence. His chief of staff for the Malayan operation was Colonel Masanobu Tsuji, a brilliant tactician and planner who was infamous for his cruelty towards the defeated enemy in China.

In the beginning of December 1941, the Allies noticed a large accumulation of military force on Hainan Island in the South China Sea. In fact, the Japanese were using the island to train their troops in tropical warfare in preparation for the invasion of Malaya, but the Japanese claimed this was part of their operation in China.

On 1 December 1941, Shenton Thomas, the Governor of Singapore, declared a mobilisation upon the request of the British military command.

Viktor Koš, as a member of the Local Defence Corp (LDC), described the mobilisation:

> *In the afternoon, after reporting for duty, we were provided with all sorts of materials, including a military rifle and 40 rounds of ammunition. Various groups were then assigned to guard the power*

plant, the radio tower, the gas station etc. My colleagues Jugas, Martinec and others were sent to their 24-hour watch immediately, but after their unit was driven to the radio tower, I was released and could go home. I was ordered to report again on Tuesday at 5 pm for my 24-hour turn. From that moment, we had to carry the full gear with us all the time, wherever we went. We were responsible for making sure that none of it got stolen. The service was organised in such a way that half of the men were on watch and the other half were off duty, and then we switched after 24 hours. Later we managed to rearrange it for our people so that we always had at least some staff from each department at work while their colleagues were with the LDC. In addition, Mr Jugas, our director, was relieved from service, and I [as chief accountant] was allowed to work during the day and be on watch only every other night.

Our biggest worry at the LDC was when we were assigned to guard the gas station. It was being watched by 15 to 17 men, a sergeant and a commanding officer. We were rotated, by being two hours on guard and another four hours on alert, in total 24 hours. It was always bad to stand there during the night because we were not used to something like that from our civil lives. I, for example, was never a soldier. Our main worries were what would happen if the gas station got bombed. The huge gas tanks would certainly explode and destroy everything left standing after the bombs. I was assigned to the gas station about four times in total, twice for 24-hour service, and twice only during the night.

The whole service felt like 'playing soldier', though we were equipped with live ammunition. Some of the LDC volunteers were handling their guns in such a way that it was a miracle that no serious injury or incident happened [...] Yes, we were armed, but our commanders were concerned that we might do something stupid, and preferred that we don't use our weapons [...] The worries about irresponsible fire were elevated after one of the LDC volunteers mistakenly shot dead two Chinese people.

After the mobilisation was declared, all the volunteers – including Silvestr – reported to their units. The next day, *The Straits Times* tried to calm the population:

> *Singapore was much less perturbed by the issue yesterday of a Proclamation declaring the existence of a state of emergency and*

calling out the Volunteer Forces than it had been on Saturday at the sight of troops pouring out of cinemas and cafes in response to an announcement whereby leave was cancelled immediately [...] it did produce a marked effect on the civilian population. As was only to be expected in the circumstances, all sorts of wild rumours quickly gained currency and produced apprehension among several of the less strong-minded members of the populace. A reassuring statement issued sometime after the event did a great deal to correct that situation.

Certainly, there is nothing in the regular news services to justify alarm. Japanese statesmen and 'spokesmen' are still yelling their heads off. But they have been doing that on and off for some years past [...] There are reports of troop movements and movements of ships. Japan has been moving troops and ships in a variety of directions ever since the invasion of Manchukuo. Reduced to its simplest form, the position is this: Japan's bluff has been called.

She may be more temporising, but even that cannot be achieved without some modification of the attitude adopted by the extremists in Tokyo. In any case, a complete showdown cannot be long delayed. Japan cannot continue to exist under the present economic pressure. She can only secure the relaxation of that pressure by abandoning her expansionist programme. The one alternative left to her is to take action which will bring war to the Pacific. To those who are inclined to nervousness at current developments we would emphasise that the very worst Japan can do is to provoke a war in which the odds will be overwhelmingly against her. That is the absolute limit of her power for evil. She cannot win such a war; she cannot secure domination of the Pacific [...]

Since that possibility does exist to some degree, it is simple prudence that we should place ourselves in the highest state of preparedness. Armed forces have been sent to and retained in this part of the world solely because of the danger of war with Japan. To go a certain distance toward meeting that danger and then to be 'caught on the wrong foot' after all the planning and scheming would be sheer stupidity.

Invasion of Malaya

When the reconnaissance airplane spotted a large Japanese convoy steaming towards Thailand on 6 December 1941, the British did not take any action. They had prepared Operation Matador, a detailed counter-attack plan for the invasion of the neutral Thailand to deny the Japanese a chance to establish a foothold for their attack, but those in command hesitated and waited until it was too late. The British authorities were still hoping that it was only a show of strength by the Japanese to which they did not want to respond with confrontation. Thus, the desire to avoid an open conflict with Japan prevailed.

Shortly after midnight on 8 December 1941, the local Indian garrison spotted a large number of invasion vessels approaching the beaches near Kota Bharu at the northeast coast of Malaya. The first wave of 5,000 Japanese soldiers was launched around 1 am local time – about 40 minutes before the first bomb was dropped on Pearl Harbour which is generally considered as the start of the war between Japan and the Allies.

When Lt Gen Percival brought the news to Singapore Governor Shenton Thomas that night, he calmly replied, "Well, I suppose you'll shove the little men off!"

The first wave of attack was indeed fended off, but it did not take long for the attackers to break through the relatively weak defence line and by the afternoon of the first day, the defenders had already been pushed inland. After securing this foothold, the Japanese moved southward along the east coast of Malaya.

Simultaneously, another wave of Japanese troops which had landed in Thailand invaded the west coast of Malaya. The British also failed to implement Operation Krohcol, an advance into southern Thailand to prevent or at least delay the Japanese.

Coinciding with the amphibious landing, the Japanese launched a massive air attack targeting the airstrips in northern Malaya. By the end of the first day, 60 British airplanes were destroyed – most of them on the ground, not even given a chance to take off. Within a week, the Japanese gained full control of the airspace over northern Malaya, exposing the British infantry to air raids without any protection.

Air Raids in Singapore

The launch of the attack on Malaya could not have been missed by the inhabitants of Singapore because the city was bombed on the night of 8 December as well. Although the first raid was symbolic, it still killed several dozen people, and its psychological impact proved effective.

This is how Viktor Koš experienced it:

In the night from 7 to 8 December, around 4 am, I was woken up by some strange sounds and then I heard explosions. We have seen from our window how every explosion was followed by a burst of fire reaching big heights, and we have heard the sounds of airplanes flying above us. Calmly, without any feeling of panic, we watched a scene that was soon to become so fearful for us on a regular basis. The streetlights were on, we could not see the searchlights in the sky nor any anti-aircraft shooting, the sirens were silent. I could not understand. Only after a long while, when the bombing raid was over, the sirens finally sounded, but the streetlights were never turned off.

Early in the morning, I received a phone call from Mr Jugas who informed me that these were Japanese airplanes and that some bombs were dropped right into the centre of the city. He also said that Mrs Červenková visited him and demanded that she be relocated, because one of the bombs fell near her apartment and she did not want to live there anymore in case there would be more bombing. Only upon my arrival to office did I learn that Japan declared war on Britain and on America.

It is clear that Singapore was caught by surprise and was unable to respond to the aerial attack on that first night. This was despite the extensive Air Raid Precaution (ARP) drills that had been carried out for two years.

The newspapers in Singapore gave extensive coverage of these air raid drills and civilian defence training in Singapore. The first one, which took place on 16 March 1939, included blackouts for when enemy bombers attacked the city. About a thousand ARP volunteers participated, their task being to work with the police to check if shops and households put out their lights or blacked out their windows from 10 pm. The *Malaya Tribune* reported that the "black-out was highly satisfactory" and that "so excellent was public co-operation that there were no instances of any of the ARP volunteers having to issue warnings to households". Those who failed to oblige were subjected to a fine of up to 1,000 dollars.

Cars were banned from the streets because of their bright headlights. Only trolleybuses and motor buses were allowed to operate during the night drill to provide transportation for civilians. Around midnight, the RAF launched observation flights above the city to check the situation from the air. And then at dawn, combined naval, army and air force manoeuvres began, during which a simulated attack of 20 approaching vessels was engaged by the aircraft and artillery. According to the news, the simulation was watched by a large number of citizens. It might have been a welcome, exciting show for many of them after the sleepless night, but for the Czechs, it was no fun since this was the day after their country was occupied by Hitler.

Similar civil preparedness and ARP training were organised in June, July and November of 1939 when multiple rescue teams – firemen, ambulances and police – coordinated rescue efforts at several sites of simulated bombing. Motor traffic was entirely stopped; only rickshaws and bicycles were allowed on the streets. The press noted that, for the first time in history, the city's bars were closed before midnight. More of such training followed in 1940: one in January 1941, to test the reaction of citizens and the effectiveness of rescue units in both day and night, lasted a full 24 hours.

Probably learning from their experiences of the raids by the Luftwaffe (Nazi German air force) on London, the British authorities established a special unit in Singapore in mid-1941.

The July editions of various newspapers announced that bomb disposal units were being formed in Singapore to search for and remove unexploded bombs as they may be buried "five to 30 feet deep in the ground". The newspapers reported that the units' vehicles "have distinguishing marks – the front mudguards are partly painted a vivid, danger red, and on the windscreen will be the letters 'BDU' – Bomb Disposal Unit". What I found very interesting was that the Volunteer Corps members of the BDU included two Czechoslovaks, Alois Čepka and Jan Mráz. Some of their war-time adventures are vividly described in a diary of their unit's commander Charles Kinahan.

Upon the recommendation of the authorities in Singapore, the Municipality constructed several air-raid shelters. Some companies, including Bata, prepared contingency plans to relocate its workers and archives to outside the city centre in order to limit the risk of being hit.

It was hoped that all these drills and preparations would be put to good use when the Japanese started bombing Singapore from the middle of January 1942. By then, they had taken control of the airstrips in southern Malaya and Singapore was within range of their bombers and fighters. Air raids took place twice or three times a day, targeting primarily the naval base and airports. This was how Viktor Koš described them:

The bombings then continued several times a day, sometimes even during the night. I have noticed that many companies moved their offices from the city centre to private houses and garden villas in the outskirts, where they assumed they would be safer. There was also a rumour going around that in northern Malaya, the Japanese were dropping leaflets calling on local people, in the interest of their own safety, to move further away from public buildings and institutions that would become targets. Because our Bata office in the centre of Singapore was in the vicinity of many potential targets, and also because the quality of the building was not the best, we did not feel very safe there. Once, the bombs were falling into the sea and on ships right in front of our building, everything was trembling, and we had to run to the basement. I have decided to move the accounting office to my apartment, and all our employees welcomed such a decision – everyone was very scared to stay in the city centre. Mr Jugas also moved the sales department to his house nearby, and in this way, we had most of the administration together again [...]

Shortly after 8 December, the Plhoň family moved to live with us because they were afraid to stay at their place and the risk appeared much less in our house since it was in the middle of a garden quarter. The Martinec family moved to the Jugas' who lived in our street, just a few houses away. Some families found a shelter at Anička's place.

In the course of a few days, there began a rush to build shelters. Construction of shelters had been recommended by the government even prior to 8 December, but few people took it seriously. But now, due to the skyrocketing demand, the prices of sand, wood and other building materials were rising, and it was also hard to find experienced construction labour. It became compulsory for all companies and employers to construct shelters. Thus, we have built one in the basement of our office building, and everyone was trying to make one at home too. We had originally thought that it would be enough to share one shelter at Anička's house, that it could serve both ours and Jugas' families, but it soon became clear this was not practical. The alarms were sounding frequently also during the night, and that would require us to stay and sleep in the shelter the whole night – as we were not allowed to move around after the sirens, and Anička's house was quite far away. We also had to keep in mind our two children [...]

The night alarms were taking place so frequently that we slowly became accustomed to them. Singapore island is quite large, and the airplanes were usually bombing military objects that were remote from the city. But because their target was never known in advance, the alarm was announced everywhere. The first alarm of the day usually came between 8 am and 9 am, and they usually continued till 4 pm – sometimes with short intervals of silence in between. While the alarms in the nighttime were quite frequent, the timings were less regular. It took one or two hours after the first alarm sounded for the emergency to be considered over […]

Also, during the night, several alarms sounded. However, we were often woken up first by the sound of bombs and explosions, and the alarms only came after that. At first, we used to run to the shelter when the alarm sounded – I grabbed our son, Mrs Plhoňová our daughter, my wife blankets for kids, while Mr Plhoň and his son kept observing where the airplanes were heading to.

When this was happening repeatedly throughout the night, we became so tired that we did not feel like going down to the shelter again. Sometimes, when I was carrying my son there several times in a single night, he would ask, half-awake in my arms, "What's happening?", and when I replied, "Japs are here!", he just muttered, "Again?" and continued to sleep in the shelter. Therefore, later on, we did not automatically rush to a shelter with each and every alarm. The Plhoňs were awake and kept guard. Only if the airplanes were coming in our direction did they warn us, and we all went to the shelter. The night air raids were offering a beautiful view in some ways: a lot of airplanes flying high above, many beams of searchlights from all angles trying to 'catch' them, and anti-aircraft artillery shooting. Regardless, the airplanes continued their majestic flight.

Once we were watching them again from our doorstep, when suddenly three loud explosions came from the street right in front of our house (there was a big garden between the street and our house). You can't imagine how scared we were. But since we weren't blown away immediately, we gradually realised that the sound was moving upwards – it was a mobile anti-aircraft gun shooting to the sky, while being positioned on our street!

Sinking of British Battleships

While the RAF was quickly wiped out of the Malayan sky by the Japanese, a blunder that further shattered the morale of the defenders and the confidence of the civilians was made on the sea.

Since the government in London was unable to send its main fleet as required by the Singapore defence plans, it decided to at least send a small fleet of three capital ships, code named 'Z Force'. This fleet consisted of a battleship *HMS Prince of Wales*, a battlecruiser *HMS Repulse* and an aircraft carrier *HMS Indomitable*. The *HMS Prince of Wales* had, in May 1941, participated in the successful hunt for *Bismarck*, the most iconic German battleship of World War II. The *Prince of Wales* was also where the legendary August 1941 summit between Roosevelt and Churchill took place.

However, the Z Force did not contribute any decisive strength; it was all the British government could afford at the time. Churchill was trying to persuade Roosevelt to send the US fleet to Singapore, but his request was turned down on the grounds that, for the Americans, the Atlantic and Europe were critical priorities.

When the Z Force arrived in Singapore, it was incomplete. *HMS Indomitable* had run aground in the Caribbean on its way to Singapore. Despite this, the arrival of the two famous warships elicited much celebration and excitement among the people of Singapore.

The following day, the local newspapers enthusiastically published headlines like "Grave Warning to Japan", "Haw Haw Tokyo" and "Japan's Hopeless Task in Pacific War". The famous *HMS Prince of Wales* was even nicknamed *HMS Unsinkable* by the press.

One of the sailors of *HMS Repulse*, Richard Smith, later recalled:

> *Everybody was told that the Japanese fleet was absolutely useless and that it was just a lot of rice paper and string. We would go up there and knock them about and cause havoc – it would be a walkover and we would enjoy ourselves.*

Just like its assessment of Japanese air power, the Allies hugely underestimated Japan's capabilities at sea. The Washington Naval Treaty, signed by Great Britain, the United States, France, Italy and Japan after World War I, limited the construction of warships. However, the Japanese navy and air force developed alternative technologies, accompanied by a focus on first-class training, to compensate for this handicap. Among the results were the 'Long Lance' torpedoes (Type 93) and the legendary 'Zero' fighter aircraft. The Long Lance torpedo, which carried half a ton of explosives and was propelled by an engine using pure oxygen, had a radius of 35 kilometres and an incredible speed of 52 knots (95 kilometresper hour). In addition, unlike other torpedoes of that time, it left hardly any trace on the water surface. It remained unsurpassed by any other throughout the war. The Zero was a top-notch aircraft with an unparalleled range of 2,600 kilometres. Its reach was further extended by modern aircraft carriers.

On 8 December 1941, the day that Japan attacked Malaya, the Z Force, accompanied by four destroyers, set off on its first Pacific mission. It was heading to Kota Bharu with the objective of attacking the Japanese transport ships and disrupting the invasion. The warships, however, did not have air cover which was to have been provided by *HMS Indomitable*. The ability of the fleet to defend itself against air attack was further reduced as the analogue system which controlled the anti-aircraft guns of *HMS Prince of Wales* failed to operate in the hot and humid tropical climate, and it was not possible to repair it before the battleship sailed out of Singapore's naval base.

When Admiral Tom Phillips, Commander of the Z Force, realised that it would not be able to intercept the Japanese invasion fleet on time, he ordered a return to Singapore the next evening. He probably realised that he had made a mistake as he is said to have told one of his officers that he would "never again put capital ships in the position we are now in". He still had the option to call for RAF support from air bases but, for some reason, did not. Perhaps he was betting on keeping a radio silence to stay hidden from the enemy.

Shortly before midnight on 9 December, the ships were spotted by a Japanese submarine. Next morning, 88 Japanese aircrafts were sent from a base near Saigon to intercept and destroy Z Force. With a well-coordinated torpedo attack, the *Repulse* and the *Prince of Wales* were sunk in the early afternoon of 10 December.

The British, unaware of the capability of the Long Lance torpedoes, were surprised that the enemy bombers could successfully drop torpedoes away from anti-aircraft fire. The Japanese pilots, on the other hand, were very surprised they encountered no enemy fighters.

The Commander-in-Chief of the Japanese combined fleet, Admiral Isoroku Yamamoto, received the news of the fate of the Z Force with a big smile. Not only had he wiped out the entire British Pacific fleet at the cost of only three Zeroes, given that part of the American fleet was lying damaged or sunk in Pearl Harbour while the rest were retreating to California, the entire Pacific had become essentially Japanese domain.

Japanese Blitzkrieg

The sinking of Z Force came as a crushing blow to the British. After losing much of its navy and air force in the region, the defence of Malaya and Singapore was now fully in the hands of the army. Percival had 90,000 men in Malaya, and an additional 50,000 men in Singapore. They were composed of very diverse units: about half were Indians, a quarter British, a sixth Australians, with the rest being locals. They also had very mixed skills, with a significant number assuming various auxiliary roles and unprepared for frontline action. Crucially, most of the soldiers had little or no previous experience of real battle; many were raw recruits sent to the Far East in haste.

Against them was a considerably smaller Japanese army of 70,000 men, half of which fought on the frontline with the other half as reserve. Although they were inferior in number, they were superior in experience. Many of them were battle-hardened from the Second Sino-Japanese War, and they surpassed the defenders in motivation and determination. Importantly, the Japanese infantry was supported by 200 light tanks – to which the British armoured cars, just over a dozen of them, was no match. The Japanese command, unlike the British, also took good care to prepare its troops for jungle warfare: planned landings and tactics were rehearsed, and every soldier received a booklet with instructions as they were transported south to their landing site.

And so, although the Japanese were outnumbered, they managed to crush the British due to the use of surprise tactics and efficient coordination among various units. The typical operation procedure started with the shelling or bombing of British roadblocks and defence points followed by fast frontal attacks supported by tanks. When required, the Japanese launched quick flanking action through the jungle, forcing the defenders to withdraw before they were encircled. Where this flanking tactic was not possible, troops were landed by sea at the rear of the defence.

The British soldiers were frustrated because they were often ordered to retreat even without having any contact with the enemy. It was enough that once information arrived about Japanese being spotted somewhere in the rear, whole companies, including artillery, were ordered to quickly abandon their defence positions. They were supposed to apply the 'scorched earth' policy during their retreat, but often in their panic and rush, weapons and depots of food and ammunition were not destroyed. To the rapidly advancing Japanese, these welcome supplies came to be known as "Churchill stores".

While the Japanese were motivated by their quick wins, the morale of the defenders basically collapsed after three weeks of defeats and chaotic retreats. The British soldiers, despite their numerical superiority, began to ascribe almost supernatural skills to the Japanese troops. The units moving to the front encountered terrified retreating soldiers. Some of them described the Japanese brutality they had witnessed: murdering the wounded, bayonetting, beheading and burning of captives alive. The Japanese, due to the speed of their advance, did not allow the Allied troops to regroup nor build robust defence lines.

This is how Viktor Koš captured the first weeks of the battle in his diary:

> *Wild news was reaching us from the north of Malaya, and even the newspapers had to acknowledge the successful advance of the Japanese army. We could observe it anyway, as new crowds of people were entering Singapore every day, fleeing from the Japanese by cars or by train. Everything alive was rushing south to seek safety in the "impenetrable fortress" of Singapore.*

For Yamashita, the quick advance was a cornerstone of his strategy. To maximise mobility, he chose to attack only with three divisions although the Japanese High Command had offered him five. This was a testament to Yamashita's military brilliance, as most commanders would have gone with a bigger force. Put in another way: he understood that he did not have sufficient supplies nor troops for a protracted war with the British.

To allow the soldiers to move fast both on roads and through the jungle, the Japanese used bicycles confiscated during the early days of the invasion. This also gave them the capacity to take more food and ammunition than if they carried them on their backs. All this was planned as special teams trained and equipped for bicycle repairs accompanied the infantry.

A remarkable, sad moment that further eroded both the morale and reputation of the British for the people of Malaya was their evacuation from Penang Island on 17 December 1941. The evacuation ships were reserved only for white people; the Asian population who also crowded the piers were not allowed to board.

The Penang drama is captured succinctly in the diary of Viktor Koš:

> *Several days after 10 of December, Mr Zelníček arrived from Penang along with other escapees. They told us horrible stories about the situation there. There have been no anti-aircraft guns and no airplanes to protect them. The Japanese pilots had a free hand to do whatever they liked: bombing and often machine-gunning people on the streets during low flyovers. The entire Penang police ran away and disappeared, with the British officers going first. Chaos, rioting and killing followed.*

Like in Singapore, the air raid protection in Penang completely failed during the first attacks. The sirens were silent, and the streets were full of people, exposed to the Japanese pilots who strafed them. More than 2,000 people were killed or injured in just the first day.

Soon after that, yet another blow shattered the confidence of people in Singapore and Malaya. Hong Kong fell to the Japanese on 25 December. It surrendered only after two weeks, contrary to what the Singaporean newspapers had written earlier.

> *Hong Kong could face a blockade for nine months. To begin with, Hong Kong is a fortress. It has a regular garrison; it has a volunteer defence force; and the Governor, Sir Geoffrey Northcote, has just passed his Legislative Assembly a Conscription Bill, giving powers to call up all British residents between 18 and 55 years of age. Hong Kong's Maginot Line, sited some five miles within the frontier, has recently been completed. It is a scientifically designed system of 'defence in depth'.*

The press in Singapore was still assuring its readers, just a week before Hong Kong fell, that:

> It can be stated unequivocally that Britain means to hold Hong Kong. And the local authorities, the garrison and the civilian population are as one in their determination to stand their ground, no matter what may happen [...]
>
> British troops have been withdrawn from Shanghai because that city could not be held against a Japanese attack. But Hong Kong has been continually strengthened. This colony has become a fortress. All the experience in coast defence of the British Isles is at the disposal of the authorities. This island, which boasts the classic beauty of Italy and Greece, has the rugged terrain of Scotland. Its granite mountains are

a powerful asset to the defenders. Artillery emplacements and air raid shelters extend deep into solid rock. In some respects, the fortifications here have the natural strength of Gibraltar.

We can imagine the reaction of the people in Singapore who were also told that Singapore was and "impenetrable fortress" and the "Gibraltar of the East".

With bad news constantly flowing in, the Governor of Singapore, Shenton Thomas, tried to boost morale in his broadcasted Christmas message:

> *Help can come to us, but not to Japan, and you may be sure that help will come to us. What we have to do, therefore, is to hold on, to hold on with every atom of strength we have. The tide will turn [...] and the time will come when Japan too will be pushed back from the scenes of her initial success.*

On 10 January 1942, the Governor and his wife visited the Singapore volunteers at the SSVF headquarters. The newspapers wrote that it was his first visit to the volunteers since the Pacific War started, and that he "spoke to a large number of men on duty, inquired if they required any comforts and questioned them about the food they were getting". It is more than likely that Silvestr was present during the Governor's visit to the Volunteer Corps.

The Governor made another broadcast on 24 January. By then, it was plain to everyone that the situation was desperate. Still, he tried to keep the unity of people and lead by example:

> *We are altogether in this war, and we are all determined – European and Asiatic – to make certain that the enemy shall not capture Singapore [...]*
>
> *I speak to you not only as your Governor but as one of you. I am a citizen of Singapore just as you are, and my wife and I are proud to take our share of the common danger and trials. Our house has been damaged by bombs. We spent our spare time visiting the wounded in hospitals, the volunteer and passive defence units, and talking to people in the bombed areas. We share your anxiety and distress. We are in the war with you [...]*
>
> *I am going to give you some simple and necessary advice which I*

ask you to follow. Go and give some of your blood [...] Go and give your help in getting away with debris [...] The shopkeepers should shut their shops and take cover during the raids, but as soon as the raiders passed, they should open the shops and carry on business as usual. Do not help the enemy by stopping business [...]

The Japanese are trying to frighten you by dropping leaflets on which are written all kinds of vague threats. I advise you to pay no attention to these leaflets. Their only purpose is to create alarm.

The gloomy atmosphere of January 1942 in Singapore was also captured by Josef Varmuža, an advertising manager for Bata in the region:

After Pearl Harbour and the fall of Hong Kong to the Japanese, we have fully realised the proximity of the enemy, their rapid advance and victory all over Southeast Asia. Singapore was the impenetrable fortress, the most important harbour. Suddenly in December 1941, the Japanese were standing just across the Johore strait, 16 miles from our city [in fact, the Japanese reached the Johore shoreline on 31 January 1942]. The bombs kept falling, airplanes were fighting right above our heads. A panic struck everyone. Hasty evacuation of women, children and men-civilians followed.

As the British retreated south through Malaya, their army destroyed the Bata factory in Klang as a part of the 'scorched earth' policy. The factory had already suffered three direct hits in a Japanese bomb attack on 4 January 1942. Despite that, the Bata factory still remained partly operational.

Viktor Koš diary provides more details:

As the battlefront was getting increasingly closer to Singapore, we started to consider transferring the goods from our shops in Malaya, so that they would not get lost. However, for such a move, we had to obtain a permit from the management [this is clearly a reference to the British custodian who was assigned to Bata in May 1941]. They did not want to grant us the permit, arguing that such a move would unnecessarily cause panic among the citizens, because it would suggest that the defence line is weak and won't hold. Several days later, when the front moved, we finally got the permit for what we requested earlier. However, by that time, our assets were already in occupied territory, and it was too late.

One of the decisions we had to make was also about our factory in Klang. The initial opinion was that, of course, our boys need to stay there, while they can send their wives to us in Singapore. One day, however, they received an order from the local authorities to destroy the factory. That meant that they could not stay there anymore, even if the factory was not destroyed entirely. They would then face a revenge of the Japanese who would be angry that the factory was purposely damaged and would see it as an act of sabotage. In the meantime, we asked the government to at least allow us to take the machinery away from there to Singapore. Again, they refused to give us the permit, insisting that the front would hold [...]

One day, Mrs Boďa and Mrs Sokol arrived in Singapore from Klang, I think it was around 10 or 15 January. They told us that the boys will follow soon, and indeed they did. The Sokols were accommodated with Jugas, the Boďas and Mr Hlobil at Anička's place. Mr Dvořák and Mr Koblížek settled in our house [...]

The day that the British troops were to withdraw, they came to Klang and requested our staff to burn it all down. The Director of Klang, Mr Sokol was thinking about it and eventually he refused. He said that he was responsible for the Bata factory, and he just couldn't do it. The soldiers then ordered him to go and destroy another shoe factory in the neighbourhood, while the army itself would destroy ours. Thus, both factories were set on fire. Immediately after that, they got into cars and drove back to Singapore, as the Japanese were already approaching.

On 31 January, less than two months after the Japanese landed in north Malaya, the last of the British troops crossed the Johore causeway into Singapore. The retreat was complete, and Malaya was abandoned.

It is very telling that during the battle of Malaya, the Allies suffered 50,000 casualties (killed and wounded), while the outnumbered Japanese counted their losses to be 10 times lower. During the two-month 'blitzkrieg' down Malaya, the Japanese fought two battles, repaired five bridges, and advanced 20 kilometres on an average day!

I have to admit that until I started my research, I had little idea about how quickly and easily the Japanese army managed to run over the British in Southeast Asia. My knowledge of the Pacific theatre of World War II was very superficial, with fragments of information pegged to

Pearl Harbour, Midway, Guadalcanal and Iwo Jima. I now understand much better what happened in Malaya and Singapore, and why it was considered such a spectacular failure for the British.

And now, we see Yamashita's forces looking at Singapore from across the Johore Strait, just one kilometre away. Here, they took a short break to regroup and prepare for their final attack.

Our poor Silvestr had only two weeks left to live.

- XI -
Battle of Singapore

COULD AN 'INFERIOR' Imperial Japanese Army really break through the defences of the mighty British forces and cause the fall of Britain's "Gibraltar of the East"? More and more, the unthinkable seemed imminent.

By now, Silvestr and his Czechoslovak compatriots – about 125 of them – would be well aware of the unexpected defeat of the British in the Malay Peninsula and would be feeling the horror and desperation of what might be coming. Yet, none could have known that the Japanese invasion and occupation would bring death to ten of them.

Viktor Koš recalled the last day of January 1942 when the retreating British soldiers blew up the causeway between Singapore island and the Malayan peninsula:

> One day we heard heavy explosions, and the following day newspapers said the connection between Singapore and the Malay mainland was successfully blown up. This causeway, an artificial embankment made at enormous expense some years ago, was about a kilometre long. It was crossed by a road, a railway and a water pipeline. Naturally, they couldn't blow up the whole embankment, so they just made holes in two sections.
>
> But another point was that as a result, they cut the water pipeline as well, and the whole island of Singapore found itself without a drinking water supply. There are some reservoirs, but they would only last for several weeks.

Singapore was indeed dependent on water brought from the mainland. Its two existing reservoirs could not collect enough water for the population of nearly a million. In the British National Archives, I found a booklet published in 1932 to celebrate a remarkable piece of engineering: a system of dams built on the Malayan rivers Pontian Kechil and Pulai, from where a 50-kilometre-long water conduit was built to bring water to Singapore. It was then accumulated in a huge cistern on top of Fort Canning Hill, its elegant arches captured in several photographs in the booklet.

As with water, Singapore was not self-sufficient in food and depended on products from farms in Malaya. In January 1942, food stocks on the island were enough for just a few months.

After the retreat of British and Australian troops from Malaya on the last day of January, the Japanese army took a week to rest and get ready for its final strike: the attack on Singapore.

Transport ships with last-minute reinforcements were still arriving in Singapore between 29 January and 5 February. They brought the 18th British Infantry Division that left the UK bound for Egypt, but as they were passing South Africa, news of the Japanese invasion of Malaya arrived and they were rerouted to Singapore. After spending several months at sea, the soldiers were practically unfit for the battles that commenced just a few days after their arrival.

One of the transport ships in this last supply convoy was RMS *Empress of Asia* which carried a vital delivery of tanks and weapons. The Japanese air force bombed it, and the ship and its precious cargo caught fire and sank just a few miles from its destination.

To protect the northern coast from a sea attack, the troops tried to build some improvised defences but the works were complicated by a lack of workers (most of the civilian Chinese labour fled in fear of the frequent bombardment), by inefficient supply of material, as well as by Japanese fire power from the opposite side of the Straits of Johore.

In mid-January, the RAF and RAAF received a cargo of 50 new and modern Hurricane fighters. They therefore managed to mount some resistance in the air above Singapore, but their performance was disappointing, largely due to the lack of experience of pilots with the new type of aircraft. Several, in fact, were destroyed in accidents. Most were knocked out of the sky by the Japanese air force. Massive attacks of up to 130 bombers at a time destroyed the main RAF Singapore airbase at Tengah. As a result, on 3 February, the Allied command decided to pull the remaining pilots out of the hopeless situation, saving – at least for the moment – the remaining aircraft by moving them to Sumatra.

At that time, it became clear to Churchill that a disaster was looming. After receiving a situational report from General Archibald Wavell, the Allied Commander-in-Chief for Far East [so called ABDACOM – American-British-Dutch-Australian Command] who was the superior of Lt Gen Percival, Churchill was astonished. He wrote in a memorandum: "I must confess to being staggered by Wavell's telegram. It never occurred to me for a moment that [...] Singapore [...] was not entirely fortified against an attack from the Northwards..."

In his reply to Wavell, Churchill stressed:

> I was greatly distressed by your telegrams, and I want to make it absolutely clear that I expect every inch of ground to be defended, every scrap of material or defences to be blown to pieces to prevent capture by the enemy, and no question of surrender to be entertained until after protracted fighting among the ruins of Singapore City.

The Japanese troops, tired after two months of rapid advancing through Malaya, had a limited stock of food and ammunition. Yet, on the other side of the Johore Strait sat a demoralised Allied army. Its nominal strength was still 85,000 men, but it was composed of various elements that did not always get along well and whose commanders found it challenging to cooperate with each other. Out of the 45 Allied battalions in Singapore, 21 were Indian, 13 British, six Australian, two Malayan and three composed of the Malayan and Singapore volunteers – including Bata Czechoslovaks.

General Yamashita decided to send 30,000 of his troops to attack Singapore. They were therefore outnumbered by the defenders by nearly one to three, which is remarkable since the usual military doctrine for amphibious assault recommends that the attacker's advantage be at least two to one. The Japanese were thus taking a considerable risk.

Lt Gen Percival, commanding the Singapore defence, was however facing the very same problems previously faced in Malaya: he lacked tanks and airplanes, his infantry was made of heterogeneous troops of dubious training, and he did not get along well with the Australians and their commander, General Gordon Bennett.

A crucial point is that Percival was also unable to predict his enemy's movements. As such, he was forced to spread his troops too thin to cover an extensive area. Though small, Singapore was an island with a coastline measuring some 200 kilometres. This gave the attackers a huge advantage as they could choose a section in which to concentrate all their power and hence break through the thin defence line.

Percival was tricked into believing that the Japanese would invade Singapore from the northeast where its coast was easily approachable. He had, therefore, concentrated his best units and equipment there. The Japanese were indeed manoeuvring there, with several hundred men transported to the small island of Pulau Ubin. But it was a decoy.

In reality, they were getting ready to invade from the northwest, where the strait was narrowest and where the Singapore shore was a cluttered tangle of mangroves, swamps and estuaries of several rivers. As such, that part of the island was least explored by the British Command, who did not seriously consider an invasion coming from that section. Percival allocated this 'unimportant' section of the coast to the Australian division whom he did not really trust and considered to be a second-rate force.

At the British National Archives, on advice of Jonathan Moffatt, I read a very interesting report by Brigadier G.C. Ballentine, commander of the Indian brigade who was stationed on the left (southern) flank of the Australians. He recalled that:

> Some 250 Chinese non-regulars, armed with anything from a rifle to knife, were sent into the area. They were used to patrol and watch the mangrove under the quite false impression they would be quite at home in such primeval surroundings. Actually, they were city-bred folks, who had never been nearer swamp than a bus might take them.

According to Ballentine, the Chinese recruits were very nervous and caused several false alarms. Eventually, in the heat of battle, several of them were shot by the Australians who had mistaken them for Japanese.

Ballentine's diary bears a broader witness about the incompetence of the British Command. He described the chaos that was already observed in January. When he, along with his three battalions, arrived in Singapore from India, the unloading of ships took several days because of the lack of personnel at the harbour. Later, when he was assigned to the southwest sector, the chaotic logistics resulted in their taking several days to gather there. And once they arrived, he discovered that almost no preparation was done in the sector. Except for a small artillery battery, there was nothing: no barbed wire obstacles, no reconnaissance. Ballentine had only two weeks to improvise some kind of defence structures and to train his men in counterattacks.

The Australians on his right wing arrived similarly unprepared, on 31 January, therefore giving them only one week to prepare. The British Command was even then turning down their request for barbed wire, and ignoring reports from Australian scouts that there was increasing movement of the Japanese on the opposite bank of the strait.

Triumph of the 'Tiger of Malaya'

Unlike the confused Percival, Yamashita had a very good overview of the positions and strength of the defenders, thanks to aerial reconnaissance as well as his spies.

After intensive shelling and bombing that, among other things, severely disrupted communication lines between the British Command and frontline units and destroyed some of the spotlights positioned along the coast, the Japanese launched their invasion at nightfall on 8 February 1942. Using dozens of small boats to cross the strait and under the cover of darkness, it was not very difficult for them to penetrate the thin defence lines as the Australian brigade of 3,000 men was covering a coastal area of more than 30 kilometres long. The Japanese soldiers thus isolated pockets of Australian defenders and attacked them from behind, eventually wiping them out. The Australians had called for reinforcements, but Percival refused to dispatch more soldiers because he still believed that the main attack would come from the east.

On that first night, over 13,000 Japanese soldiers landed in the Australian sector, and 10,000 more followed at the break of dawn. After the first day of fighting, they managed to push the defenders back to establish a strong foothold in the northwest of Singapore. They started to land their light tanks there and, not facing much resistance, regrouped for further advance.

The disintegration of the Allied forces was fast. Ballentine wrote about how the supplies for his Indian brigade had already been totally cut off on the first day:

> From the commencement of the Japanese offensive on 8 February, all supply arrangements broke down and completely ceased, nor was any alternative method substituted despite strong demands by headquarters of the 44th Indian Infantry Brigade who [...] depended solely on their own skill of scrounging.

Another example of the paralysis of British Command is revealed in the recollection of Colonel G.G.R. Williams, which I came across in the British archives. Williams, with his 1st Malayan Brigade, was also positioned in the western sector, but more inland as a backup. He heard the heavy bombardment on the night of 8 February, but only learnt about the Japanese landing when he listened to the BBC News on his private radio the next morning.

This chaos and confusion also impacted the volunteers. Herman Marie de Souza, commander of a company from the SSVF Malacca battalion, recalled how his company was moved to Singapore shortly after the mobilisation and was accommodated in St. Patrick's School on the east coast of Singapore. He immediately noticed the lack of preparedness. He spent several days digging trenches and helping with some improvised defences on the beaches.

On 11 February, he was ordered to cover the retreat of British units from Changi at the coast, but shortly after that, another instruction came for him to take a defensive position along Farrer and Adam Road which was far inland. Once he got there and confirmed his position with the command, he received an order to retreat. How demoralising it must have been.

The Singapore coastline near the causeway, being in the northwest, was also the responsibility of the Australians. They achieved some success by creating a wall of fire after setting ablaze oil flowing into the sea from nearby depots and causing havoc among the Japanese Imperial Guards who were trying to cross the strait there. Their divisional commander Nishimura was already considering a retreat when another mistake in Allied communication caused an early withdrawal of the Australians.

The shore was thus left undefended, allowing the Japanese to take it. Once they gained control, Japanese engineers repaired the damaged causeway, giving smooth access to Singapore for Japanese tanks, soldiers and supplies.

Churchill was furious – he was not able to comprehend how a relatively small Japanese army could score such a quick success against the British defenders. On 9 February, he sent a telegram to Wavell:

> I think you ought to realise the way we view the situation in Singapore. It was reported to the Cabinet by the Chief of Staff of the Imperial General Staff that Percival has over 100,000 men. It

is doubtful whether the Japanese have as many in the whole Malay Peninsula. In the circumstances, the defenders must greatly outnumber Japanese forces who have crossed the straits, and in a well-contested battle they should destroy them. There must at this stage be no thought of saving the troops or sparing the civilian population. The battle must be fought to the bitter end at all costs. Commanders and senior officers should die with their troops. The honour of the British Empire and of the British Army is at stake. With the Russians fighting as they are and the Americans so stubborn at Luzon, the whole reputation of our country and our race is involved.

However, despite some localised successes where the defenders managed to mount determined resistance against the enemy – such as at Bukit Brown cemetery, where the uneven terrain among the graves gave the Australians good cover and allowed them to hold the Japanese back considerably, although at a great cost – the front in Singapore was moving quickly eastwards toward the city.

Contrary to many myths about the massive 15-inch naval guns which protected Singapore from the sea, and which some sources claim were not able to be turned around, I have learnt that they actually did play a role by shelling the Japanese positions. Their support was however limited because they fired armour-piercing ammunition designed to destroy warships and not high-explosive shells that would cause massive damage to infantry and other land-based targets. These guns fired several hundred times, mostly between 10 and 12 February, after which the British destroyed them so that they would not fall into the hands of the Japanese.

On 11 February, the Japanese took control of the central food and ammunition stores at Bukit Timah and water reservoirs in the area. Given that they were running out of both, it gave them a significant boost – while it was an equally significant loss for the defenders. On that day, Japanese airplanes dropped 29 wooden tubes marked with a white-red ribbon behind the British lines. They carried a message for Percival, urging him to surrender. He did not – yet.

Interestingly, the Czechoslovak Press Agency ČTK in Nazi-occupied Prague, probably repeating the Axis' propaganda narrative, jumped the gun and was already reporting a Japanese victory in Singapore. This inaccurate news would have surely caused Silvestr's parents a great deal of anxiety:

BATTLE OF SINGAPORE

SINGAPORE FIRMLY IN JAPANESE HANDS. Tokyo, 12 Feb (ČTK). The street fighting in the last pockets of resistance in the city is virtually over. The whole city and the large commercial port buildings in the southwest are firmly in Japanese hands, according to the latest reports from the battlefield on the island of Singapore. The number of prisoners continues to rise. Although no further official communication has been published since the last official report, issued on Thursday [12 February 1942] evening, announcing the capture of the city, military circles here point out that the capture of the city of Singapore, and especially of its harbour area, has practically sealed the fate of the whole island fortress. It goes without saying that further fighting and cleaning operations on a larger scale are to be expected in various sections, especially in the area of the Naval Base and Seletar Airport, until the island is completely liberated from the enemy. This opinion is justified by the fact that, in addition to the immense will of the Japanese troops to win, and in addition to their superiority in men and material on the ground, the fighting morale of the remaining enemy troops is fundamentally shaken. It may be said, these circles emphasise, that the fate of the whole island fortress, viewed from the military point of view, must be regarded as sealed from the moment when the Japanese shock troops captured the highest point controlling Singapore and the strong enemy garrison of Bukit Timah. This small hill may be compared with the famous 'Hill 203' which has become a part of military history and whose capture in the Russo-Japanese War led to the fall of Port Arthur.

The fact is, fighting continued on 12 and 13 February, although the perimeter was getting closer and closer to the city.

One of the most famous battles in which truly heroic resistance was mounted took place in the southern sector, around the Buona Vista village and on the nearby hills of Pasir Panjang. This is one of the crucial parts of our story, because this is where, according to Josef Vyhnálek, Silvestr was last seen on Friday 13 February.

A day later, on 14 February, the Japanese managed to break through and invade this area, which included Alexandra military hospital at the outskirts of the city. In the afternoon, their troops entered the hospital and committed one of the infamous massacres, murdering several hundred patients as well as medical staff. Silvestr was probably among these victims, although there is (to date) no hard evidence of that.

On that day, *The Straits Times* was published on just a single, one-sided sheet of paper. It stated that 13 February was "probably Singapore's worst day since fighting began in Malaya", with "almost continuous shelling of the area, while air bombardment was heavy". However, the slogan under its title still carried the Governor's appeal "Singapore Must Stand – It SHALL Stand!".

The position of the defenders was desperate: the water supply had been cut, and they were running out of ammunition and fuel. The numbers of killed and wounded civilians were also rising, as about a million citizens were now jam-packed into a small area exposed to artillery shelling and bombing.

On Sunday 15 February 1942, *The Straits Times* was published for the last time before the Japanese Occupation, during which it would be renamed to *Syonan Shimbun* (*Syonan Times*). It still carries the Governor's 'credo' in the title, but the main headline reads "Strong Jap Pressure – Defence Stubbornly Maintained – Volunteers in Action". The article indeed praises the role of volunteers:

> British, Australian, Indian and Malay troops, and including now men of the Straits Settlements Volunteer Force, are disputing every attempt by the Japanese to advance further towards the heart of Singapore town. There was a strange diminution of activity during last night, with little shelling and no bombing of the city area. Reasons for this were still unapparent when we went to press at 7 am. British guns had been heard again from 8 am and after a while there was another lull [...] It is understood that our artillery engaged some of the enemy forces with considerable success, inflicting about 100 casualties.

On the morning of 15 February, Percival outlined two options at his headquarters, now located in a bunker on Fort Canning: immediate counterattack with an objective to regain control of the water supply and supplies at Bukit Timah, or surrender. His demoralised commanders and staff opted unanimously for surrender. After a short negotiation with Yamashita, the official capitulation was signed by Percival at 5 pm. Subsequently, as was agreed, all fighting ceased by 9.30 pm. Singapore had fallen.

In relation to the surrender, I came across a very interesting piece of information in one of the books, although I failed to verify it elsewhere. It suggests that Percival's delegation, in order to be on time for the surrender at the Ford Factory, had to borrow (or more likely confiscate) a Ford V8 car that was owned by the Bata Shoe Company.

Percival did not know that Yamashita was playing a big gamble. On 15 February morning, he had received a report from Colonel Tsuji that his soldiers have on average only a hundred bullets left, and that the ammunition for heavy machine guns is even at a more critical level. Yamashita later came up with his famous quote:

> *My attack on Singapore was a bluff – a bluff that worked. I had 30,000 men and was outnumbered more than three to one. I knew that if I had to fight longer for Singapore, I would be beaten. That is why the surrender had to be at once. I was very frightened all the time that the British would discover our numerical weakness and lack of supplies and force me into disastrous street fighting.*

The Japanese plan to make an impression on the British and create an illusion of a much bigger force than they really were, worked perfectly. *The Straits Times* wrote, at the end of January 1942, that according to military estimations, the Japanese have at least six divisions and 100,000 soldiers. The truth is it was just half of that size.

It's no wonder that Winston Churchill later said that the fall of Singapore was "the worst disaster in British military history". In Singapore and Malaya, the Japanese captured 130,000 Allied soldiers – that's more than the number of Germans captured by the Soviets at Stalingrad. Despite fighting an enemy three times its size, the Japanese army successfully invaded and captured the "impenetrable fortress" in exactly one week, and their own losses were only five thousand men: of this, one-third died, and two-thirds were wounded.

General Yamashita's victory earned him the nickname "Tiger of Malaya", while a lifetime of shame was awaiting Percival.

Through the Eyes of Batamen

The fall of Singapore, especially the two weeks leading up to it, must have been a terrifying experience for all its citizens. The city was exposed to regular aerial bombing that claimed up to 2,000 victims a day. The civilian hospitals were overcrowded, and the exhausted doctors did not have time nor material for proper surgeries – the patients often just got their wounded limbs amputated.

Several of the Bata Czechoslovak men were assisting in the relief work. When I found a war diary by Charles Kinahan in the archives of the Imperial War Museum in London, I was excited to read about his involvement with the SSVF volunteers, more specifically their Royal Engineers company which was, at the start of the war, converted to the already-mentioned Bomb Disposal Unit. Kinahan writes about "two Czechs and a Dane" in his squad: those were most likely Alois Čepka and Jan Mráz, who were – as I found out from the SSVF yearbooks – with the volunteer Royal Engineers. Therefore, I believe they experienced the following with Kinahan:

> We were mobilised a few days before the invasion actually took place. Coincident with their landing, the Japanese did a night bombing raid on the Singapore Naval Base [about 12 miles east of Singapore Town – facing South Johore] and on Keppel Harbour of Singapore. So, the next day, off we went to deal with our first lot of unexploded aerial bombs – not having a clue what a Japanese bomb looked like! We had been trained on German bombs with their booby traps. Fortunately for us, unexploded Japanese bombs proved simply to be duds. No booby traps were found [...]
>
> My first bomb was in the yard at the back of a Chinese shophouse near the civilian jail. To dig it out would have involved the structure of the house, so in the end we decided to leave it. The next was in a pigsty behind a Chinese atap house near the Tiong Bahru Housing Estate. Five piglets were running around in the bomb hole! We dug a shaft centred on the hole made by the bomb, which we finally uncovered. I held the bomb whilst David Waters extracted the fuse with the rest of the team at a safe distance. We then drove back to camp in triumph with me sitting astride the bomb [...]
>
> The next bomb for my section was in swampy ground off Thomson Road on the way to the Naval Base. The nature of the ground made this an extremely difficult task; it was finally abandoned after much waste of time. Our final bomb was in a rubber estate close to Tengah Aerodrome.
>
> The last few days before Singapore surrendered were spent collecting unexploded artillery shells. By this time the Japanese were closing in on the town. After extracting the fuses, we dumped the bombs in the harbour.

The memoirs of Viktor Koš provide more vivid details about the bombings:

> *One Dutchman had a shelter near his apartment – a simple trench, in which he was hiding with one other woman. Once, the bomb scored a direct hit on that shelter, ripped everything apart, and rooted out a big tree nearby. They later found the head of this poor Dutchman on that tree's branches – that's all that was left of him and the lady [...]*
>
> *Once, when Zdeněk Plhoň [the 17-year-old son of Klement Plhoň] was arranging something for us in the bank downtown, an air raid took place. He felt sufficiently safe in the bank, it was a solid building, and everyone present went to hide in its basement. The bombs were falling so close that they could hear them loud in the shelter. As soon as the raid was over, while he was rushing home, he saw many dead bodies and limbs scattered along the street. He was so terrified that he never went back to town, and he rather quit working for us.*

Koš also recorded that his colleague from Bata, Dr Eugen Straussler – the father of Tom Stoppard – was slightly injured during an air raid:

> *One day, around 5 February 1942, soldiers brought wounded Mr Straussler to my home. He was also a member of LDC, and as he stood guard at the backup telegraph central, a bomb fell nearby. While he stood behind a pile of sandbags, the explosion ripped out a large chunk of soil and it flew in an arch over the bags and directly hit Sträussler, who was thus smashed to the ground. His face was grazed from the fall, and he couldn't move too much, because he was hit hard in the back. A moment later, a military doctor arrived and took him to the hospital. Luckily, it was nothing serious and he was back home in five days.*

Especially for the Bata staff, one of the most traumatising experiences was when their Singapore factory got bombed on 30 January 1942. This is how Koš recalls it:

> *That day, Mr Klement Plhoň, who usually arrived regularly at noon, did not come. We had actually not noticed until he rushed in around 1 pm, all covered in black dirt. He reported to us that our factory had been bombed.*
>
> *When the air raid siren went off and they observed that the bombers were heading towards the factory, all employees were requested to go down to the shelter. Only one local worker was 'playing the hero' and standing outside. When the bomb exploded, he lost his arm. One of our*

boys – I think it was Lebloch – was also 'playing the hero' but suddenly ran into the shelter. As soon as he jumped in, the bomb detonated.

After the bombing was over, we all rushed outside to inspect the factory. The local workers, especially girls, were crying. In tears, they just collected their belongings and ran for home. They never came back to work again.

The building received three direct hits, one in the centre and two above the shoe storage. Its roof was made of steel beams, and all three bombs hit those beams as they were falling, exploding above the ground and scattering the roof to pieces. Lots of damage was done also beneath them. There were big holes in the roof, so we covered our goods with tarp. The cars of our employees, parked outside, suffered a lot of damage from the splinters. Most of the local workers quit immediately and never returned. Because nobody wanted to work anymore in the factory, our production was reduced to hand-craft shoemaking on the first floor of our administrative building.

Starting from 7 February, Singapore city was also exposed to artillery shelling.

> On the morning of 7 February 1942, we heard several explosions in short intervals near my apartment. We went out, and as we were looking, we heard a whistling sound and then boom! These were the first artillery shells flying above our heads. The pounding lasted for about half an hour [...] On Monday 9 February, the shells started to fly above my house from 6.30 am. When it was over, they called me from Mr Jugas' house nearby to say that one of the shells had hit them. When I arrived, I was surprised to see how much damage could be done by a single shell. There was a tree standing next to their house, the shell hit its branches and exploded; the splinters flew in through the window, damaging lots of furniture and accessories. There was a big hole in the middle of the office desk of Mr Heim. Luckily nobody was harmed because no one was present that early.

As a result of the bombing, the water mains in the city were damaged and caused intermittency of supply to homes. Koš noted:

> In the afternoon of 9 February, an employee from the waterworks dropped by and told me that he was ordered to close the water supply

to my house. He said that all the houses on our street would be disconnected, and the same was happening in other parts of the city. He showed me a copy of the order, which said that the water would only remain available to hospitals and public institutions. Before he disconnected us, we filled up all the containers we could find.

A panic broke out among the citizens. The Czechoslovaks were especially scared that there were Germans coming along with the Japanese army. Koš wrote that "our local workers kept talking in fear that once the Japanese entered the city, they would keep shooting and killing everyone for at least two weeks. Many of the Chinese were digging holes in the gardens to hide their jewellery, because the Japanese soldiers were advancing so fast." Clearly, the horrors of the Japanese brutality in Nanking, which became known internationally in 1938, were terrifying and causing everyone to think that the same might happen to Singapore.

The desperation and hopelessness were further exacerbated as the streets of the city were increasingly roamed by bands of deserters, often drunk on whatever they scavenged in the shops and bars. Occasionally, some of them resorted to violence as they tried to force entry into hospitals, where they wanted to take shelter. A large group of armed Australian deserters also boarded the evacuation ship *Empire Star* but were removed at Batavia.

According to estimates I came across, almost a third of the Allied army deserted in the final days of the battle of Singapore. One of the indicators of the lack of loyalty to the British was that after the surrender of Singapore, nearly half of the Indian troops switched sides and joined the Indian National Army that was promised by the Japanese to get an opportunity for a war campaign on Delhi. The scale of the desertion is clearly illustrated in another note by Brigadier Ballentine: he recalls that after the surrender, as he was taken prisoner of war, suddenly 700 soldiers were claiming to belong to a unit that had in fact only seen 200 of its men in battle.

The appalling scale of desertions was also experienced by Viktor Koš:

After our wives were evacuated, we decided to go to the cinema – me, Mr Strangfeld and Mr Plhoň. I think it was on 7 February. It was an interesting scene: the cinema was full of soldiers who came here primarily because there was a bar inside. They were all terribly drunk [...]

> Many soldiers were wandering across the city, alone or in small bands – these were the deserters. They were mostly without their rifles and concentrated around the docks, hoping to sneak onto one of the departing ships. Once, two such individuals came to my apartment, already quite drunk, and were asking me for food and drinks. I offered them some salami, but they were not really interested. Although already drunk, all they wanted was more alcohol. It was a big trouble for us to get them out of our house eventually [...]
>
> Another day, Mr Heim sent his driver to arrange something somewhere, and after a long while, the driver returned on foot. He said that two soldiers stopped him and requested for the car. When he refused, they pulled out a pistol and pointed it at him. Of course, he then obliged. There were many cases like that. It was done by the deserters – all they wanted was to enjoy the last days, drinking and driving around [...] Once I witnessed a soldier who shot through his own arm in order to avoid being sent to battle.

I found several other witness accounts from the Singapore volunteers who also recall the chaos associated with the deserters.

One of the SSVF officers, 2nd Lieutenant Middleton-Smith, describes vividly in his diary how, as the end was coming, various officers were popping up on his section of the beach, looking for boats they could use to escape Singapore. He recalls that he arrested one of them and handed him over to the superiors.

Another volunteer, Major Taylor, writes about how one of the SSVF battalion commanders, who was decorated for bravery during World War I, psychologically collapsed, leaving him to take over the command.

Middleton-Smith also mentions how in the last days before surrender, practically all services stopped working, including air raid protection, removal of debris from the streets and rescue of people from the ruins, burying the dead and even firefighting.

Anarchy and the decay of order also invited the settlement of old scores. This sealed the fate of the infamous spy Patrick Heenan, a British Indian army captain who secretly worked with the Japanese and was passing them information about air force infrastructure and Allied operations during the battle of Malaya. When he was caught, the British put him into detention and transported him to Singapore to await a court martial there. As the Japanese were approaching, Heenan's self-confidence grew and he started to threaten his guards, claiming that in a few days, he would be set free while they would, in turn, end up as prisoners. On Friday, 13 February, his guards decided to take justice into their own hands. They took Heenan to the harbour and shot him dead, dumping his body into the sea.

The impression of a total disaster was further fuelled by the decision of the British Command, made on 9 February, to launch a systematic destruction of infrastructure and supplies in order to deny the Japanese access to them. The authorities, with the help of some volunteers, began to wreck machinery in factories and destroy stocks of raw materials, especially in the harbour. This included confiscation of binoculars and other devices, potentially useful for military purposes, in shops. The documents also mention a destruction of vast amounts of alcohol, some 1.5 million bottles; only minimum reserves in the hospitals were spared. The British soldiers also eventually set fire to the huge oil depots around Singapore. As they continued to burn for several days, they created massive clouds of black smoke above the island, even reaching the city.

Evacuation of Bata Families

Most wives and children of the Batamen managed to escape Singapore in the first evacuation wave in January. Zdeněk Plhoň describes this in his memoirs:

> *The management of Bata – after overcoming a lot of bureaucratic obstacles – arranged places on the evacuation ships heading to Australia and to England [with a stop in India] for most family members of the Singapore-based staff. Considering the daily bombing and shelling of the city, all the chaos and difficulties, this act deserves utmost respect.*
>
> *Finally, a group of 18 Czechoslovak women and a comparable number of children boarded an evacuation ship* Empress of Japan *[how ironic!] on 31 January. In total, the ship took about 3,000 women and children, mostly of English citizenship. A smaller ship nearby took an additional 1,500.*
>
> *Both ships left under the darkness of the night. Because the strait to the north of Singapore was already under control of the Japanese, there was only one option left: sail south, towards Java Island, and then turn around the southern tip of Sumatra westward, into the Indian ocean. During the daytime, both ships were bombarded by the Japanese*

airplanes near the Bangka islands. The second smaller ship was hit and damaged; it had to be taken to Jakarta's dry dock for repairs. Its 1,500 passengers were eventually captured by the Japanese, because the repair was not finished before the Japanese took over Java as well.

A group of the 18 Czechoslovak women with kids finally arrived at the Colombo harbour in Ceylon [present-day Sri Lanka], and from there continued on another ship to Bombay. Here, the Indian branch of the Bata company took care of them.

A much more detailed account is provided in the diary of Viktor Koš, a top member of the Bata management in Singapore:

> The events were unfolding quickly and the bombing continued day and night. That's why in early January I suggested to my wife that she should leave Singapore with our kids. The kids were very scared. But my wife kept refusing the idea, saying she would stay with me no matter what – and that if something bad were to happen, it should happen to all of us together. However, one day, she changed her mind. It was around the middle of January, on Sunday, when my wife was with Mrs Jugas in the garden next to the tennis court, while the children were playing in the corner of the garden, near the road. Suddenly an alarm went off. Our son Paloš yelled: "The Japs, the Japs!" and started to run home, Jarka [wife] went after him. I was shouting at him from the tennis court not to be afraid, that the Japs are not here yet, but he did not stop and continued running. Because I was behind the fence that surrounded the court, I was not able to stop him and comfort him. [...] Right on Monday I started to inquire about the options for my family to evacuate. The immigration office told me that they can't grant me a visa for Australia nor a permit to leave Singapore unless I first get an official statement from another country that would agree to accept me and my family. At that moment, a large-scale evacuation of women and children from Singapore was not considered yet, although a number of them were leaving on their own. However, many obstacles were created for people to leave, especially for foreigners like us.

It was indeed not easy to flee from the upcoming war. One of the reasons was that Australia, in particular, was hesitant to accept refugees from Singapore. In his quest, Koš approached the colonial officer who was in charge of supervising the operation of the Bata company and

LEFT: *Singapore Naval Base in April 1941. Despite its ceremonial "opening" in 1938, it was still unfinished at the time of the Japanese attack.*

SECOND LEFT: *Soldiers of the British Argylls regiment undergoing armoured vehicle training. Singapore volunteer forces posted to armoured regiments, including Silvestr, used the same type of car.*

BELOW: *British troops training in Malaya, 1941*

AUSTRALIAN WAR MEMORIAL

LEFT: *A formation of the Imperial Guards – Japanese army's elite corps – advancing in Kedah, 12 December 1941.*

BOTTOM LEFT: *An Australian crew of a two-calibre anti-tank gun guarding the Causeway connecting Singapore with Johore. The tower of Sultan Ibrahim's palace, used by Japanese General Yamashita as an observation post, is visible.*

BELOW: *The Bata factory in Klang, damaged by Japanese bombing. It was the largest and main shoe production facility of Bata in British Malaya. In late January 1942, it was completely destroyed by the retreating British army as a result of its 'scorched earth policy'.*

ABOVE: *Ruins in the city of Singapore after a Japanese air raid in January 1942*

LEFT: *The Bata shoe factory in Singapore was first damaged after several direct hits by Japanese bombs, and eventually destroyed to deny Japanese access to its machinery.*

TOP RIGHT: *A pall of smoke rising from the fires at the Naval Base blankets Singapore city.*

RIGHT: *Japanese tanks passing Bata's office building, February 1942.*

ABOVE: Aerial view of the Alexandra Military Hospital complex showing the large oil depot in its vicinity and Pasir Panjang Ridge in the background.

RIGHT: A map of the fighting front and Japanese troop movements across the Pasir Panjang ridge between 12 and 15 February 1942. Silvestr was last seen alive by his comrade Josef Vyhnálek on 13 February during the battle where Bata volunteers fought alongside the Malay regiment. The Alexandra Military Hospital is on the bottom right where the railway turns and crosses Alexandra Road.

RIGHT: *British soldiers surrendering to the Japanese army in Singapore*

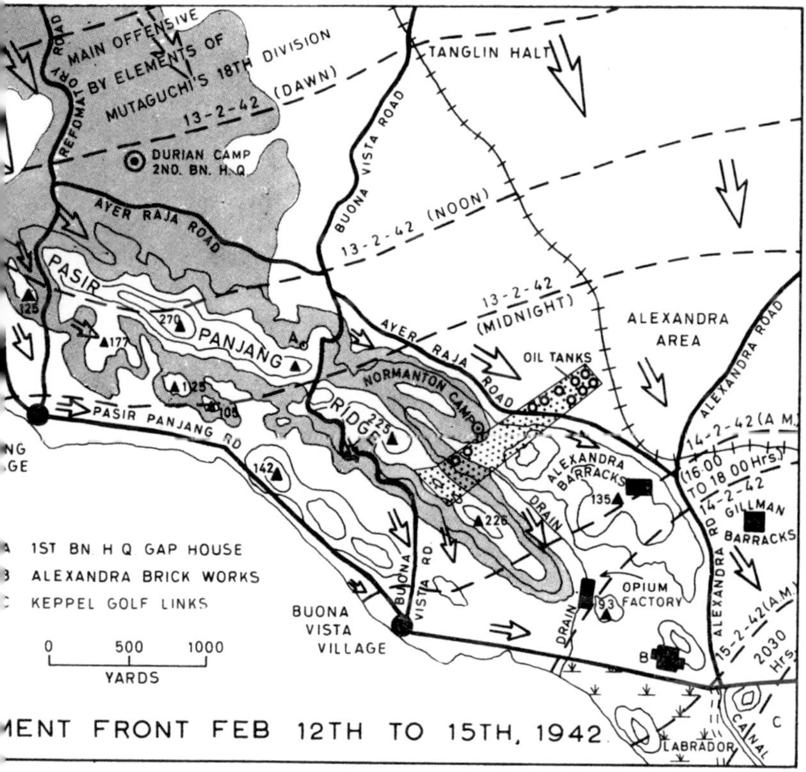

ABOVE: *The frontpage of Batanagar News from October 1945 running a detailed story describing the wartime events as experienced by the Czechoslovak Bata employees in Singapore.*

LEFT: *The Czech translation of Silvestr's Certificate of Death, officially sent to his family by the British authorities in July 1947.*

with whom he had good personal relations. From him, Koš learnt that:

> [...] as far as he knows, there are considerable difficulties in obtaining permits to leave the island, but that possibly women with small children could somehow be prioritised. The following day, he also told me in confidence that neither Australia nor India wants to accept the Singapore refugees because these may include a larger number of Chinese and Asiatics. This can't be communicated publicly though, otherwise they would riot. As a result, the permits are considered on an individual basis and there are certain criteria that an applicant has to meet.

Eventually, all wives of the Batamen applied for Australian visas, but the Australian government was hesitant in granting them. Koš writes:

> I was going to send my family to Australia, because that's where most people went. There weren't even any ships going to India. The deposit for Australia was then reduced to £300 and so all the wives of our employees applied individually for a visa to Australia. There was a little bitterness about it in the end, because many of them could not make this deposit and expected that they could get it from the company, since generally the company should take care of their evacuation. However, we could not arrange this collectively for all of them because our British supervisors refused to help. They were pointing out that other companies also did nothing about it, and there was no evacuation since there was no reason for it – and if someone left, it was his or her private matter. Besides, it was also made clear to us that we should not have any discussions with our employees about this matter. We were supposed to point out that English women with children were not leaving either. Despite these obstacles, many of our wives somehow managed to find money for the deposit, often by borrowing from Miss Anička. All the wives of our employees eventually applied for a visa to Australia, but no reply was coming from there.

Let's just imagine how unnerving the uncertainty must have been for the civilians, who – despite daily bombings and battlefront approaching quickly – were left in limbo and were not allowed to evacuate, even if they took their own initiative. The atmosphere of despair was further aggravated because of the reports of Japanese brutality with which they handled both captives and civilians in occupied territories.

Thankfully, with the intervention of Jan Bartoš, the company's director in British India, the families of Czechoslovak Bata employees were rescued. He managed to arrange the necessary visas for India in exchange for his guarantee that the company would take care of everyone. Based on these visas, the Singapore colonial government finally granted them permission to leave.

Let's get back to the diary of Viktor Kos:

For many days, our wives had their suitcases packed, but a new problem emerged – there were no ships available. As soon as the women and children got their Indian visa, we requested tickets to get them on board one of the ships heading for India. However, they told us that nobody could guarantee whether or when there might be a suitable ship. The telegram sent from Batanagar to the Immigration office was to guarantee visas for 20 people. The plan was to send 19 wives plus Zdeněk Plhoň who was under 18 years and could travel along with his mother. No man above 18 years was allowed to leave Singapore. All these permits were arranged by Mr Jugas, who put in a lot of effort to gather them.

Finally, one day, Mr Jugas was informed that a suitable ship might be leaving in few days. I couldn't tell how he'd learnt of this, but it must have been unofficial – such news was not released publicly due to security reasons, but also to prevent masses of people coming to the harbour and trying to board it. It was on 28 or 29 January 1942. Of course, Mr Jugas rushed to reserve tickets, however there were already many others requesting them. He had to wait throughout the night, but finally – thanks to his assertiveness – he managed to get them. The departure was set for the afternoon of 30 January.

On that day, boarding started early after lunch. At about 2 pm, a company car came to pick the luggage of those who were leaving. When we approached the gate to the harbour, we saw that a number of depots were on fire and heavy smoke was darkening the sky. There were already many cars and people crowded around the gate, but nobody was allowed to pass through. A storage house right next to the ship was burning.

Officials standing at the gate were sending everyone back home, saying it's futile to wait and it's better to come back in the evening when the fire would hopefully be put out. They said that there was no other access to the boat [...]. After a while, someone suggested that we try another gate on the opposite side of the harbour. When we got there, again there was a traffic jam and a chaotic crowd. Military vehicles were being repaired on this side of the harbour, and the soldiers did not like to see the civilians around, so they were pushing us out. However, when they spotted my uniform and helmet, they allowed our car to pass through – and some other cars used that opportunity and followed behind.

It was dangerous to be in the middle of the melee at the harbour. There were thousands of people crowded there, and we were scared of what might happen if the Japanese airplanes came to bomb us. Around 4 pm, indeed an air raid alarm was sounded and people began to panic, as there was no shelter in sight. There was an anti-aircraft battery nearby, and its crew was carefully observing the sky. Suddenly, several airplanes started approaching. The anti-aircraft gun was getting ready to get them in its sight when the alarm stopped. What a relief, as it turned out that those were ours! The front was already so close that nobody could be certain if the airplanes belonged to us or to the enemy, therefore an air raid alert was announced even when our own pilots were returning.

[My son] Paloš was asking whether I would go together with them. When I replied that I would follow later, he said, "I see, you will stay here and shoot the Japanese, right?" However, when I went to give him my farewell, he burst into tears and wanted me to take him home, "I want to go home, I won't stay on this ship, I want to go back to our beautiful house." I was not able to calm him down, and as I bent towards him, he grabbed me around my neck and locked his knees around my body. In the end, I had to use force to push him away. When Jaruška – who had been playing with other kids around – saw this, she also began to cry. In the end, all of us were crying like kids until finally, I said goodbye and ran away.

Most of the Bata wives and children safely reached India in February 1942. Several others who were not in this group evacuated individually, even to Australia.

Bata company arranged asylum accommodation for all of them in Nainital in North India. There are documents showing evidence that 16 of them lived in the Petersfield School, three in Jubilee Grove, and five in Edwinstown House. Several men who also managed to escape from

Singapore, got new jobs with Bata at Mumbai, Batanagar or Batapur – and their families, of course, followed them there.

The last convoy from Singapore

Many people who did not evacuate in January were desperately trying to flee Singapore during the horrible first two weeks of February 1942. Last-minute evacuations used whatever vessels were available, but they came with great risks. Japanese radio broadcasts from Penang kept warning people that all ships leaving Singapore would be sunk; and it was not an empty threat as indeed, many were destroyed attempting to sail away.

The last wave of evacuees took their chances on the night of 13 February, when a loose fleet of about 44 vessels left Singapore, trying to reach Java. Most of them did not make it and were destroyed after being torpedoed, bombed or shelled by the Japanese. Lucky survivors from the sunk ships were collected by the Japanese and interned for the rest of the war. That was the fate of a number of Czechoslovaks, including Viktor Koš, who recounts in his diary:

> On Sunday 1 February, we all gathered in the apartment of Mr Jugas to discuss our situation. Also, our consul attended. It looked like Singapore would be captured soon – our employees in the office also felt that. At the meeting with the consul, we wanted to agree on our next steps. He was assuring us that there was nothing to worry about because it would take months before Singapore might fall. Also, it would be transformed into a military fortress. Because of that, the British would minimise the number of civilians, in consideration of their safety, as well as reduce the supply needs. His speech reminded me of a talk that our consul held at Calcutta in October 1938 [that is, after the Munich Treaty]. He, too, was trying to console us by making various promises about what the army would do [...] It did not take long before the consul himself abandoned Singapore on 6 February.
>
> On the morning of 9 February, Mr Jugas took our passports and using French visa, obtained transition permits via India for us. Although he arranged these papers for everyone, including himself, a day later [10 February] in the evening, he and a couple of others decided to stay in Singapore, no matter what.
>
> On the evening of 10 February, someone brought us our passports

with French visa attached. Mr Wodak was not seen around, and someone mentioned that he had managed to get on board some ship that very evening, along with one or two other Czechoslovaks who were not our [Bata's] employees. A rumour went around that also yesterday, several Czechoslovak people left on another ship. Mr Strangfeld got very angry that while others had already left, we were not told anything.

When I arrived at our office on 11 February, Mr Varmuža was just reporting that several of our boys managed to get on board a ship that left just an hour ago. The passengers on that ship were picking up some soldiers even after it had already left the harbour.

In the chaos of the last days, before the fall of Singapore on 15 February, it became impossible to keep track of who managed to get on which of the evacuation ships.

The diary of Koš contains a list of 18 Batamen who, to his knowledge, seized the opportunity to leave Singapore with the last evacuation convoy. Including Koš himself, that would make a total of 19 men. But given the chaos described above, there could have been more. But what we do know from records is that at least five Bata Czechoslovaks made it to *SS Redang* – an obsolete cargo ship built in Denmark in 1901. It was about 50 metres long and had a carrying capacity of 500 tonnes; its maximum speed was only nine knots (about 16 kilometres per hour). The British authorities confiscated it on 9 December 1941 upon its arrival to Singapore.

The *SS Redang* and its passengers were among the unlucky ones. It left Singapore on 12 February around 7 am and carried about 100 people on board. This figure and a partial list of names have been researched by Michael Pether, a historian from New Zealand who spent years digging through archives and collecting information about the evacuation ships from Singapore. His detailed work on *SS Redang*, and some others, is available online at the website of the Malayan Volunteers Group.

About 100 kilometres south of Singapore, halfway to Bangka Island, *SS Redang* was attacked, probably by the Japanese destroyer *Asagiri*. As it was shelled, most passengers were killed; the ship caught fire and eventually sank. One of the shells scored a direct hit on a cabin in which two women were just typing up a passenger list.

Among the victims were Klement Plhoň, Oldřich Smržák, and probably Eugen Straussler and Bedřich Heim, who were likely on board as well. Three other Batamen who were at the foredeck at the time of attack managed to get into a lifeboat: Hynek Červinka, Vladimír Zelníček and Josef Strangfeld. However, Strangfeld suffered a heavy injury on his leg and died shortly after in the lifeboat as a result of bleeding.

Only 30 passengers of SS *Redang* survived on one of the three lifeboats on the ship. On the afternoon of 14 February, they reached the coast of Sumatra, where a British minesweeper HMS *Tapah* picked them up two days later. However, soon after that, the *Tapah* herself was captured by the Japanese. The survivors from SS *Redang* eventually spent three-and-a-half years at an internment camp on Sumatra.

This story of Batamen from SS *Redang* was told by Červinka to Viktor Koš, who wrote it in his diary:

> On 11 February, Zelníček found out in Singapore's 'small harbour' that there was a chance to get onto one of the ships. He asked one soldier to bring in Strangfeld and also to tell the others. In exchange for the favour, Zelníček offered the soldier his car. The soldier indeed found Strangfeld and several others, and they quickly came to Zelníček. Those who brought along a few items and boarded the ship were Strangfeld, Plhoň, Smržák, Červinka and Zelníček. However, this ship had been waiting – anchored out at sea, not far from Singapore – the whole night. They left only on 12 February in the morning. As they sailed, they spotted a distant ship on 13 February and soon started to be shelled. A great chaos broke on board as the splinters were flying around and hitting the ship. Zelníček was a good swimmer and quickly jumped into the sea. In the meantime, one rescue boat was lowered on the water, so Zelníček swam towards it and tried to get into it. Its passengers however did not want to let him in, as it was already overcrowded. Zelníček was holding onto the boat, but people were beating him over his fingers to make him let go. Finally, however, they allowed him in. Červinka and Strangfeld were among the survivors on that lifeboat.
>
> Strangfeld, as soon as the shelling began, climbed into one of the lifeboats while still on board the ship. However, a splinter wounded him in his leg. Because he was not able to walk, Červinka pulled him out of that boat and helped him into another one, which was successfully on the water. As their lifeboat was leaving the ship, Červinka noticed that an officer was trying to lower another lifeboat, but the ropes were entangled, and it was impossible. Plhoň and Smržák were seen heading

towards that other lifeboat. The third lifeboat available was made useless as it was damaged by the shelling.

The only surviving lifeboat carried 33 people. The crew was rowing to get as far as possible from the ship, which caught fire in the meantime. None of them saw the other lifeboat around, so it probably never successfully left the sinking ship. They were taking turns in rowing. Strangfeld was sitting with his head down and had his briefcase by his legs. His neighbour was however complaining about it, and after a while he threw it into the water. Strangfeld died on the afternoon of 13 February, and it took a while before the others realised it as he was sitting motionless with his head down. The captain, who was present in that boat, decided to throw the body overboard.

Before they did it, Červinka cut off a small pouch that Strangfeld had around his neck and kept it. They did not search Strangfeld's pockets though. While they were rowing, another man and a child died. They rowed all day and night, before they reached a beach on 14 February [...] They were picked up by a minesweeper [...] Later, on 16 February, that minesweeper spotted another group of survivors and took some of them on board – among them, George Tarry who married Vlasta Šebová, a Czech seller from the Bata shop in Singapore. The minesweeper was however captured on the night of 17 February by a Japanese ship. The survivors were taken to Banka Island on 18 February and accommodated overnight in a local cinema before they were brought to the camp where they met Červinka and Zelníček.

Viktor Koš himself got on board another ship named *Mata Hari*, which too was captured by the Japanese near Bangka Island. That's how and where he eventually met Zelníček and Červinka, who told him their story of *SS Redang*.

Here is how Koš described his own departure from Singapore:

> We approached one of the transport ships, but it refused to take us on board, arguing that they didn't have capacity to take any more people and that already many passengers didn't have life vests available. So we went to another ship, but it was the same story.
>
> Eventually, we were allowed to board a third ship. People were brought in on small boats, and then they scrambled in all possible ways to get on board the bigger ship. It was crowded everywhere. There were no cabins on that ship because it was a freighter. I learnt later that all

three ships had been out of commission for several years, being used just for training of the Malayan navy. Once the anchor was lifted, we slowly sailed out.

About half an hour later, it stopped for a reason unknown to me. It was already dark. We looked back at Singapore, and what a view it was in the night: big fires all around the city, and also on the small island nearby, as the depots of oil and gasoline were ablaze. The whole sky looked as if it was covered by dark clouds, but in fact it was the black smoke from the fires.

Most Czechoslovaks, however, were lucky and reached their destinations safety when they escaped from Singapore. The exiled government in London counted 90 evacuated citizens (30 men, 34 women and 26 children), 48 of which were related to Bata. The majority (58 of them) sailed to Colombo in Ceylon and from there, further on to India. Another 21 reached South Africa, and then 19 of them continued to London. Of the evacuees, 11 reached Australia.

But there were also a number of Czechoslovaks who had remained behind – among them, Silvestr. When Singapore surrendered to the invading Imperial Japanese Army on 15 February 1942, those Czechoslovaks were not spared from the brutality of war.

- XII -
Czechoslovaks During the Occupation

WHILE I WAS trying to reconstruct what happened to my granduncle Silvestr during the Japanese invasion of Singapore, my research also brought to light the fate to other Batamen and Czechoslovaks who were in Singapore at the time. These accounts will help us understand not only what they went through and what was their role in defending Singapore, but also help us better visualise what Silvestr could have experienced in his last days.

Shoemaking During the War

I identified 126 Czechoslovaks present in British Malaya and Singapore at the time of the Japanese invasion. The majority of them succeeded in evacuating to safety. But 32 ended up in the Japanese internment camps for civilians, and four men became prisoners of war (POWs).

Most of the Czechoslovak volunteers either serving in SSVF or LDC were lucky as, shortly before the surrender, they were instructed to switch to civilian clothes and leave their units. As such, they were treated as civilians by the Japanese. Although they did eventually end up in the internment camps in Changi and Sime Road, they were still much better off than those who were captured and became POWs.

The story published in 1945 in the *Batanagar News* describes this critical moment:

> On 15 of February, the battle seemed lost. Surrender was in progress. The commander of the Volunteer Corps called the Czechoslovaks and told them: there is no certainty whether with the Japanese, there are no German officers or at least German-controlled

intelligence personnel. *If they catch you with arms, you will be treated as traitors – considering your country is occupied by the Germans – and as such mercilessly hanged, not to think of worse. Keep your soldiers' books and better leave the lines, go home and change into civilian clothes. It will be safer.*

Coming home to change, the men found their houses ransacked by thieves. In the corners of the Bata building, those who were lucky to evacuate had their trunks which they could not take with them to India. The soldiers helped themselves to the civilian clothes, and lay on the ground for a long, long sleep.

In the following weeks, when the Japanese were rounding up the Europeans and sending them to an internment camp at Changi Prison, the Czechoslovaks once again found themselves in a strange position. Since Czechoslovakia was technically a Nazi territory by then, the Japanese were not sure how to treat them: were they German subjects and therefore allies, or were they allied to the British and therefore enemies? Unsure of what to do, the Japanese allowed them to roam freely but ordered them to wear a visible red star symbol – indicating they were 'enemies of Japan' – and their apartments were marked in a similar way.

The Japanese also realised that the Bata managers and workers could become useful for the war economy, since they were professional shoemakers. So, they were instructed to resume the production of shoes, which were in high demand by the Japanese army.

Shoemaking then became their little act of rebellion. As a result of resistance and acts of sabotage by the Bata Czechoslovaks, as well as the extensive damage to machinery in the previously bombed factories, the quality and quantity of the shoe production was not satisfactory at all. A story reported in the *Batanagar News* in 1945 elaborates:

> *A Jap officer came daily with more and more threats, supplemented with kicks and slaps if the Batamen did not bow right down to the earth to him – a deep humiliating bow to every Jap soldier, officer and even civilian. It was almost a miracle, in the chaos of Japanese-occupied Singapore, that they got together some tools and materials for at least a few hundred pairs of shoes […]*
>
> *Placed as they were in such danger – surrounded, guarded, watched and controlled – the Singapore Batamen refused to give in, refused to*

work for the Japs. Had they done it openly, there would be no Batamen left to tell the story today, so they found their own way: for each pair of shoes supplied to the Japanese authority, they made four pairs of footwear and secretly gave them to the Chinese, Indian and Malay population whose plight was indescribable.

In reward, the Singapore people helped them with foodstuff and materials. And the shoes for the Japs were specially marked, indicating 'made specially for Japs'. They were made 'so special' that complaints were received after every dispatch.

The Batamen also delivered hundreds of pairs of shoes to an internment camp for women and children. Besides shoes, they also secretly supplied the civilians in the camp with quinine and other badly needed medicine. The *Batanagar News* article adds:

Such activity could not be hidden for long, even with the best precautions. Military police once came to the Bata house and took away the manager, Mr Jugas, along with Mr Chudárek and Mr Ambrož, for interrogation at the Military Police headquarters – some sort of Japanese Gestapo. This office was a prison and torture chamber, situated in the former YMCA building in Singapore.

These three came out after one week, all at the point of collapsing. Only after the victory day was it possible to get out of them bit-by-bit what had really happened [...] Apart from the brutal interrogation they had to suffer themselves, they also had to witness the terrible and indescribable torture of other prisoners, including women and young boys and girls.

Finally, the Japanese lost their patience and took over the shoe production themselves. All the remaining Batamen and other Czechoslovaks were then put into the Changi internment camp in December 1943 – nearly two years later than other European nationals. This was a group of 14 Batamen, one of whom – Alfred Mizia, a Bata supply manager – was still accompanied by his wife Růžena and two little children, because they had earlier refused to evacuate when they could. Another 12 Czechoslovaks shared the same fate, having previously worked in Singapore as artists, priests or for other companies than Bata.

According to *Batanagar News*:

On the 6 December 1943, the Japanese police surrounded the premises and gave them 30 minutes to dress and pack some belongings. Then they threw all the Czechoslovaks into a van and took them to the prison in Changi [...]

Bohman and Jedovnický have given us an account of life in the camp: the shortage of food there is now widely known. In the surrounding grass and ever-green bushes, there were plenty of slimy slugs. Some of the inmates tried to cook and eat them – they proved to be edible and at least stilled their hungry stomachs. Joint collection of slugs was then organised, and they were primarily given to the sick.

Death was stalking in the camp. There were deaths from torture, deaths from exhaustion, malnutrition and diseases. There were nervous breakdowns, illnesses, suffering. How did the Batamen withstand it all?

[...] Coming back from work, they set out to learn thoroughly the King's English; others went with Malay. Matuš was the cook, Mizia and Varmuža were hospital orderlies; Jugas himself, Pospíšil and Martinec were cultivating the allotment of earth, and so on.

The community of Bata Czechoslovaks held closely together during the internment, helping each other and organising joint production of food at the prison's yard. In May 1944, they were all relocated to an internment camp in Sime Road, where they survived until the liberation.

Bata Volunteers and Prisoners of War

We know from the memoirs of Viktor Koš that among the Batamen in Singapore, 11 were in active service as volunteers in SSVF and fought in the battle in February 1942: Pavel Ambrož, Matěj Bohman, Alois Čepka, Rudolf Janeček, Stanislav Jedovnický, Rudolf Kožušníček, Emil Matuš, Jan Mráz, Silvestr Němec, Josef Vyhnálek and Vojtěch Zamara. We can, for certain, add Karel Vítek to this list as well since he was captured and became a prisoner of war. That would make a total of 12 names.

I have gathered from the SSVF yearbooks of 1938 and 1939 that Čepka, Koblížek, Mráz, Stásek and Zamara were with the volunteer Royal Engineers. What I found interesting was that neither *Batanagar News* nor Viktor Koš mentioned the names of Koblížek and Stásek. Further research revealed that Koblížek managed to evacuate to India while Stásek had died before the war, sometime in 1941, in Saigon where he contracted typhus.

We will delve into greater detail about what the 12 Bata volunteers experienced during the battle of Singapore when we explore the possible scenarios of Silvestr's death in the next chapter.

At the time of surrender, eight managed to return home and change into civilian clothes, but at least three of them – Josef Vyhnálek, Vít Janeček and Karel Vítek – were captured in battle and became POWs. As we will explore in the next chapter, there is a slight possibility that Silvestr Němec was also captured as a POW.

Initially, POWs were put into several smaller POW camps around the island, but most of them ended up in Changi. Although the name of the area 'Changi' has become synonymous with the largest POW camp in Singapore, the captured soldiers were in fact kept in the British Selarang Barracks, a military compound in the vicinity of the actual Changi Prison (or Changi Gaol), which was – for most of the Japanese Occupation – used as an internment camp for about 3,000 European civilians from Singapore.

Here is Vyhnálek's recollection of the chaos and brutality that followed the fall of Singapore, and in which Silvestr may have found his end:

> *For those of us who became prisoners of war, a death march followed to the concentration camp at Changi Barracks. Why do I say a death march? As we were walking through the city in endless columns, at every street crossing, a Japanese officer pulled one prisoner out. That unfortunate person was then tied to a pole or chair and bayoneted to death in the eyes of his fellows. It was argued later that the Japanese did this as a warning to the other prisoners, and also to show the natives that the white men are no longer in charge of the island.*

Although historians question the reference to the "death march" because there are no other records of this particular brutality committed by the Japanese in Singapore (in contrast with the Philippines), it is apparent that there was mayhem and violence in the days and weeks following the surrender, during which more killings were taking place, and the wounded were dying.

The duties of POWs in Changi, during the first few months, were mostly to clean up Singapore. This is how Vyhnálek, one of the four Czechoslovaks who became POWs and the only one who survived, described his experience:

> *Our first job was cleaning up the rubble and burying the corpses of the dead. The decay was very fast in the tropical weather, so there was a terrible stench spreading to a perimeter of one kilometre, and when we approached the dead body, [there were] swarms of flies [...We had] rice and rice only for food. The rations were small, completely inadequate. We were making salt out of the sea water. We boiled soup from the grass, it was hardly digestible [...] When we worked outside the camp, we sometimes managed to collect wild green limes or coconuts, because they are plentiful in Malaya. Sometimes we managed to find snails – we boiled them together with rice, but again, not everybody was able to eat them.*

The conditions in the Changi POW camp were tough, especially as time went by and the Japanese supplies of food and medicine dwindled to far below what was necessary. The POWs are pictured – amongst many other documents and artworks – in a famous book, *King Rat*, which was also made into a film in 1965. It's a story of a selfish and corrupt Corporal who becomes a boss in the informal hierarchy of the prisoners in the camp and enjoys a relatively luxurious life, while his comrades are starving and living in tatters.

But even if life in the Changi POW camp was hard, it was still a friendly place in comparison to the working camps in Burma and Borneo, where most POWs from Singapore were later transferred. And so, while only about 1,000 out of some 50,000 POWs died during captivity at Changi – meaning the mortality was some two percent – the average death rate in those working camps reached over 30 per cent.

The Japanese started to send POWs from Singapore to the working camps in Burma and Borneo in March 1943. This is how Vyhnálek remembers it:

> *About a year later [after being at the Changi POW camp], we were divided into three groups: the first one went to Burma to build a railway and road there, another one to Labuan in Borneo to build an airport, and the third, to Japan.*
>
> *We as Czechoslovaks wanted to stay together. I was therefore very unhappy when a Japanese officer pulled me out of our group that was*

heading for Borneo and assigned me to Burma.

Soon we realised what kind of a hell we arrived to. Tropical ulcers, skin diseases, malaria and the worst, cholera, were haunting us all the time. Some camps perished to the last men due to cholera, in some others only a third of the men survived. The infected dead bodies were often left in the open without burials, so when the rains came, the water was contaminated, and the disease spread.

The Burma Railway – often also referred to as the 'Death Railway' – was designed by the Japanese and stretched from Bangkok in Thailand to the western coast of Burma. Its main purpose was to enable supplies to the Japanese army during their operation in Burma and the planned invasion of British India (at that time, it included today's Bangladesh, a neighbour to Burma). Without this railway, the Japanese would have to rely on transport ships that would need to go several thousand kilometres around the whole Malayan Peninsula – that long journey would have made them quite vulnerable.

In contrast, the railway supply route was only 400 kilometres long, but it had to cut through wild and mountainous inland. Its construction was therefore a very challenging task as it required – among other feats of engineering – building more than 600 bridges.

The price of making it happen was paid by the POWs and locals who were assigned to do hard manual labour under horrible conditions. The Japanese interned about 250,000 workers in numerous camps along the railway and they were forced to work in the hostile jungle with less than minimum supply of food and medicine, and no real infrastructure. The railway was built practically without any machinery, just simple shovels and picks. Jonathan Moffat edited a book that elaborates on this: *Baba Nonnie Goes to War: The Memoirs of a Singapore Volunteer on the Thai-Burma Railway*, written by POW survivor Ron Mitchell.

After it was finished in late 1943, the railway served the Japanese until the end of war – except for several brief interruptions due to Allied attacks. This is captured in another movie that was legendary when I was growing up, *The Bridge on the River Kwai*.

Out of about 60,000 prisoners of war who worked there, 20 percent did not survive. In total, approximately 100,000 people died on the construction of the 'Death Railway' in Burma as a result of malnutrition, mistreatment and diseases. Most of the surviving prisoners were sent to different locations, and the Japanese only kept several small camps there for maintenance and repair of the railway.

In Vyhnalek's memoirs, he recounts:

> The Japanese then decided to focus on defence and to build an air base at Singapore's Changi Point. The remaining prisoners from Burma were assigned to it. Therefore, we were going back to Singapore – that was in the middle of 1944. After two months there, we realised that all the skin diseases that infected us in Burma were gone – a miraculous Singapore climate!
>
> But as we got rid of one disease, another hit us badly. Epidemy of beriberi spread quickly among us, and many prisoners died of it. Our legs first got swollen and painful. When the swelling and pain extended to our stomachs, we knew it was bad: the patient was not able to eat anymore and died within two weeks.

It was because of beriberi that two of Silvestr's friends and colleagues died in the spring of 1945: Karel Vítek and Rudolf Janeček. They were less lucky than Vyhnálek: both were transferred from Changi POW camp in March 1943 as a part of the 'Force E' to Borneo. It was there, in Batu Litang/Kuching camp that Vítek died on 18 March 1945 because of malaria and beriberi. Rudolf Janeček was in the same group of prisoners and died in the same camp as a result of the same diseases a month earlier, on 13 February 1945.

There is a third Czechoslovak POW who lost his life during the Japanese Occupation. His name was Wieslaw Sienkievicz. He was of Polish origin and came from a border city of Český Těšín. Like Silvestr, he was also a volunteer with the Armoured Cars Unit (SSVAC). He died in one of the camps in Borneo on 15 August 1944. Although Sienkievicz himself was not a Bata employee, his name occurs several times in the memoirs of the Batamen, indicating that he was somehow close to their community.

The Road to Liberation

According to a report dated July 1943, which I found in the archives of the Czechoslovak Ministry of Foreign Affairs, there were 37 Czechoslovak men, five women and three children left in Singapore after the evacuations. A letter from the British Red Cross, written on 5 September 1945, has a different headcount of the liberated Czechoslovak internees: 23 men, seven women and three children.

The biggest difference in figures is for men. There is a possible explanation for this: the Foreign Ministry was probably unaware of the unsuccessful evacuation attempts of six Czechoslovaks or the four taken as POWs, and therefore counted those who died on evacuation ships or in POW camps as still being interned in Singapore.

My own headcount of the interned Czechoslovaks, compiled from a number of documents, probably gives the most accurate picture. There were 24 men (16 of them working for Bata), four women (one married to a Bataman) and four children (two offsprings of Batamen). The only Bata wife and children who did not evacuate – and who ended up in the internment camps – was Růžena Mizia with her little son Alfred (born in March 1941) and daughter Iva (born in 1936). They were all interned first at Changi Prison and later moved to the Sime Road internment Camp.

The Czech archives hold some wartime correspondence, indicating that the Czechoslovak government was not passive and had tried to find out more information about its citizens in Singapore during the Japanese Occupation. There were also attempts to exchange some of the interned citizens with Japan – this was facilitated by a Swiss ambassador in Tokyo. Eventually, such a deal was made in 1942 between Britain and Japan, although it only included diplomats and civil servants who were interned in the Far East.

From the documents that I found in the archives of the Military History Institute and of the Ministry of Foreign Affairs in Prague, the number of people included in the exchange was limited due to the capacity of the ship that the Japanese assigned for the operation. The limit was 1,700 Allied citizens, and the British authorities agreed to establish a proportional quota for various nations. The documents mention that there were about 12,000 British and 3,000 other European Allied citizens interned by Japanese in Southeast Asia.

I was surprised that the second most common nationality was Polish with some 850 citizens, followed by 800 Belgians and 620 Norwegians. Czechoslovakia, whose exiled government was registering 234 to 300 interned citizens in the region, finally got a quota for 18 that could be exchanged. They were released and sent back to Europe in the middle of 1942. Apparently, this exchange did not involve those in Singapore but included Czechoslovaks in Hong Kong, Shanghai, Philippines, Borneo, Sumatra and Java.

It was not just the Czechoslovak government that had been trying to find out what happened to their citizens in Singapore. The wives of the Batamen – after they had been evacuated to India – were also putting effort into finding out about their husbands throughout the war. They were sending inquiries and interventions, pleading with the exiled government to do something to get them released. One of the remarkable documents I found in the archives is a telegram from Nainital in India, signed by 12 wives of the Bata workers in Singapore, and sent to London in April 1942.

Two months later, Mrs Marie Košová wrote a letter on their behalf to the exiled Czechoslovak President Edvard Beneš. She listed the names of the 12 respective husbands in her appeal.

Her husband, Viktor Koš, had an adventurous journey through the war. After an attempted evacuation on a ship that was captured by the Japanese near Bangka Island, he ended up in an internment camp in Muntok. Four weeks later, they were transported to Palembang on Sumatra.

In July 1942, Koš and two other Czechoslovaks, Červinka and Zelníček (both Batamen from Singapore), whom he met at Muntok as well as several Argentinian and Swiss internees, managed to convince the Japanese and the Governor of Palembang that they should be released, since they were citizens of countries that were not at war with Japan. Koš and his two colleagues then tried to find a way to one of the cities with an operating Bata branch in Batavia.

At that time, Director of Bata in Singapore, Mr Jugas, helped them and sent them some money (since he was still not interned in Singapore); they also got a loan from the Bata office in Medan in the north of Sumatra. Eventually, on 28 December 1942, they reached Medan and spent the rest of the war there in relative peace. This was also where Viktor Koš wrote a detailed diary in 1943 from which I frequently quote.

Although the tide of the war in the Pacific started to turn in the second half of 1942, with Japanese defeats at Midway and Guadalcanal, it took another three years before the Japanese announced their unconditional surrender on 15 August 1945.

The news reached the Czechoslovaks in Singapore only at the end of August 1945, when the Allied Forces dropped leaflets above the Sime Road Camp – where they were interned at the time – informing everyone that the war was over, and Japan had capitulated.

Shortly after liberation, most of the Batamen went to India, where the Batanagar operation had avoided major disruptions during the world war. Some, however, decided to stay in Singapore and to start on the restoration of the Bata company: these were Jugas, Martinec Kožušníček, Pospíšil, Sokol and Mizia. As for the rest, upon arrival in India and after health checks, all but Bohman and Jedovnický were in such a bad state that they were immediately sent for recuperation. After this initial recovery, Bata granted them a long holiday.

Josef Vyhnálek, the only surviving Czechoslovak POW, was transported along with other liberated British soldiers to England where he filled up his 'liberation questionnaire'. It was a special moment when, 75 years later, I held the original document in my hand during a visit to the UK National Archives.

From the accounts above, it is evident that the Japanese Occupation of Singapore and the region was a period of tremendous hardship. By understanding what the other Batamen and Czechoslovaks went through during the war, I could better envision what Silvestr himself might have faced in each of those circumstances.

With that, I have now arrived at the hardest part of this story. By pulling together all the research and personal accounts I've gathered, I will finally attempt to reconstruct the scenarios of Silvestr's last moments.

- XIII -
Scenarios of Silvestr's Fate

IT TOOK ME three intensive years of research and networking to gather key documents and facts, and a couple more years of piecing them together, to reconstruct the story of the fate of my granduncle Silvestr.

For me, this process has been so much more than impersonal historical research. It inevitably elicited deep, personal emotions, which were sometimes overwhelming for me – particularly as I was drawing closer to the most painful part of the story: Silvestr's death.

After thinking it through many times, it seems to me that there are four possible scenarios regarding Silvestr's fate.

Scenario 1: His evacuation ship was sunk

The first possible scenario of my granduncle Silvestr Němec's fate is that he somehow managed to escape on one of the evacuation ships from Singapore shortly before the British surrendered but had perished when the ship was sunk by the Japanese.

This is a rather hypothetical scenario, even though one of the documents from Ivan Procházka's collection, which appears to be notes made in the 1990s by a certain Mr Martiš from Zlín, says:

> Němec Silvestr, born 20 October 1919, Zlín, died on 13 February 1942 in Singapore. After Japanese attack, Silvestr left for England on an evacuation ship that was sunk by the Japanese. According to another version, murdered in hospital.

Mr Martiš, like Mr Máčel, was one of the Zlín patriots who – after the 1989 fall of the Communist regime and Iron Curtain that isolated

Czechoslovakia from most of the post-war world – invested time and effort in the 1990s to gather information about the Batamen scattered abroad. Unfortunately, he has passed on too. Therefore, it is impossible now to find out the source of his note about Silvestr leaving Singapore on an evacuation ship.

Although there is no direct evidence for this scenario, it cannot be entirely ruled out. In fact, as we have seen in the previous chapter, many other Czechoslovaks – including some of Silvestr's colleagues – attempted evacuation from Singapore. This was also how several of them lost their lives.

As you might recall, even after the Japanese launched their attack on Malaya on 8 December 1941, the British officials in Singapore were partly in denial regarding the seriousness of the situation. As a result, the evacuation and retreats from Malaya were delayed until the last moment, and then they happened in chaos. This also explains why very few civilians managed to get away from Singapore in December 1941. The government did not recommend evacuation as they feared it might create mass panic; they argued that it was not necessary because Singapore would hold its ground. The number of people on the island was in fact increasing, as the European and some Eurasian civilians, as well as Allied soldiers, were fleeing from Malaya and pouring into Singapore – a particularly big wave of these 'refugees' arrived when Kuala Lumpur was finally evacuated.

It was only in early January 1942, as the battlefront was quickly approaching Singapore, that the authorities rushed to evacuate some of the civilians. As with what happened earlier in Penang, the evacuation effort prioritised the thousands of Europeans living there and was never meant for the large population of local people.

Dozens of ships of all kinds were then leaving Singapore: old merchant ships, liners as well as auxiliary navy vessels. They were heading west to British India and then to Britain, or south to Java and Borneo, then on to Australia; and a few also travelled to British South Africa.

The colonial administration created a special evacuation commission, which was tasked to organise the available ships. This commission was also in charge of the paperwork, including decisions on permits to leave Singapore. Priority was given to women and children.

As described previously, this was how most wives and children of the Batamen managed to escape in the first evacuation wave in January

1942. It is documented that most of them reached India safely in February 1942. Several others who were not in this group evacuated individually, some eventually ended up in Australia.

The last wave of evacuation ships departed from Singapore between 11 and 13 February. About 44 vessels went out to sea – this is however only an estimation; the exact figure is not known because the documentation did not survive the war.

By the time that last convoy left Singapore, the Japanese had already gained full control of the air as well as the sea surrounding Singapore, therefore any escape was very risky. They announced that all evacuation vessels would be destroyed, determined "not to allow another Dunkirk". Indeed, most of those vessels were destroyed or captured, only six of them eventually managed to escape and reach safety. The British Command then suspended all evacuations on the morning of 14 February.

The full lists of those on board the evacuation vessels were compiled only after departure, and because most of the ships eventually sank, those documents have been lost. Therefore, we will never learn the names of the thousands who boarded those ships and later perished at sea – they ended up being officially declared as 'missing'. So, in the event that Silvestr did manage to find his way onto one of those vessels – as the note by Mr Martiš suggests – he might be amongst those.

The survivors who managed to escape from the sinking ships and save themselves were later captured by the Japanese and interned in camps in Sumatra. This was the fate of Viktor Koš, the main Bata accountant in Singapore.

In his war diary, Koš listed 18 Batamen who, to his knowledge, were part of the last evacuation convoy. But given the chaos around the evacuation vessels, there could have been more – possibly also Silvestr.

However, the chances that Silvestr somehow managed to escape from Singapore are nearly zero. As a volunteer in active service, he would have never received the required permit, although it was not impossible to sneak aboard one of the ships during the chaos. Also, he certainly was not leaving with a group of other Bata people, as otherwise, they would have remembered him.

When I was searching through the 'FindMyPast' portal for persons with his name, there was even a moment when I thought that miraculously, my granduncle might have indeed survived the war, moved to the United States and lived there, and for some reason, did not want to inform anyone from the family. This was when I found a record of "Sylvestr K. Nemec", born just like Silvestr in 1919 and registered in Wisconsin, who died in March 2000 at the age of 81. This, as you might expect, turned out to be the wrong person, and hence, a dead-end.

Scenario 2: He died as a prisoner of war

A second possible scenario is that Silvestr was captured and died as a POW. What makes me consider this as an option?

The main lead was provided by Josef Vyhnálek in his 1946 article:

> *Several Czechoslovaks were captured by the Japanese just a day before capitulation. These were Rudolf Janeček, Karel Vítek, J. Sinkievicz, J. Vyhnálek and wounded Silvestr Němec, whom we have not seen ever since, and he is still missing.*

Vyhnálek also wrote in his letter to my family that he last saw Silvestr fighting at the Gap in Pasir Panjang on 13 February, after which they got separated; later that day (that is, two days before the surrender), Vyhnálek and others were captured by the Japanese in that area.

If Silvestr was captured and was not seen by his friends thereafter, he must have died shortly after capture, maybe a couple of days or weeks following the surrender of Singapore. It surely would be before the Japanese finished identification and registration of all their prisoners as – unlike Josef Vyhnálek or Rudolf Janeček, whose POW cards I found – I couldn't find Silvestr's.

Vyhnálek's POW card was written on 15 August of the 17th year of the Hirohito's era, which corresponds with the year 1942 of the Christian calendar – that is exactly six months after Singapore's capitulation. It's recorded that Vyhnálek became a POW on 17 February 1942.

As there is no trace of Silvestr's POW card and there seems to be no witness accounts of him being in captivity, if he did become a POW, he must have ended up in a prisoner camp separated from the rest of the Czechoslovaks. But even then, his name does not appear on any of the publicly accessible nominal rolls and records of POWs in Singapore – with one remarkable exception.

There is one unique historical document suggesting that Silvestr did indeed become a POW. It has become known as the 'Jeyes List', a nominal roll secretly written up sometime in 1942 by Jack Bennett, a salesman from an export company based in Borneo, who ended up being detained in Singapore's internment camp for civilians at Changi Prison. It was here that Bennett compiled a list of all known Europeans from Malaya and Singapore that were not interned at Changi, and therefore were either known to be POWs elsewhere or were considered missing. Bennett was systematically collecting and verifying his information from other people in the camp or from those who were transiting through it.

Bennett's list is written in small script on 18 sheets of folded toilet paper – that's where the name 'Jeyes List' comes from as Jeyes was a brand producing toilet paper. It was the only 'paper' available in the camp as it was forbidden to keep any documents or records. He attached a code to each name: 'M' meant missing, and 'POW' indicated prisoner of war.

I have received a digital scan of the 'Jeyes List' (along with other invaluable documents) from Jonathan Moffatt from the Malayan Volunteer Group. It is a low-resolution copy, but still readable enough to clearly recognise this record: "NEMEC – CZECH – BATA – POW".

So indeed, Silvestr might have been captured alive, maybe wounded, and became a prisoner of war. According to historians, the 'Jeyes List' is considered a highly reliable source, with some 95 percent accuracy. Of course, Silvestr may fall under the five percent of cases where Bennett's information was incorrect; but we can't rule this scenario out.

However, there is another historical document, created directly at the POW camp, that suggests otherwise. The administration of the main POW camp in Singapore, set up at the Selarang Barracks in Changi, was headed by an incredibly diligent SSVF Captain, David Nelson. With his small team, he compiled many records of POWs present or passing through the camp, including their movements to various labour camps in Burma or Borneo. At a big personal risk, he managed to keep hiding and preserving these documents throughout the war.

Some of his records can now be found in the British archives. One of them is Nelson's copy of the Malayan Directory. This is a printed directory of British citizens living in Malaya before the war, into which Nelson wrote short notes, updating information about these persons' whereabouts during the Occupation. And in it, we can also find Silvestr's name! His record was added to a margin of the paper in pencil and says, "M/V NEMEC S 1/SSVF". The letter 'M' stands for 'missing', and 'V' indicates that he was a volunteer; there is also additional information that he was with the 1st Battalion of the SSVF ("1/SSVF"). So, in this Nelson's directory, Silvestr is not recorded as a POW, but as 'missing'.

Finally, there is also one small discrepancy that might indicate Silvestr's survival during the fall of Singapore by a few more days. The date of his death in the online record of the Commonwealth War Graves Commission (CWGC) is 17 February – that would be two days after the capitulation.

This is in contrast with the official death certificate that states that he died "on or around 15 February 1942". I was trying to get to the bottom of the CWGC's dating, hoping that some other interesting document or reference might emerge. Unfortunately, my inquiries with CWGC on this matter have so far failed and I have not learnt what is the source of their information.

But even if Silvestr was able to stay alive till 17 February 1942, this second scenario suggests that he probably lost his life before he could be registered at one of the POW camps. As for how he lost his life in this scenario, we may never know.

Scenario 3: He died in battle at Pasir Panjang

A third possible scenario is that Silvestr was killed in battle at Pasir Panjang, the hilly ridge in the southwest of Singapore island.

The main information suggesting such a fate is a letter from Josef Vyhnálek to Silvestr's parents, dated on 21 August 1947.

> *I remember vividly how we were attacking the Japanese, he [Silvestr] was very pale, so it seemed to me that he might have felt that something would happen to him. It was when we were attacking the hill CAP [correct reference is Gap Hill] near Pasir Panjang in Singapore and was about halfway up the slope when thousands of airplanes spotted us, and we were heavily bombed and fired upon by machine guns. During that bombing, we ran and scattered into the rubber plantations and that was the last time I saw your Silvester. Throughout the time of my captivity, I thought he might have escaped to India or Australia, but after the liberation, I have unfortunately learnt that nothing is known about his fate.*

As mentioned previously, we know from the memoirs of Viktor

Koš that the following 12 Batamen in Singapore were in active service as volunteers during the Battle of Singapore: Pavel Ambrož, Matěj Bohman, Alois Čepka, Rudolf Janeček, Stanislav Jedovnický, Rudolf Kožušníček, Emil Matuš, Jan Mráz, Silvestr Němec, Karel Vítek, Josef Vyhnálek and Vojtěch Zamara.

This perfectly fits the post-war article in the *Batangar News* from October 1945 where the following 12 volunteers from Bata are named:

Ambrož, Bohman, Kužušníček, Matuš and Jedovnický
   (machine gun unit)
Čepka and Mráz (bomb disposal unit)
Němec, Janeček, Vítek and Vyhnálek (rifle unit)
Zamara (heavy artillery unit)

The SSVF battalions, including our 12 Czechoslovak volunteers, were initially positioned in the southeastern sector of Singapore – the opposite side to where the Japanese eventually landed. Besides various references in literature, I found first-hand accounts of that in two documents at the Imperial War Museum's archives in London. Both Lance Corporal James Hodgson (4th SSVF Battalion) and Private Richard Middleton-Smith (1st SSVF Battalion) mention that in early February, they were assigned responsibility for defence of the beaches close to the city, where they manned small pillboxes and prepared obstacles against invasion from the sea.

How is it then possible that Josef Vyhnálek participated in the battle at the Gap in Pasir Panjang, which is in a different sector of the island? I found several pieces of evidence indicating that some volunteer units from SSVF were moved to that area, probably to reinforce the Malay troops facing the Japanese advancing towards the city along the southern coast.

The first piece of evidence is from Josef Vyhnálek himself, since he mentioned fighting at Pasir Panjang in both his letter and memoirs.

The second is Jan Baroš' article in the *Batanagar News*, where he wrote:

> *The volunteer units were posted for beach defence all along the coast [...] On 2 February, the commander of the Volunteer Corps, in which the Batamen were serving, put the whole force on the frontline to face the Japanese assault.*

Third is when Lance Corporal Hodgson wrote in his diary that as fighting began in the western side of the island, the volunteers were gradually dispatched there.

Fourth is the story of Middleton-Smith of SSVF, whose unit was ordered to move from the beaches to a machine gun post in Tanglin, which is just a few kilometres north of the Pasir Panjang ridge.

Fifth is a recollection of Pancheri from 1st SSVF Battalion that "our three companies, S, B and D were deployed in the Holland Road area and towards Ayer Rajah Road". We already know that the B company was the one to which the Czechoslovaks were attached.

Sixth, Dol Ramli in his 1965 work, *History of the Malay Regiment 1933-1942*, wrote:

> By the 12th, the danger of a tank breakthrough into Singapore town had caused Percival to decide on a close perimeter defence of the town to include the Pierce MacRitchie Reservoirs. All beach-defence troops stationed in the north and east part of the island were, therefore, withdrawn and deployed accordingly.

Last, and perhaps the most significant account, is from *Marshall of Singapore*, a biography of David Marshall by Kevin Tan. It says:

> The 1st Battalion (companies A, B, C and D) had been assigned to defend the beaches on the southern side of Singapore island, from Bedok to just past the Singapore Swimming Club at Tanjong Rhu. The defence of the stretch of shore from Bedok eastwards to Changi was in the hands of the Manchester Regiment […] When it became quite clear that the Japanese were not going to land on Singapore's southern beaches, the high command decided to move the SSVF troops northwards to halt the Japanese attacks. On 11 February 1942, B Company was moved to … the middle of the island, to reinforce an Australian battalion.

While getting there by driving up Holland Road, it got under heavy fire. Kevin Tan writes:

> It was a frightening experience for the volunteers, who had never experienced anything close to this, not even in the most realistic of simulated battles. They were dodging mortars and enemy fire and staring mortality in the face.

We will soon find out – from an account included in the fourth scenario – that Silvestr suffered shell shock. Could this be the event that caused it? It might be, since it happened on 11 February, the day on which he is recorded to have been treated for it.

Finally, the B Company made another move:

> B Company spent the next 24 hours on the tennis court, securing Holland Road from elevated ground. Later, the men moved further towards town into Ridout Road, where they spent four days supporting the troops in front.

Ridout Road is two-and-a-half km from the Gap (and Alexandra Hospital is just about midway). Since the B Company arrived there on the 12th, it is probably from there that some of the volunteers were sent to support the Malay Regiment fighting the Japanese in Pasir Panjang – just as Vyhnalek recalls it. There is a possibility that Silvestr was one of them.

Heroes of Pasir Panjang

Having established that at least some of the SSVF volunteers, including several Czechoslovaks, participated in the fighting at Pasir Panjang, let's now examine what happened there. What kind of battle they were joining? What do we know about the Japanese advance and tactics in that sector? Knowing this may help us reconstruct the last hours of Silvestr's life – if he had indeed perished at the battle of Pasir Panjang.

In this area, defence against the advancing Japanese 18th Division of General Mutaguchi was placed on the shoulders of two battalions of the Malay Regiment, combined with Malay volunteers and parts of the 44th Indian Brigade. Together, it was about 1,400 defenders. Against them was a significant part of the 13,000-strong Japanese division.

The defenders at Pasir Panjang were plagued with the same problems as the overall British operation: confusion, disarray, indecisiveness and chaotic orders from the main command, as well as difficulties with communication. The morale of the defenders was certainly not helped by the flow of deserters and stragglers retreating through their positions. One of the war diaries I read describing the battle of Pasir Panjang was written by Colonel A.G. MacKenzie who, as a lieutenant during the battle, single-handedly eliminated a Japanese infantry gun crew – for which he was awarded the Military Cross. He remembers that as he was moving to his position, a soldier he was passing was shouting at him that it was "suicide to go on".

Despite the many obstacles, the Singapore defenders managed to mount quite a strong and heroic resistance at Pasir Panjang.

While we now know that the main battle of Pasir Panjang took place between 12 and 14 February, the advanced units of the defenders actually made contact with the enemy at dawn on 10 February 1942. Overnight from 11 to 12 February, the Allied positions there were under intensive artillery shelling and bombardment. On 12 February, the defenders succeeded in repelling several enemy attacks. After nightfall, they fell back to a new line which was going through the Gap – a strategic point in the middle of the ridge, through which a winding road offered access to the Singapore suburbs, including to the Alexandra Hospital area.

It was here, around the Gap, that fierce fighting took place on 13 February – matching what Josef Vyhnálek described, when he placed his last sighting of Silvestr here on that day. It was again preceded by concentrated Japanese bombing and shelling. The precise artillery firing was guided from an observation balloon released by the Japanese near the western coast a day earlier. MacKenzie recalls that "the mortar barrage was so thick and fast that it was more like heavy machine-gun fire than mortar shelling". This would have been an absolutely terrifying moment for Silvestr, whose short military training with the Singapore volunteers could not have prepared him for such experience.

After the intense Japanese fire, a main frontal attack supported by light tanks and the air force followed at 2 pm. Despite fierce resistance by the Allied soldiers, the Japanese managed to break through the line about two hours later, and the defenders had to engage in hand-to-hand combat. Most of the B Company of the Malay Regiment were then captured. It is quite possible that alongside them, Josef Vyhnálek and several other Czechoslovaks were also captured, as he clearly wrote in his memoir that it happened "two days before the surrender". Was Silvestr among them? Again, we will probably never know.

On the evening of 13 February, the defence line moved closer to the city again, reaching the immediate vicinity of Alexandra Hospital. This is where the story about the infamous massacre connects.

Seen from a military perspective, the battle at Pasir Panjang was insignificant. Even if the defenders succeeded, it would not have changed the outcome of the Battle of Singapore. That is probably why these events never made it into the "bigger history".

However, one of the moments of the battle at Pasir Panjang became a legendary story of the heroic last stand of the Malay Regiment's C Company on Bukit Chandu, which means 'Opium Hill' in Malay. It got its name from a British opium factory that was once located at the foot of the hill.

It happened a day later, on 14 February. The C Company, composed of about 50 Malay soldiers, was led by a brave and charismatic Lieutenant Adnan Bin Saidi. That day, they found themselves cut off from an escape route and, unable to retreat, decided to fight to the last man. Shortly before it, Adnan adopted a motto for his Company, "*Biar putih tulang, jangan putih mata*" which, translated, means "Rather death than dishonour".

At first, the Japanese tried to fool the defenders of Bukit Chandu. A group of their soldiers put on some Indian uniforms and marched towards the hill, pretending they were coming as reinforcement. However, the Malays noticed it was a trap: the disguised Japanese were marching in the columns of three, as the British would do, but the Indians/Punjabis actually march in four columns. First the Malays let them come close and then opened fire from Lewis machine guns and killed at least 22 of the Japanese; the remaining ones crawled back to safety.

Two hours later, the outraged Japanese stormed the hill with a frontal banzai charge, supported by several tanks. The defenders, heavily outnumbered, fought fiercely in a hand-to-hand combat but did not stand a chance. The Japanese captured their commander Adnan, who was injured in the battle; they beat him brutally and finally stabbed him with bayonets.

After that, they put his body into a sack and hung it upside down from a tree (some versions of the story say that he was hanged from the tree alive and was only bayoneted then). In the following days, nobody was allowed to cut his body down and give him a proper burial.

The Japanese, infuriated by the resistance of defenders and by the death of their soldiers, did not take prisoners and murdered most of the survivors. Only five of the Malay soldiers, led by Lieutenant Abbas, managed to escape by jumping through the wall of fire from burning oil – two of them suffered bad burns.

One of the last successful actions of the Pasir Panjang defenders – and undoubtedly also a little sweet revenge – took place around dusk of

14 February. Shortly after 6 pm, two Japanese companies were spotted approaching the crossing of Alexandra Road and Pasir Panjang Road, where the Malay Regiment's D Company was hiding in a defensive position. What followed is captured in MacKenzie's diary:

> Imagine our surprise and delight when the Nips appeared marching straight down Pasir Panjang Road – in fours! We let them get to within 100-150 yards of 'D' Headquarters and let them have it with machine-guns first and then mortars. Almost every man of their first company was slaughtered and a lot further back too. An officer up on the right counted 94 bodies on that part of the road that he could see alone.

This incident took place in the vicinity of Alexandra Hospital, and I can see that that might have fuelled the anger of the Japanese, who then massacred their captives from Alexandra Hospital the following morning. We will explore what happened in greater detail in the fourth and final scenario.

Other Accounts of the Battle

During my research, I managed to collect about two dozen war diaries, written by soldiers who personally participated in the Battle of Singapore. I made copies of many of them from the UK National Archives and archives of the Imperial War Museum in London; and obtained some additional pieces from Jonathan Moffatt of the Malayan Volunteer Group.

These diaries not only provided a personal perspective of these battles, but also details that have helped me understand the circumstances of the Singapore defenders. I especially appreciate their varied personal comments and observations.

One of these personal accounts illustrates a situation Silvestr might have found himself in. It was written by Hugo Hughes from the Malay Regiment. On 13 February, he was seriously wounded in the battle of Pasir Panjang: he lost his leg and was rushed to Alexandra Hospital. Hughes, who was one of the lucky few who survived the massacre a day later, writes:

> The last of the overwhelmed RAF had packed up about the time the Japs landed, and Jap planes in the past few days had become appreciably

bolder. In fact, they appeared quite indifferent to the seemingly point-blank fire of our Bofors. Outside the village, I skirted amongst the scrub as one damned plane flying at well under 2,000 feet almost appeared to be stalking me. Having reached our right flank platoon, I lay on the ground and chatted with the Malay officer [...] A tense atmosphere – mortars and shells bursting on the ridge behind us, that infernal aeroplane flying around lower than ever, a jumble of battle noises in the distance. Everything became suddenly intensified. Shell and mortar explosions came nearer – so near that I was screwing my eyes closed and gasping as one would from a solid punch on the body, with each successive burst. I am in no position to compare that barrage with the devastating artillery hits of the last war or with any other kind of war. Knowing fellows declare that the Jap missiles are noisy but barely lethal. To me the concentration and frequency of explosions was terrific – perhaps 50 shell bursts within 200 yards of me in a few minutes [...]

I cannot say which one of those bursts hit me; I can't describe the sensation. It was not painful – feeling was a passive thing. Blood was gushing from a gaping wound in my leg, the torn flesh and muscles hung outside my trousers. Horrible to look at, and I had the sickening realisation that I would soon bleed to death at this rate and called to the Malays, crouching face to the ground, for some string and tied a lanyard after the fashion of a tourniquet. A Malay clung to my foot – from terror or from blank mindedness. Hell on Earth! One of these crumps would be the end.

A short let up and Rix appeared, and I asked him to get me out [...] It could not have been many minutes later when a Eurasian orderly came over. He immediately improved the tourniquet and staunched the blood considerably. A racing carrier disregarded his shouts to stop. He cursed and bullied some Malays on to their feet, and between them I hobbled to the road trailing my shattered leg. A car, the C.O.s, came along and I got piled into the back. Directed by the orderly, the driver shot up Reformatory Road and into Ayer Rajah Road at breakneck speed and pulled up in front of Alexandra Hospital. We must have come very close to, if not through, the Jap lines.

This firsthand account provides us with a vivid picture of what happened. I can't help but imagine Silvestr in a similar agonising situation, since many sources have mentioned that he was wounded at the time and hospitalised.

Finally, there are also details about the Pasir Panjang fighting in the memoirs of Josef Vyhnálek – Silvestr's colleague, friend and co-fighter:

> The section assigned to our unit to defend was Gap Hill, quite a strategic section [of Pasir Panjang]. During the night of 12 February, we heard a great deal of noises from airplanes above our heads. The spotlights came to light up the sky and we realised that it was a massive Japanese paratrooper operation. Our artillery shot several airplanes down. The fighting began at dawn. We soon found ourselves surrounded by the Japanese on all sides. After four hours of heavy fighting, when the rest of our unit was driven into the rubber plantation, we concluded that further resistance was futile. Our losses were about 50 percent, and we were running out of ammunition. Therefore Hunter Grey, the commander of our company, ordered us to surrender. The Japanese immediately disarmed us and tied us, one by one, with ropes to the rubber trees. They left us like this, without food or water, for three days, till the capitulation of Singapore on 15 February. Several Japanese soldiers with machine guns were on guard. Perhaps the capitulation saved us. We learnt only later the horrible destiny of those who were captured by the Japanese earlier. They were suffering from hunger and thirst, and at the end, were bayoneted to death so that the Japanese units could advance forward with the rest of their army.

Experienced historians have warned me on multiple occasions that individual personal war accounts are often confused and inaccurate, especially in details – therefore they should not be taken as a reliable source unless they are independently confirmed by other evidence.

In this case, Vyhnálek is apparently wrong when he describes an enemy paratrooper operation: the Japanese in fact did not use parachutist operations in Malaya or Singapore. Vyhnálek however seems to be quite accurate in other details, including the correct dating of the main battle at Gap Hill (13 February) and the name of the commander Hunter-Gray, except for the understandable spelling mistake.

Hunter-Gray hailed from London's Woolwich and as a boy enlisted in the Royal Tanks Corps. In Singapore, he worked as a high-ranking police inspector. He was married (and later divorced) to a car racer, and during the 1930s, also led a local police musical band. It's therefore quite plausible that he, being a senior police officer and knowledgeable of Singapore, was at some point put in charge of commanding a volunteer unit in a field.

Vyhnálek is also correct in his description of Japanese brutality towards their captives in battle, like how they would kill them with bayonets. Indeed, he and his companions were probably lucky because the capitulation took place only two days after their capture.

If Silvestr did indeed participate in the battle of Pasir Panjang, he might have been injured, captured or killed there. In the case that he was injured, he would have – like Hughes – been taken to nearby Alexandra Hospital.

Scenario 4: He was killed in the Alexandra Hospital Massacre

The final scenario is that Silvestr Němec died as a victim of the Alexandra Hospital massacre. This possibility is mentioned most frequently in the documents I have seen. To reconstruct what likely happened, I will provide a recap of these references in chronological order.

First, "The story of Batamen in Malaya" is an article published in the *Batanagar News* in October 1945. It was written by Jan Baroš, chief editor of the *Batanagar News*, based on the stories told to him by the first two Batamen – Mr Bohman and Mr Jedovnický – who reached India from Singapore after liberation:

> *It cannot be ascertained now who and how many were wounded, so far as we know, Kožušníček, Vitek and Němec were wounded. Němec was sent to the military hospital. When the Japanese later captured it, in the rage of animal brutality, they mercilessly killed all the wounded soldiers lying in beds. Here, Němec met his end.*

Second, the letter from Pavel Ambrož, Silvestr's colleague, to the Němec family. It's dated 21 December 1945:

> *About three days before the occupation of Singapore by the Japanese, Silvestr was wounded and moved to a field hospital. After the fall of Singapore [15 February 1942] I was searching for him in all hospitals but did not find him. Now that the British have taken over Singapore again, I have gone through the military records and found that he has been listed as 'missing'.*

Third, another worrying letter to Silvestr's anxious parents: this one written by Antonín Jugas, director of Bata Shoe Co. in Singapore, on 22 January 1946:

> It was only after the capitulation that we learned from our other people that your son was injured and taken to a hospital. Since then, nobody has ever heard of him.

Fourth, a recollection by Josef Vyhnálek, Silvestr's colleague and friend. He captured this information in his memoirs, written long after the war, in October 1966:

> Silvestr Němec, originating from the Brno region, was wounded when our positions were bombed at the beginning of the battle. He was taken to the hospital on Alexandra Road. This hospital was stormed by the Japanese several days later. All its personnel, doctors, nurses as well as patients were killed; Silvestr being one of them.

Finally, the fifth mention is from an unpublished section of the memoirs by Marie Bohman, daughter of Matěj Bohman (one of the Singapore Batamen):

> Mr Larry Kent, former Singapore resident, recalled that a Czech boy was among those cold-bloodedly bayoneted in their hospital beds.

I was lucky to get an independent confirmation about the story told by Larry Kent, formerly known as Ladislav Kvapil. One day, I received an email from Australia, sent by Mrs Helena Staroba-Giglietti. Her father, František Staroba, worked for Bata in Batanagar in India and then was sent to Java just before the war. The family managed to escape on an evacuation ship *Deucalion*, which was pursued and hit by a Japanese submarine, but eventually reached Australia. Another connection with our story is that Helena's sister, Líba, married a son of Antonín Jugas, the head of Bata in Singapore when Silvestr was there.

Helena's parents, who then lived in Australia, maintained a close relation with Ladislav Kvapil. In his old age, Mr Kvapil was taken care of by Helena, and she listened to many of his stories. She wrote me to say she still remembers Mr Kvapil telling her about a young boy from Bata who was stabbed to death at the Alexandra Hospital. Helena could not remember his name, but it's highly likely that it was Silvestr as he was the only "Czech boy" mentioned by name in other sources.

There are further references to Silvestr being murdered in the hospital, such as the article by Emil Máčel in 1993 or by Ivan Procházka in 1996; but they are secondary sources, most likely citing from the above-mentioned 1945 article by Jan Baroš. Therefore, I do not consider them as adding more weight to this scenario.

There is, however, a very important document that was first pointed out to me by Jonathan Moffatt from the Malayan Volunteers Group. It is a page from a list of missing soldiers in Singapore, and there is an entry about Silvestr. According to this document, he was "shell-shocked" on 11 February 1942, and then "missing before 15 February 1942". Since this was recorded, we can assume that he was treated for shell shock on 11 February, and possibly taken to a hospital.

Shell shock is not a direct physical wound, but a post-traumatic stress disorder caused by a nearby explosion of an artillery shell. Poor Silvestr, who left his country for Singapore at the age of 19, probably did not have a chance to go through a regular military training in Czechoslovakia before departure. As a boy growing up in Vémyslice, all he probably experienced were public demonstrations of military training, which were entertaining and exciting for a young lad in a small town. Thus, his only preparation for the war was the training of the Singapore Volunteer Corps. The concentrated artillery shelling and bombing, targeting the positions of defenders – as described so graphically by those directly engaged in the Pasir Panjang battle in the previous section – must have been absolutely terrifying for him.

The record of Silvestr suffering shell shock on 11 February perfectly fits with the other historical documents quoted above, suggesting that Silvestr was wounded several days before the fall of Singapore.

It is not known whether Silvestr suffered some other injuries. It is possible that he returned to his unit following a medical treatment on 11 February. That would be less likely if he had suffered shell shock, but it can't be entirely ruled out – notably as Vyhnálek remembers in his August 1947 letter that the last time he saw Silvestr alive was when they were both fighting around the Gap in Pasir Panjang on 13 February. Vyhnálek also mentioned that Silvestr was "very pale" – this might have in fact been due to the shell shock.

If Silvestr had been inflicted with a physical injury during that battle, it's almost certain that he was taken to Alexandra Hospital because it was nearest to the Pasir Panjang battlefield. And if Kožušníček and

Vítek were injured around the same time as Silvestr – which is what several accounts tell us – then they would also have been admitted to Alexandra Hospital. This scenario would explain how they ended up witnessing Silvestr's murder and why they became the source of the stories that would later spread among the Batamen.

Back then, Alexandra Hospital was named British Military Hospital. As its name suggests, it was the main hospital for the British forces, to which the Czechoslovak volunteers were attached.

The construction of the British Military Hospital was completed in 1938, shortly before the war. Built in the colonial style, it's a magnificent and spacious complex located on an elevated area and surrounded by a garden and auxiliary buildings. It still serves as a hospital to this day. Around the time of World War II, the hospital boasted modern interiors and state-of-the-art facilities, with a nominal capacity of 356 beds.

Witness Accounts of the Massacre

The most comprehensive publication about the massacre at Alexandra Hospital to date is Peter Bruton's *The Matter of a Massacre: Alexandra Hospital Singapore 14th/15th February 1942*. Published in 1989, it is based on witness accounts of about 20 survivors. At the beginning, Bruton acknowledged some of the challenges he faced: all original documentation of the hospital had been lost, and what people recalled or wrote down after three-and-a-half years in harsh prisoner camps is fragmented and sometimes contradictory.

As it is very difficult to get hold of Bruton's publication, which he released himself in a limited edition, let me provide you with an abbreviated version of how he reconstructed the events:

> *The civilian staff of the hospital was disappearing during the last days of the fighting. On Friday 13 February, the command of the hospital ordered the remaining eight local nurses to leave as well. They were concerned that following the capture by Japanese, a similar violence towards the medical staff could occur as it did recently in a hospital in Hong Kong.*
>
> *There were about 900 patients in the hospital at this moment – mostly British, but also some other nationals. It was well over the designed capacity, and therefore was very crowded. To accommodate so many patients, the wards originally designed for 24 beds each, were*

holding 72 injured who were lying on stretchers between the beds. A number of patients were also outside of the rooms, along the corridors. New wounded soldiers were still arriving, mostly during the night when the risk of bombing was limited.

The number of hospital staff was around 180 people.

The hospital was well marked with red crosses: there was a Red Cross flag on the pole, additional flags dropped from the windows and spread on its roof. On the lawn outside, a big cross was made of the white and red bed sheets.

On the evening of 13 February, the Japanese managed to penetrate the Pasir Panjang defence line and reach the vicinity of the hospital, thus turning the surrounding area into no man's land. The following morning, the hospital became the site of a crossfire, as artillery of both sides were firing above and across it.

On 14 February, around 1 pm, a line of Japanese soldiers was spotted passing by. Suddenly one of these soldiers appeared in a gap between the overlapping blast walls near the hospital entrance. A British medical captain approached him, pointing to his Red Cross armband and saying "hospital". They stared at each other for a moment, then the Japanese soldier fired his rifle on him, possibly considering his camouflaged helmet as a threat. Luckily, he missed and the captain ran back to hospital; the soldier did not pursue him inside.

Then around 2 pm, a group of Indian sappers were passing through the hospital. They took advantage of its roof and were firing from it on some Japanese soldiers around. Some of the patients later recalled that they even heard a firing sound of a light machine gun from somewhere within the building.

It does not matter whether the Indians ignored the neutrality of the hospital because of fear, panic or just stupidity. What they did soon proved fatal to the hospital.

Shortly after the Indians rushed out of the hospital, around 2.30 pm, Japanese soldiers stormed in in pursuit. They were coming in three separate groups, each approaching the hospital from a different direction. The Japanese soldiers seemed to have spent quite some time on the battlefront, based on their appearance: unshaven, dirty, in full gear, armed with rifles and bayonets, and heavy camouflage made of grass and twigs.

First group, approaching from the railway, scared hospital staff that was in a nearby laboratory building. As they started to run towards the hospital, the Japanese opened fire. Two were killed and one, wounded, crawled towards the main entrance, calling for help.

Another group of Japanese soldiers entered the building in the direction from which the Indian soldiers initially came. As they got to the corridor, the first place they saw was an improvised intake room that was crowded with about hundred wounded soldiers. One Japanese soldier took a broom and used its stick to beat them on their heads. Lieutenant Weston, who was in-charge of this room, took a white bed sheet as a sign of capitulation and held it next to the door. Another Japanese soldier stabbed him with a bayonet and killed him. It might have been this moment that triggered the outburst of atrocities that lasted for the next half an hour.

More Japanese soldiers rushed to the intake room and began to shoot and stab the patients there. Some of them tried to escape out of the room, gimping to the corridor and towards the main entrance, but there they got shot down by a machine gun. Some others were rushing through the corridor to the back of the building, where they eventually ran into another Japanese unit that also began to shoot or bayonet them. Several Japanese soldiers entered two of the wards, where they killed some patients and forced the others, who were able to walk, to stand up and move to the corridor.

A third Japanese group climbed up the verandas between two surgery sections. Here, six medics and doctors started a surgery around 2.30 pm despite the fact that the building was under fire. In order to get a better cover, they were performing it outside of the operating theatre, in an adjacent corridor. At the moment the Japanese reached them, they had just finished one surgery and were waiting for the next patient. The Japanese started to shoot, and the medical team ran into the operation theatre where they stopped, standing with hands raised above their heads. The Japanese ordered them to go out again, and as they did, they were stabbed and most of them got killed. Also, the patient, still lying in anaesthesia following the surgery, was bayoneted to death.

In the meantime, some other Japanese soldiers from this group went to the two surgical wards and were having sadistic fun torturing the patients there: twisting their bandaged arms and legs, beating them with rifle butts, and slinging the weights that were holding some patient's arms or legs in fixated positions. Later they went out to the main corridor, where they were randomly shooting or bayoneting the patients around.

In another room, two Japanese soldiers were robbing the patients of watches and other valuables, stabbing several of them along the way. Suddenly a Japanese officer came in, kicked them out and apologised in English: "I am sorry, but my men are tired and hungry – they have been fighting without rest for many days."

The frantic slaughter lasted for about half an hour. Fifty people were killed, both patients and staff. Many more were wounded, left lying on the floor, bleeding.

Yet, the worst was still to come.

The soldiers rounded up about two hundred people, mostly staff, but also patients from the ground floor – the intake room as well as the corridor – who were capable of walking. Their hands were first tied behind their backs, and then they were tied together in small groups. After that, they were ordered to march out of the hospital – patients in their pyjamas and bandages.

The captives were then led away, guarded by the Japanese soldiers. They had to duck for cover several times as the artillery fire was going on around them. After walking about a kilometre, they were crammed into an old building of the Sisters Quarter, which the nurses used for accommodation. The building was divided into three small compartments. The biggest one, 10 feet by 12 feet, held about 70 captives. One of the smaller ones, nine-by-nine feet in size, had 57 people in it. The Japanese then blocked the windows and doors from outside with wooden planks. Two machine guns were placed next to it, guarding the building.

The poor captives had to stand all the time, as there was not enough space for most of them even to sit inside the tiny rooms. As the time passed and they had to relief themselves, they were urinating on each other. The Japanese did not loosen the ropes with which they were tied, nor did they provide them with any water. Everyone was terribly thirsty, because after the water supply was cut on 11 February, the hospital was rationing water at strictly limited amount of one pint per person per day. In the suffocating heat and stench, and with no fresh air or any water, people began to break and collapse, screaming out of desperation and calling for water. The moaning and screaming continued throughout the whole night. Several patients reached a state of delirium, and in one of the rooms, seven people were reported to have died overnight.

Next day, shortly before noon, the doors finally opened and one

Japanese officer told the captives that they would be moving to a different location, further away from the battlefront, and he promised them some water along the way. The Japanese then started to take the captives out in small groups of two or three, and they were seen going out and around the building. There was a lot of shooting and shelling going on outside continuously, so for a while, nobody suspected anything wrong. At some moment, however, the captives recognised distant screams such as "Oh God!", "Mother!" and "No, no!" from the outside. Their suspicion that the Japanese were killing them one by one was confirmed when one of the soldiers came in, wiping blood from his bayonet. In the horror, few of the captives tried to kill themselves, one cutting his own wrist and another hanging himself. Several others seized an opportunity to escape when one of the shells hit a corner of the building and created an opening in the wall – they climbed out and started to run for their lives. Most were mowed down by a machine gun outside, but five escaped and hid, ultimately reaching the British troops for help.

Because of those five survivors, we have several witness accounts today about the slaughter that happened outside the hospital on 15 February 1942.

Of the approximately 50 killed in the hospital, Bruton managed to identify the names of 28. From the roughly 200 who were murdered in cold blood a day later, he was able to recover the names of 90. Thus, the majority of the victims are still not identified by name. We can only speculate that Silvestr was one of them.

As a follow-up to Bruton's publication, I found several originals of the witness accounts he used for his reconstruction in the British archives. Thus, I discovered some additional details, for example, that the patient under anaesthesia who was murdered was a Lance Corporal Robert Veitch, who – just like Silvestr – was a volunteer with the FSMVF's armoured cars company. His story, therefore, seems very similar to Silvestr's.

The archives also has a letter from Bill Cowan to Dorothy Young, a sister of his friend who was also killed in the Alexandra Hospital massacre. It is very moving:

My dear Dorothy, [...] I am finding this letter a very difficult one to write. You have asked me to tell you what I know, and I feel very uncertain whether I should do so or not.

Mother thro' kindness, didn't inform you correctly of what happened to your brother and my very dear friend Hal. If you impart her information to the War Office, they will know it is incorrect. Alexandra Hospital was never bombed. The Jap airmen, right till the end recognised it as a Military Hospital. They had that much decency, which may seem strange, comparing their chivalry with that of the Japanese Fighting Forces.

Well here goes Dorothy and pray God that I am doing the right thing [...]

Three days before the capitulation he was ordered into Alexandra Hospital for treatment and that was the last time I saw Hal. The next day some of our Indian Troops, like idiots, retreated through the hospital and some of them fired on the Japs from the roof... They [the Japs] followed on into the hospital and went berserk, killing patients and medical personnel alike.

But that is enough of that, Dorothy, maybe already I have said more than I should.

Besides Cowan's short summary of the massacre, there is one thing that struck me. The young Dorothy was told – after the war – that her brother died in the hospital after it was bombed. This is exactly the same narrative as what I heard in my family. I now think that this was really a "merciful lie", told by the British authorities or soldiers to the families of the massacre's victims, to spare their loved ones the horrific details. Even for me, reading the description of the massacre was so disturbing that I found myself wishing that Silvestr was killed quickly and did not have to endure the horror night in the Sisters Quarter barrack.

Another historian I got in touch with, specifically for the Alexandra Hospital massacre, was Ian Richardson. Ian's father, like Silvestr, had volunteered but was with the Malayan Volunteers (FMSVF). He also happened to be hospitalised at Alexandra during the time of the massacre. Luckily, he was among those who survived.

Ian has been following up on the work by Peter Bruton, who abandoned the subject shortly after publishing his document in 1989. I have learnt from Ian that Bruton was driven by a desire to learn more about the fate of his uncle, John Bruton. So, it might have become too emotionally charged for him, or perhaps he got frustrated by how much the individual accounts contradicted each other.

Ian wrote me, saying he managed to gather a wealth of new information and was preparing his own publication. According to him, he managed to reconstruct a list of 342 names of people who were in the hospital that day – that is, about one-third of those believed to be present. Silvestr is not on Ian's list, but then again, this does not mean he is not one of the victims.

There is no original documentation because the management of the hospital decided to destroy it shortly before the Japanese came. Ian's most recent estimation was that 56 people were killed during the initial rampage, and another 160 to 170 people were massacred a day later. Sadly, we may never know the full results of Ian's meticulous work as I found out, after he stopped replying to my emails, that he had passed away in August 2022.

When I was sharing the information available about Silvestr with Ian, he also made a judgment that Silvestr was very likely among the victims. His line of thought is that if Silvestr was admitted on 11 February with shell shock, he would likely be sedated and as a patient with comparatively light injury, placed on stretches in the main corridor, because the wards were overcrowded. This would also make him directly exposed to the first wave of brutality, as the Japanese soldiers were storming through the ground floor of the hospital building.

Also, as the Japanese likely ordered the patients to raise their hands, Silvestr might have been confused as a result of the drugs and not followed orders quickly enough or he might have been agitated or thrown into a state of panic since he was shell-shocked. Either way, he might have attracted attention and provoked the Japanese to kill him.

The day after the massacre, on Monday 16 February 1942, General Mutaguchi who was commanding the division that was fighting in the Pasir Panjang area, paid a visit to the hospital. He apologised for any inconvenience and as a symbolic gesture, is said to have fed some of the patients peach compote with a spoon. He said that he was directly representing the Japanese emperor, which is the greatest honour to the patients.

When the massacre was investigated by the War Crimes Tribunal, Mutaguchi gave a statement that he had no knowledge of it:

> *I did visit the Alexandra Hospital. My visit was one of goodwill and I took with me my chief of staff and senior medical officers. I discovered that the hospital was in good order and there did not appear to me any*

trouble. I never had any slightest knowledge of a massacre that you refer to. I wish to add that I never found any necessity to apologise for anything to the patients in the hospital, on the other hand, I did express in a polite Japanese way my regret for any possible inconveniences which they may have experienced.

It was fascinating for me to go through the investigation protocols related to the case, which include statements of several Japanese officers and soldiers. They all describe in quite some detail the movements of Mutaguchi's 18th Division, including its position in the area on 14 and 15 February.

For example, Ito Kojiro describes how his 55th Regiment was positioned in the morning of 14 February at Pasir Panjang, and around noon, started to descend towards the city. Kojiro, who was with the 2nd Battalion, specified that his unit was heading towards the main road, and was followed by the 1st and 3rd Battalion, with the 56th Regiment following.

It appears that it must have been soldiers from either the 55th or 56th Regiment, who were at the vanguard of the division, who attacked the hospital at the foot of Pasir Panjang. None of the soldiers remember approaching the hospital, although some of them recall the building in their testimonies.

The Seventh Investigation Team of the War Crimes Tribunal eventually issued a verdict in June 1947, concluding that it was not a war crime for which any individual could be sentenced. One of the legal advisors said:

Even if we can establish what troops and officers were responsible for the affair (a very difficult matter as it took place in the heat of battle) the case would still be a weak one as there was undoubtedly firing by our own men from the hospital building.

General Mutaguchi was acquitted from responsibility for the massacre because there was no evidence that he knew about it or that he might have prevented it. He was sentenced to jail time for some other war crimes but returned to Japan in 1948. He died in Tokyo in 1966.

Considering all four scenarios and the evidence supporting them, I believe that most likely, Silvestr was murdered during the Alexandra Hospital massacre. Reading the detailed and vivid accounts of Japanese brutality and the suffering of the victims has caused me countless sleepless nights. I still shudder when I come across a reference to it or recall its horrors. In a way, I rather wish that my granduncle died during the battle of Pasir Panjang, as it would seem less traumatic and gruesome.

- XIV -

Tracing Silvestr in Today's Singapore

IN RECONSTRUCTING the events of my granduncle Silvestr's possible fate, I knew that my quest would not be complete without a visit to the very place he spent the last three years of his life. Singapore. For various reasons, I have long postponed my trip there. Among other things, I wanted to be as prepared as possible, being clear about where exactly I wanted to go, who I wanted to meet and what else I wanted to try and find out.

In the end, this final 'expedition' took place in May 2019. It provided me with a long-awaited opportunity not only to gather more information from the National Archives, the National Library and the local branch of Bata, but also to stand at the places where Silvestr lived and where – according to several possible variants – he eventually died. In addition, I finally got to meet some of my compatriots who have been remotely helping me with my search. And last but not least, I also wanted to use the trip to give a final and dignified farewell to my granduncle – on behalf of the whole family – 77 years after his tragic death.

When I wrote to Pavel Hajný and Olek Plešek about my planned trip, both Bata enthusiasts and researchers were excited to join me. This was absolutely wonderful news: I finally had the opportunity to meet Olek, my closest research partner, who would travel to Singapore from Australia. The two well-read gentlemen were the most competent company for my trip. And so, finally, the three of us took the last steps in the search for Silvestr and other Czechoslovaks in Singapore.

Today's Singapore is hugely different from the Singapore before World War II. After the war, the British had failed to restore their lost authority and respect from the local population, who were increasingly demanding an end to colonial rule and for their own self-determination.

The case escalated further when the Communist guerrillas – whose armed resistance led to the declaration of a state of emergency in Malaya in the 1950s – also fought against British rule.

Britain was eventually persuaded to grant independence in all areas except defence and foreign relations to Singapore's leader Lee Kuan Yew, who won the 1959 election to become Singapore's first Prime Minister. Four years later, Singapore joined the newly formed Federation of Malaysia, which included the other former British colonies of Sarawak and Sabah, two Malay provinces in northern Borneo. However, in 1965, the Malaysian parliament decided to exclude Singapore from the federation due to disagreements. Singapore thus became, not by its own choice, an independent country on 9 August 1965.

Thanks to this, however, it was able to achieve enormous economic success and become a modern, economically advanced country – in terms of GDP per capita, it now ranks in the top 10 globally. The population has increased sevenfold since 1942, when Silvestr lived there. And while three-quarters of the population is Chinese, the government has an intentional policy to ensure that the ethnically and religiously diverse society lives in peace and harmony.

As a result of its post-war population growth, economic boom and modernisation, Silvestr would not have been able to recognise Singapore today. The island, which in its time was mostly covered by jungle and rubber plantations, is now almost entirely a vibrant city. That old city, which was an area of just a few square kilometres in the southeastern corner of the island, has been pretty much rebuilt through modern development. Modern high-rise construction, shopping malls and housing estates keep growing across the island.

I therefore did not have many expectations about finding the historical places I learnt about through my research on events in the 1930s and during World War II. In the end, it turned out to be really exciting and the result by far exceeded my expectations.

In Silvestr's Footsteps

Thanks to a prior arrangement, we were met at the Singapore airport by a Bata driver and their sales manager Tiago Solca, who offered us some initial advice about Singapore and with whom we also agreed to meet later at the company's office. We stayed with two Czech friends who have been living and working in Singapore for several years:

Lukáš Černý and Pavla Schneuwly. Pavla, who at that time worked as a professional guide and knows Singapore and its history very well, provided us with invaluable support in the following days.

We were staying in the Siglap district. This was where, according to various documents, Silvestr used to go for training with his armoured car unit. Back then, it was a small fishing village, but today it is a residential area. It is about 10 km from the SSVF headquarters on Beach Road, where the armoured cars were based.

The very next morning, we went downtown where I had an appointment with Mary Anne Schooling. She is the daughter of one of the local volunteers and had written about the Singaporean Eurasian volunteers. She now lives in Australia but grew up in Singapore and has witnessed its incredible transformation. Mary Anne showed us several key sites in the centre of the old town.

The first was the Catholic Cathedral of the Good Shepherd. It was here in July 1941 that Singapore's Bata workers gathered for the funeral of their director, Václav Rojt. Silvestr, although not being on good terms with him, attended the farewell ceremony in person, as was reported by the newspapers.

This church also played an interesting role in the story of the Singapore volunteers at the beginning of the Japanese Occupation. The *Syonan Shimbun* newspaper printed a propaganda article on 23 May 1942 with the headline "A Generous Gesture by the Victorious Army". This is part of its text:

> *I have just witnessed one of the most inspiring spectacles in the everyday life of post-war Syonan. The spectacle takes place every Sunday in a certain Catholic church in the heart of the city. To this church each Sunday, two lorry loads of war prisoners arrive. The majority of them are members of the former Singapore Volunteer Corps and in real life they were well-known businessmen, holding good positions in the previous Government and Municipality. A very generous gesture to these prisoners of war by the victorious Nippon army [...] they are permitted to attend the mass and incidentally see their relatives and families in church.*

Our next stop just down the road was the magnificent Capitol Building at the junction of the North Bridge Road and Stamford Road. It was here that the Bata company opened its first shop in 1931 and

ABOVE: The original war memorial in Vémyslice, Silvestr's hometown. It shows his name as "Němec Sylva" and states that he "died in a foreign army".

LEFT: The memorial after renovation in 2017. My granduncle's name is now on the memorial to the left.

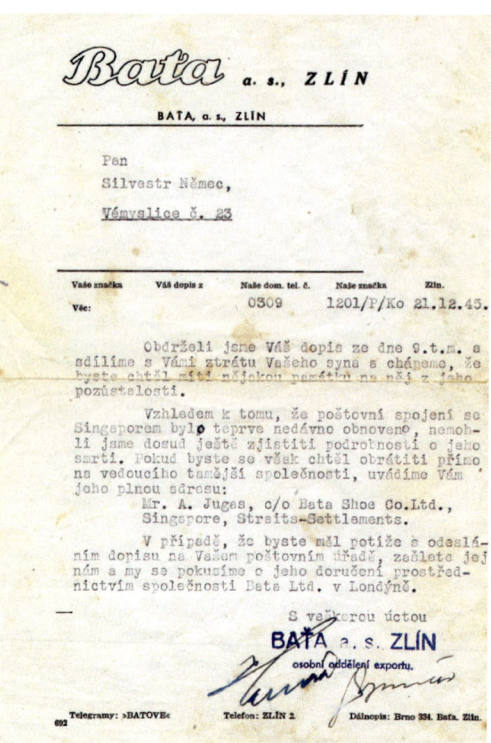

LEFT: *The letter from Bata headquarters in Zlín to Silvestr's parents, written in December 1945. They informed the family that no information was yet available from Singapore and that if they wished, they could write directly to Antonin Jugas, the director of Bata Shoe Co. local branch there.*

BOTTOM: *Telegram of 29 September 1945 from Antonin Jugas in Singapore to Bata in Zlin about the situation of Bata and its employees after liberation.*

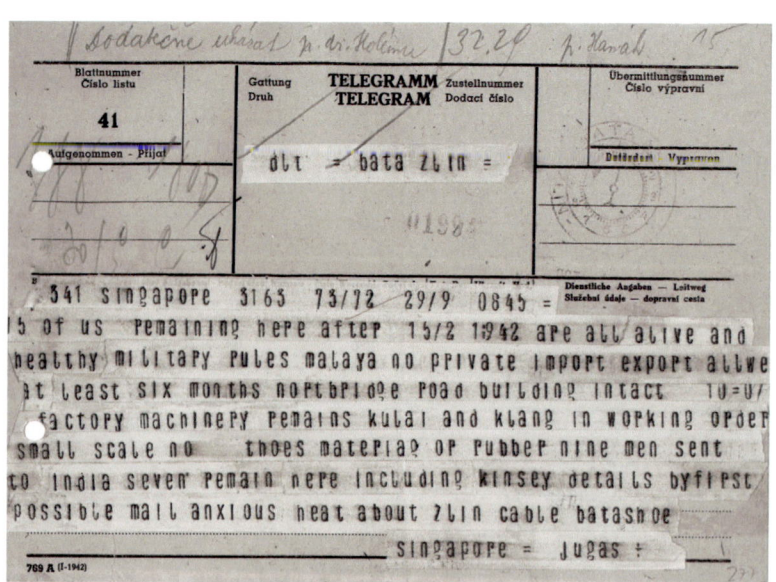

```
Communications on this subject
should be addressed to—
THE UNDER SECRETARY OF STATE,
       COLONIAL OFFICE,
              LONDON, S.W.1.
and the following
Number quoted 10001/47 (S. NEMEC)
Your Reference
```

Downing Street.

4 July, 1947

Sir,

   With reference to your letter of the 22nd of May regarding the fate of your son, Private Sylvester Nemec, I am directed by Mr. Secretary Creech Jones to inform you with regret that no information is available in the Colonial Office other than the fact that he was reported missing on the 15th of February, 1942.

   Your letter has, however, been referred to the Governor, Singapore, as all such enquiries are now being forwarded to the Far Eastern territory concerned for investigation. The authorities in Singapore will take all possible steps to obtain information and they will communicate with you direct.

   Mr. Creech Jones desires me to express his deep sympathy with you in your anxiety and it is hoped that information may now be available in Singapore.

                    I am,
                      Sir,
                    Your obedient servant,

FRANTIŠKA NĚMCOVÁ, ESQ.

ABOVE: *The letter from the British Prime Minister's office to Silvestr's mother, Františka Němcová. It is dated 4 July 1947, just two weeks before the British colonial office in Singapore issued a Certificate of Death for Silvestr.*

Statement of the lost of house-hold goods, furniture and personal belongings of missing Mr. Silvester Nĕmec, in Tiong Bahru Flat, 10, Room No. 3. Guan Chuan Street		15.2.42	Missing from the date capitulation in Singap Was serving in S.S.V.F
Furniture/bedroom:			
1 single bed	40.—	"	"
1 side bed table	8.—	"	"
1 mattress	20.—	"	"
1 Small table lamp	10.—	"	"
1 Wardrobe	60.—	"	"
1 dressing table with mirror	40.—	"	"
1 Ceiling lamp shade	5.—	"	"
1 Curtain	15.—	"	"
1 Carpet/small size	30.—	"	"
Personel. 1			
1 Camphor Wood Box	60.—	"	"
6 Europeans Suits	400.—	"	"
1 doz. white suit	110.—	"	"
2 doz. white shirts	85.—	"	"
3 doz. popelin shirts, 3 silk	220.—	"	"
2 doz of socks	15.—	"	"
4 doz handkershiefs	24.—	"	"
3 doz Singlets	46.—	"	"
1 doz Neckties	24.—	"	"
1 doz. Woolen Stocking	36.—	"	"
6 pairs of shoes	72.—	"	"
3 doz. of pans	72.—	"	"
1 doz bedsheets	46.—	"	"
2 doz. Towels	60.—	"	"
3 leather Suit cases	52.—	"	"
Total private Chatttels	**1675.—**	"	"
Miscellaneous.			
1 Camera "Leica"	400.—	"	"
Tota Miscellaneous	400.—	"	"

ABOVE AND LEFT: *The list of Silvestr's lost property, prepared by his colleagues and friends, to help the family seek some compensation from the British authorities. It records Silvestr's last address: Flat 10, Room 3, Guan Chuan Street, Tiong Bahru.*

RIGHT: A nice welcome organised by Bata Shoe Co. upon my arrival in Singapore with Pavel Hajný in May 2019.

BELOW: From left, Pavel Hajný, Olek Plešek and the author at the Bata store on North Bridge Road, the site where Bata Shoe Co built its main office building in 1940 and where Silvestr went to regularly.

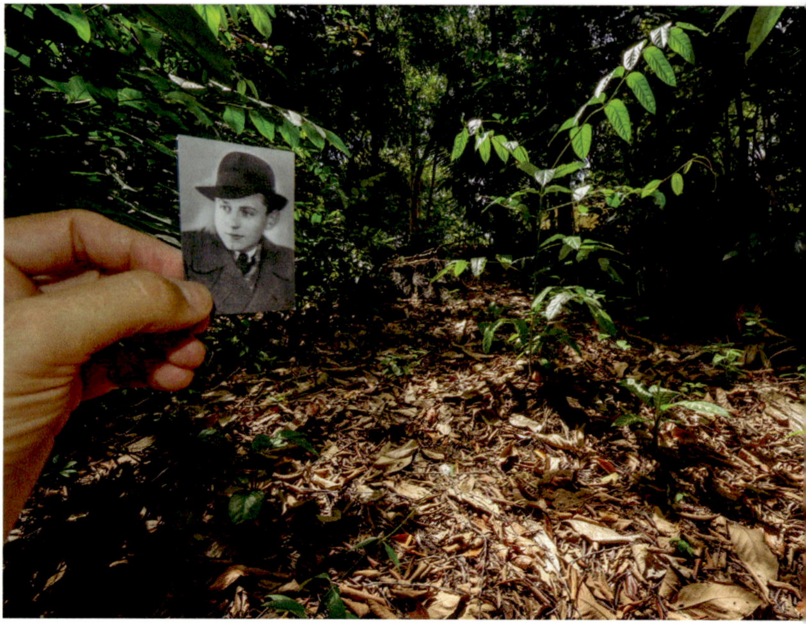

Level
1
Auditorium
Clinic A
Clinic B
Rehabilitation 1
Pharmacy
Ambulatory Surgery Centre
Clinical Measurement Centre
Endoscopy Centre
Care & Counselling
2
3

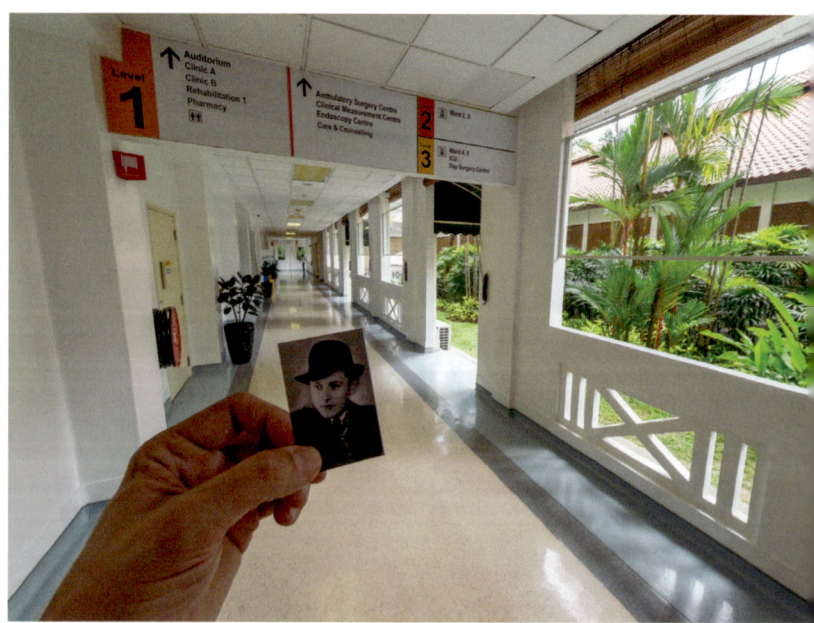

LEFT: *The Gap, Pasir Panjang Hill. It was somewhere here that on 13 February 1942, the Czechoslovak volunteers fought heroically against the advancing Japanese army, and where Silvestr was last seen alive.*

BOTTOM LEFT: *Alexandra Hospital, where on 14 February 1942 Japanese soldiers slaughtered dozens of hospital staff and wounded patients including, very likely, Silvestr.*

ABOVE: *The family of František "Frank" Wakerman, Silvestr's close friend and Bata colleague. From left: son David, wife Daisy and daughter Jane. Olek Plešek is second from the right.*

BELOW: *War memorial in Zlín. The top entry of the second column is that of Silvestr Němec.*

The 1939-1945 Star, the Pacific Star, the Defence Medal, and the War Medal 1939-1945 awarded to Silvestr in memoriam by the British government.

where its Czechoslovak sellers and chiropodists worked. However, shoes are not sold anymore on the premises where Silvestr worked for three years: I found some luxury brand shops selling jewellery, watches and designer home accessories in its place.

Today, you can buy Bata shoes just a minute away, in a big store on the ground floor of a modern high-rise building, Peninsula Plaza, whose architecture reminded me of the Czechoslovak socialist style from the 1980s. This is also where the local branch of the Bata company now has its offices on the 19th floor. By comparing the layout with old maps and photographs, I came to the conclusion that the company's own building, inaugurated in June 1940, once stood on this very spot. This is where the employees, and therefore also Silvestr, came once a week to collect their pay.

Sadly, my hopes that the Bata company might keep old archival records and that I might be able to find a pre-war document – Silvestr's pay slip would have sufficed – were unfortunately dashed. We soon found out, during our office visit hosted by the management a few days later, that they did not have any archived records that could be relevant.

But the fourth place I explored in downtown Singapore was worth it. Almost miraculously, three two-storey colonial buildings that were used by the Volunteer Corps before the war are still in place, crouching in the shadow of the new high-rises on Beach Road. Standing side by side were the former headquarters of the Malayan SSVF battalions, the SSVF armoury, and most importantly, the SSVF headquarters with its drill hall and what used to be the basement garage for armoured cars.

The scenery around has changed beyond recognition. The sea is now several hundred metres further away, due to land reclamation, so even the name of the street – Beach Road – captures just a memory of the time when these SSVF buildings were a stone's throw away from the sea, separated only by an open area which served as a parade ground and drill yard for volunteers.

Three of the original buildings now serve different purposes: one is a Marriott Hotel, another is a café (its name "Armoury" references the past) with an art gallery and the third – most important to me and the story of Silvestr Němec – serves as a multi-purpose venue for weddings, congresses and similar events.

Its original structure and façade have been preserved, with a large, beautifully rendered 'SSVF' sign and a flagpole. Beneath it, there is also a bronze plaque that reads:

TRACING SILVESTR IN TODAY'S SINGAPORE

> *In memory of all ranks of the Singapore Volunteers Corps who lost their lives during the Malayan campaign and as prisoners of war 1941-1945. They fought not in enmity against men but against powers of darkness enslaving souls of men.*

If we take away the surroundings, the building of the former SSVF headquarters looks exactly like in the old photos. We already know that Silvestr used to come here every Thursday afternoon for training, and sometimes also for weekend camps. The former basement that used to be a workshop and garage for armoured cars, is now a social hall.

At the time of my visit, a wedding reception was being prepared there. The main room, with its unmistakable arched vault, is one floor up. It was formerly used as a drill hall, and we know from old photographs that social events, such as the annual Volunteer Corps dinner, were sometimes held here. The original arches of the high ceiling are now almost hidden in clusters of tubes of various lengths hanging bizarrely from it like stalactites. I was told by the staff that it was an installation of thousands of modern light fittings called the "Forest of Lights". In my view, it rather ruined the impression of the unique space, but I was still grateful that the whole building had been preserved to this day. In any case, I felt a great thrill at the thought of standing at a place where Silvestr spent a lot of his time during his last year.

On my way out, I fastened one of the three commemorative wreath ribbons I had brought with me to Singapore to the flagpole on the outside of the building. One ribbon was a typical combination of Czechoslovak colours of white, red and blue; the other was black and said in golden letters: "Silvestr Němec, volunteer – remembered by family and friends".

Finally, the fifth place in downtown Singapore that I visited was the Cenotaph, the memorial to the victims of World War I located in a park by the Padang, a large field surrounded by important landmarks. The memorial was where the Czechoslovak community used to gather every year on 28 October to celebrate the national holiday and anniversary of the creation of independent Czechoslovakia. My granduncle Silvestr stood on the steps of the Cenotaph, in the small crowd of his compatriots, silently remembering his homeland and his family in Vémyslice. Now I was standing there too, warmly remembering our dear Silvestr.

I also visited the headquarters of the National Library of Singapore, where I borrowed another treasure – a unique publication by Bata, on its 20 years' anniversary in Singapore, published in 1951. It is the only available copy I have been able to track down. Then I went to the National Archives of Singapore, where they have some pre-war documents related to the volunteers and architectural plans of old buildings that were of interest to me, including one Bata workshop and the apartment blocks of Tiong Bahru where Silvestr last lived.

What surprised me most, on my first day in Singapore, was probably the weather. I found it nearly unbearable: so hot and humid, especially in the direct sun; I was barely able to be active for more than a few minutes before I had to seek some shade. It made me wonder again how Silvestr and the other Czechoslovaks could have functioned in such a climate – not to mention the physically demanding military training and then several days and nights of continuous fighting. Yes, of course, the Europeans had longer time to acclimatise after arrival, and the rhythm included a longer break through the midday, but still! Now I understand a little better the complaints I was reading in the memoirs of several Czechoslovaks.

During the next few days, we visited more distant places. We started with the Bidadari cemetery, where Bata's director Rojt was buried and where the funeral procession of Singaporean Czechoslovaks said their final goodbye. One of the old photographs that I now have in my personal collection shows a delegation of Bata managers led by Jan Bartoš from Batanagar, passing through the old, decorated gate of the cemetery.

Bidadari used to be a really large cemetery, divided into sectors according to different nationalities. When I included this site in my itinerary, my friends who live in Singapore were sceptical whether it still existed. And it really took us a while to find it: we had to drive back and forth through a construction site several times before we managed to find this old gate. We arrived literally at the last minute – a sign on gate announced that in less than two weeks (that is, in June 2019), the remaining fragment of the former cemetery would be closed, and its old gate moved to a public park somewhere else. I was very grateful that we still made it – today, visitors will only find a large, new housing estate at that spot.

We also tried to explore the former shooting range in Rafle Range Road at Bukit Timah, where Silvestr and SSVF volunteers used to practise rifle and machine gun shooting. However, it was not possible to get there, since the area has become the Temasek Club for officers of the Singapore Armed Forces.

Not far from there is Adam Park and a vast Chinese cemetery on Bukit Brown, where some of the most vicious fighting between the attacking Japanese and defending Australian troops took place – on the hillside and between the tombstones. A fascinating archaeological excavation of the site was carried out a few years ago by an English historian, Jon Cooper, and he published a great book about it, entitled *Tigers in the Park*; it is now part of my library, thanks to Pavla.

One of the most important locations for me to visit was Tiong Bahru. It was a grandly conceived housing project built in the late 1930s by the Singapore Improvement Trust as part of the creation of modern and affordable urban housing. The area has several streets with rows of apartment blocks in the style called Streamline Moderne, a late development of the Art Deco movement, creating a pleasant historic oasis of fine architecture of human proportions in today's megacity.

Because Silvestr's colleagues included his last-known address on the list of lost property that they made after the war, I knew that Silvestr lived in flat 10, room 3, Guan Chuan Street in Tiong Bahru. I was very excited when I walked through the shared entrance to Blocks 10 and 12, and climbed the staircase, which Silvester used to use daily, up to the third floor to the front door of his former apartment. Unfortunately, it was locked and no one answered the bell, so I couldn't ask whether I might look inside. Still, it was one of the highlights of my visit to Singapore – I was on the doorstep of Silvestr's very apartment!

Later, thanks to the kindness of a real estate agent, Mr Alvin Yeo, I at least got hold of a plan of that particular floor and apartment.

I noticed there was another point of interest in that building, which is an underground air-raid shelter that was part of the original architectural plan for Tiong Bahru – it was apparently one of the first shelters for civilians that the government began building in the late 1930s. I can imagine that Silvester also got to see this shelter, although he probably never used it himself: the full mobilisation of volunteers took place on 1 December, seven days before the first air raid on Singapore, by which time he and his SSVF unit were already gathered in a provisional field accommodation in the Geylang English School.

Eventually, I even got an opportunity to travel to southern Malaysia and follow Silvestr's footsteps to one of his favourite destinations on weekend trips with friends: the Kota Tinggi waterfalls. Thanks to an old photograph, I managed to identify the exact pond in which the young Batamen frolicked and imagined a happy and carefree Silvestr in that place. It was a really beautiful moment for me.

Rest in Peace

Most important for me were, of course, the locations where Silvestr could have died.

I was very impressed by a tour of the Alexandra Hospital, which was offered to me by their own historian, kind and sympathetic student, Tan Ding Xiang. He had studied and collected an impressive archive of documents related to the Japanese massacre, and occasionally gives relatives of the victims a tour of the hospital grounds – just like he did for me.

In the little park in front of the entrance, on a meadow where a small memorial commemorates the events of the massacre, I prayed for Silvestr and attached a second memorial ribbon to one of the bushes. We then walked through the main hospital building, where we stood in the exact same corridor in which, on that fateful day, a group of Japanese soldiers went berserk and bayoneted dozens of patients and medical staff. When I realised that I was standing right where Silvestr might well have taken his last breath, I almost cried.

We then saw other areas of the hospital which, until then, I could only imagine after reading several witness accounts describing the horrible events: the staircase where the officers descended from the upper floor, and the location of the former operating theatre where the Japanese had stabbed the anaesthetised FSMVF volunteer, Robert Veitch.

Then we walked through the area behind the main building, where the Sisters' Quarter might have been and where the unarmed captives taken from the hospital spent an agonising night before the Japanese slaughtered them the next day. Tan also showed us two places where their mass grave might be hidden under the green vegetation.

After my visit, I have learnt from Tan Ding Xiang in 2021 that an archaeological survey was conducted in an attempt to identify potential locations of a mass grave of the victims of the 1942 massacre. I was very excited that something new could come out of this work, but I had to manage my hopes and be realistic about the chances of them finding anything, let alone identifying the remains of Silvestr. When I checked a year later, he updated me that no human remains were found at the two places that were surveyed. With these negative findings, the archaeological project seems to have been phased out.

After the tour, we drove to another potential site of the 15 February massacre. It lies a few hundred metres southwest of the hospital, behind the embankment of the former railway. Here, on what is now a rundown site, stands a derelict building once occupied by the Eton House school. According to some historical reconstructions, it may have been the site of those long-gone Sisters' Quarter huts.

Finally, I could not miss the Pasir Panjang ridges near the Gap, where Josef Vyhnálek last saw Silvestr when their unit of volunteers fought the Japanese. Today, the forested crest is called Kent Ridge Park where there are popular walking trails. I picked out a nice spot on one of the hillsides just off the road and symbolically remembered Silvestr there as well.

What They Died For

An additional stop that I originally did not plan in Singapore was suggested to me by Mrs Pavla Williams. She has lived in Singapore for eight years and was intrigued by my blog and Silvestr's story. Mrs Williams asked her husband Ben, who is a psychic, to try to find out more using his special skills. And when I was finally coming to Singapore in person, she arranged a meeting for us.

We met at the place that Ben identified as the site of Silvestr's death, based on his dreams in which he said he had connected with Silvestr's soul. It was on the hillside of Fort Canning, which is also a site of a bunker in which General Percival had his last headquarters before the fall of Singapore (Australian soldiers ironically nicknamed the place "Confusion Castle"). Percival had moved here after the strategic hill of Bukit Timah had fallen. Before that, the bunker housed the command of the southern sector of Singapore's defences – the sector under which the Volunteer Corps fell.

According to Ben's visions, wounded Silvestr was in Alexandra Hospital with another Czech friend. When the fighting came nearer to the hospital on 13 February, the two discussed quietly during the night that maybe it would be better to leave the place. On the morning of Saturday the 14th, they sneaked out of the hospital and crawled in a direction they thought would lead them to a safer area. After some time, however, they were ambushed by a Japanese patrol, a short clash ensued, and then they split up and ran in different directions. Silvestr suffered a stab wound somewhere behind his right shoulder but dragged on for the next few hours. His destination was Fort Canning, where perhaps he wanted to inform the commander of the imminent threat to the hospital. But near the final destination, on a slope of the hill, he collapsed and succumbed to his wound and general exhaustion.

We walked around that place and then Ben also performed a brief ceremony, in which he said he let free the energy that remained at the site as part of Silvestr's trapped soul, helping him to finally leave in peace. He added that he felt Silvester was thanking me for allowing him to finally return home.

Personally, I am very sceptical about these things, but it was an impressive and magical moment. It's an interesting hypothesis and given the uncertainties of all the other variations of Silvestr's death, something like this might have happened. I even read in one of the war diaries, by Colonel Williams of the Malayan Brigade in Singapore, a reference to the fact that the defending units in the southern sector sometimes sent messengers ("runners") with messages directly to Fort Canning because of the broken telephone lines – heading here with a warning about Alexandra Hospital would have been a common practice for Silvester.

Our final stop in Singapore was the war memorial at Kranji. It is located on the northwest corner of the island. On a gentle green slope lie thousands of graves, arranged in rows, of those whose bodies were found and identified, allowing a proper burial.

Walking further up the hill, we finally reached the memorial. Its walls are covered with the names of more than 24,000 soldiers and volunteers who died in the battle of Singapore or in the Japanese prison camps, but whose remains have never been found.

Silvestr's name is engraved among them on one of the many panels.

Seeing those 24,000 names on a virtually endless list is very chilling. I could not help but think that behind each one of them, there is a story like Silvestr's. At some point, it becomes impossible to imagine the thousands and thousands of lives and to comprehend their loss. And when one considers that World War II had even thousand times more victims, the consideration turns into sheer horror.

There is an obelisk rising above the tombstones at Kranji War Memorial. On it are carved these words in a number of languages: "They Died for the Freedom of All People". I stood there for a moment to let the words, and this whole journey, sink in. Then, on behalf of my family and our friends, I left the third and last memorial ribbon for Silvestr there.

- Epilogue -
A Living Story

DURING MY TRIP to Singapore, I also organised a meeting for those interested in the stories of Czechoslovaks present there during World War II. About 20 people turned up to hear about the findings of my research and talk with our trio – Pavel Hajný, Olek Plešek and myself – about the history of Bata in the region. It was lovely to see the diversity of the participants: the oldest lady was over 90 years old, but there was also a group of young enthusiastic students. Most of them were Czechs, but a few Singaporeans attended too.

Perhaps the most amazing aspect was the attendance of relatives of Silvestr's colleague, František (Frank) Wakerman – he was also a chiropodist and left for Singapore on the same day as Silvestr, so they must have spent time together during the voyage.

Wakerman stayed in Singapore after the war, married a local women and started a family there. After many decades, I managed to track them down, thanks to a tip from Ivan Procházka. They were very surprised that after such a long time, someone reached out to them and was keen to learn more about the Bata Czechoslovaks, including František. He is unfortunately no longer alive, but his wife Daisy, daughter Jane and son David came to the meeting. Their presence made it really special for everyone.

They brought with them some pictures from the family archive, and it was breathtaking for me when František's son David recalled during the evening that his father sometimes talked about Silvestr at home. "When my dad would tell us about his Czechoslovak friends, he would mention six names and one of them was Silvestr," David said. "I vividly remember us driving through Pasir Panjang together when he suddenly told me that there was a massacre near this place and that his friend named Silvestr died there. I clearly remember these two names linked together: Silvestr and Pasir Panjang."

Also, Olek Plešek had a very touching surprise for me at the end of our trip. On the eve of our departure, he ceremoniously presented me with a precious original of the famous book, *Czechoslovaks on the Banks of the Ganges: From the Earliest Times to the Present*, written by Jan Baroš and published in Batanagar in 1946. It is a detailed chronicle of the activities of the Bata people in the Far East during the 1930s and during the war. What's more, Olek wrote a personal dedication in the book, signed by 14 descendants of the Bata families who, like Olek, live in Australia today. They collectively gave me this precious gift as a gesture of appreciation of my years-long work on a subject so dear to them.

I am grateful to have gotten to know Olek and many other wonderful people, both in person and remotely, during my journey of discovery. I have made many wonderful friends and expanded my own horizons over these years of my research. Most importantly, I am grateful that I was able to give – at last – a symbolic farewell to Silvestr, on behalf of my family, at the place where he probably died 80 years ago.

Looking back, I find it almost unbelievable how much information was recoverable about a forgotten story from a relatively distant past. Because of this, I have managed to reconstruct Silvester's life and fate in interesting detail, which helps me to picture my forgotten granduncle in a much more substantive, vivid way.

It is also a very moving and powerful feeling that with the interest expressed by so many people, Silvestr is now being remembered again.

But my journey of "Searching for Silvestr" did not quite end with my trip to Singapore or with this book being published. I will continue to read interesting documents about the wartime events in Singapore from time to time, and perhaps new information will emerge somewhere. As it has happened to me several times in recent years, I may unexpectedly hear from someone who knows more or has an interesting tip on where to look.

If you want to learn how the story developed since I handed over the manuscript of this book to the publisher, I invite you to visit the website http://silvestr.janberanek.cz or the Facebook page https://www.facebook.com/SilvestrNemec1919. And if you have a comment, question or information to share, you can contribute there and become part of this continually unfolding story.

For me, this journey has been filled with serendipity, wonder, heartbreak and exhilaration. It has also gifted me with many new and wonderful friendships. I realise, too, that many other people have built a special connection with my granduncle Silvestr Němec. He is no more a nameless, forgotten boy who disappeared during the horrors of the war. I hope that wherever he is now, he is at peace and smiling.

- Appendix I -
DRAMATIS PERSONAE

In my research on my granduncle Silvestr, I have come across the names of many other Czechoslovaks who were in Singapore around the time he was there, just before the Japanese Occupation. For the benefit of others researching their lost loved ones, here is a list I've compiled together with Olek Plesek.

This list (presented here in alphabetical order) is based on the following sources: *List of Bata Employees Overseas* (1944); the Nominal Roll of Czechoslovak Citizens in Singapore as prepared by the Czechoslovak Consulate in India (1942); the archive of personal files of Bata employees stored in the State Archives in Zlín; the Singapore press (1935-1960); list of the European citizens interned in Changi Prison during the Japanese occupation of Singapore (1945); documents available on the online portals of the National Archives of Australia and findmypast.co.uk. Important contributions were also made by Jonathan Moffatt and Michael Pether. Some of the information was provided by the families – descendants of the Bata employees involved.

The Bata Czechoslovaks

Adamík, Jaroslav (b. 1910) was trained as a shoemaker and graduated from the Bata School of Work (Baťova škola práce). He joined the company in July 1927, working as a storekeeper. In August 1938, he was sent to Singapore, his new position there being a unit head. He evacuated on 11 February 1942 to India, where he subsequently worked for Bata factory in Batapur (Pakistan). His wife, Božena, and son Jaroslav were evacuated to India, along with 30 other Czech and Slovak women and children, on 1 February 1942 aboard the *Empress of Japan*. They were provided asylum in the Petersfield School in Nainital. According to a report from 1946, Adamík left the company and was employed by Janda Co. in Lahore. In December 1956, he travelled aboard the *Queen Mary* liner from London to New York, together with his wife and daughter Pavla.

APPENDIX I

The passenger list has their last country of residence as Pakistan. In May 1960, he and his wife travelled from London to Montreal, Canada, aboard *Ivernia*. He later settled in the United States. His daughter Pavla currently lives in Texas.

Ambrož, Pavel (b. 1912) was born in Vyškov and was trained as a shop assistant. He joined Bata in October 1936 as a supplier and later became a salesman in Jihlava. There is also a record of him working as a short-term construction worker for Bata in 1935. He left for Batanagar in India as a supplier in November 1938. At the outbreak of war in the Pacific, he was based in Singapore. He joined the Straits Settlements Volunteer Force (SSVF) on 15 November 1940. After the capitulation, he managed to avoid being captured as a POW by changing to civilian clothing. He worked in Singapore until he was interned in December 1943 at Changi Prison under number 3365, occupying cell 4.4.25. In 1944, he was transferred to the Sime Road internment camp and was in hut #114. After the liberation, in October 1945, he sailed to India for recovery. He returned to Czechoslovakia in October 1947 and remained there.

Bleha, Josef (b. 1916) joined Bata in November 1932, graduated from the Bata School of Work and worked as a seller in a store. His last departure for Singapore was in May 1939, to assume the position of deputy head of a store, but we know that he had been there before: he was mentioned in the local press in 1934 and 1937, and also by Josef Kramoliš as being there in 1932. When the war in the Pacific started, he was stationed in Siam (Thailand), and as such, was not directly impacted. In March 1947, he and his wife, Božena, sailed from Liverpool to Bombay on *Franconia*. At that time, he was working for the London branch of Bata Shoe Co. and had put down Indochina as his destination.

Boďa, Jan (b. 1912) lived near Bratislava with his family and joined Bata in September 1927 as a rubber laboratory technician. He left for Singapore with his wife and son Jan (b. 1937) in March 1939. His new position was head of production of rubber shoes and director of the company's factory in Klang, Malaya. As the war approached, he signed up for the Local Defence Corps (LDC) and served under registration number 180. On 11 February 1942, he managed to evacuate to India. His wife, son Jan and daughter Helena (b. 1940 in Klang) had travelled there ahead of him. Another son Zdeněk was born to him and his wife in September 1942 in India. Boďa got a position with Bata in Batapur, and later moved to Lahore, where his second daughter Věra was born in 1945. In 1956, the company moved him to Batanagar. Three years later, he was sent to the Bata factory in East Tilbury in England where he died in 1971. His daughter Věra was married in 1970 to Olek Plešek, the son of a Bata employee from Batanagar. Both Věra and Olek now live in Australia.

APPENDIX I

Bohman, Matěj (b. 1911) joined Bata in August 1925, graduated from the Bata School of Work and worked as a supplier. He left for Singapore in August 1938 as a seller. There, he joined the SSVF. He saw action during the Battle of Singapore and fought alongside an Australian named Edward. During the Japanese Occupation, in December 1943, he was interned at Changi Prison under number 3368, occupying the cell 4.4.26. Thereafter, in 1944, he was moved to the Sime Road internment camp and was in hut #114. His wife, Marie (b. 1912), with their two children, Milan (b. 1937) and newborn Marie (b. October 1941), were evacuated on 1 February 1942 to India. There she was given a place in an asylum house in Nainital. After the liberation, in October 1945, he sailed to India for recovery, along with his other colleagues. He also visited Czechoslovakia. Bohman died in 1990 in Singapore. Marie divorced him in the 1940s and was remarried to Petr Havrlant, the manager of the Bata tannery in Mokama Ghat, India. The family moved to Australia in 1947.

Čepka, Alois (b. 1910) was born in Moravská Ostrava and joined Bata in March 1936 as an accountant and correspondent. He later served as a tyre seller. It was in that position that he was sent to Singapore in February 1938. There, he joined the SSVF as Private #12973. First, he was attached to the Singapore Royal Engineer Volunteers (SREV), which was later reorganised; Čepka then joined the Bomb Disposal Unit under the command of Charles Kinahan. In December 1943, he was interned in Changi Prison under number 3369 and placed in cell 4.4.25. When he was later moved to the Sime Road internment camp in 1944, he occupied hut #114. Following the liberation, Čepka sailed to India in October 1945 for recovery along with his other colleagues. In 1946, when he was on vacation in Czechoslovakia, he filed a request for "certificate of nationality and reliability". He is recorded to have sailed with his wife, Jaroslava, and their two children (Alice and Eduard) on a French ship *Liberté* from Southampton to New York. He died in Canada.

Červinka, Hynek (b. 1906) was trained as a shop assistant and a tailor. He joined Bata in July 1929 as a seller. He left for Singapore in August 1938 as a chief of the department. His wife and two children, Ludmila and Tomáš, were successfully evacuated on 1 February 1942 to India and accommodated in Petersfield School in Nainital. Červinka tried to escape on the ship *SS Redang*, which was sunk on 12 February. He survived but was captured and interned at a camp in Palembang, Sumatra. However, he was soon released and together with Koš and Zelníček (see below), travelled to Medan where he lived out the rest of the war. In October 1945, he passed through Singapore on his way to Batanagar, India. Shortly after, he was employed in a different Czechoslovak company. In November 1947, he applied for a position at Bata but was not accepted. He remained in Malenovice, Czechoslovakia, where he died in 1984.

APPENDIX I

Chudárek, Stanislav (b. 1914) was born in Polešovice na Moravě, and joined Bata in December 1928. He worked as a regional controller of Bata shops – the same position he was sent to Singapore to fill in September 1938. During the Japanese Occupation, in December 1943, he was interned at Changi Prison in cell 4.4.18, under number 3370. In 1944, he was moved to the Sime Road internment camp and placed in hut #114. After the liberation, in October 1945, he sailed to India for recovery, along with his colleagues. In 1946, he returned to Czechoslovakia where he married Hedvika Sloupská in July. In September 1946, he worked in Calcutta. Two years later, they moved to Singapore where, in 1962, he took over the director position from departing Antonín Jugas. In 1963, the company directorate was moved to Klang in Malaysia where Chudárek died in 1969.

Dufek, Antonín (b. 1911) was born in Slavičín in Moravia and trained as a locksmith. He joined Bata in November 1929, graduated from the Bata School of Work and got a job as a turner in Bata factory. In 1937, he worked for the Bata Aviation Zlín Company which was building airplanes. He left for Singapore in August 1938 as chief of machinery in the unit of Jaroslav Adamík (see above). He evacuated to India on 11 February 1942, following his wife, Anna, and daughter Marie, who had both left earlier on 1 February. They later lived in Bombay (Mumbai). After the war, he worked for Bata in the Belgian Congo from 1947 until his retirement in 1971, save for a few years in the 1960s, when he was on mission to Burundi. He became a Belgian citizen.

Dvořák, Vladimír (b. 1915) was born in Polička, joined Bata in August 1930, graduated from the Bata School of Work and worked as an accountant. The company sent him first to England in 1933, and then to Vienna in 1935. He was sent to Singapore in March 1939 as an accountant. During the Japanese Occupation, he evacuated to India but returned to Singapore after the war and also lived in Thailand.

Goldmann, Artur (b. 1911) was born in Moravská Ostrava, joined Bata in 1936 as a correspondent, and later became a seller. He was sent to Singapore in December 1938 as a controller of samples, under Bata's export company Kotva. When World War II began in Europe, he decided to return and fight; later he served as a commander of an Allied military unit. After the war, he worked for the Czechoslovak Ministry of Defence. According to a record from 1945, he changed his family name to "Gonda".

Gromnica, Bedřich (b. 1916) was born in Dobratice, near Český Těšín, and trained as a shoemaker. He joined Bata in August 1931 and later worked as a chiropodist in Mladá Boleslav and Vítkovice. In July 1937, he was sent to

Singapore as a supply manager. He successfully evacuated on 27 February 1942 and arrived in Australia on board *Marella*. There, he applied for citizenship in May 1950, which was granted in April 1951. He lived in Australia until his death in 1976.

Heim, Bedřich (b. 1909) started working for Bata in August 1929 as a shop controller. In December 1936, he was sent to New Zealand as a wholesale manager. In June 1940, he signed up to join the LDC in Singapore, where he served under #311. He died during an evacuation attempt in February 1942, probably on the *SS Redang* which was attacked and sunk by the Japanese. His wife, Elsa, was evacuated to India on 1 February 1942 and was accommodated at the Edwinstown House in Nainital. After the war, she returned to Zlín and married another Bata employee Kilián. The name of Bedřich Heim is engraved on the Kranji War Memorial in Singapore.

Hlobil, František (b. 1912) was born in Bystřice pod Hostýnem and joined Bata in July 1927. After induction, he was appointed head of maintenance. In August 1934, he was sent to the Netherlands for a year, then in May 1936, to East Tilbury in England. In November 1938, he departed for Batanagar, India, to work as a chief machinist and instructor. He moved to Singapore before June 1940, and joined the LDC, serving under #181. After the war, he lived in Batanagar and Bombay. In August 1953, it was recorded that he was on a flight from Frankfurt to New York. He eventually settled in the United States.

Hrbek, Jan (b. 1910) was trained as a locksmith and joined Bata in October 1935 as a mechanic in the stockings factory. In August 1938, he was sent to Singapore as a director in charge of stockings production. During the war, he was listed in Red Cross documents as a POW.

Janeček, Rudolf (b. 1919) was trained as a shoemaker. He joined Bata in January 1934, graduated from the Bata School of Work and worked as a seller. In January 1939, he left for Singapore as a seller-chiropodist – likely travelling on the same ship as Silvestr Němec. Together, they enrolled in SSVF, Janeček as Private #13778. Shortly before the war, Janeček and Němec lived together at the same address in Tiong Bahru. Janeček was captured, became a POW, and died in February 1945 due to beriberi in the Labuan POW camp in Borneo. His name is engraved on the Kranji War Memorial in Singapore as well as on the war memorial in Zlín.

Janečková, Marie (b. 1920) was born in Všetaty, joined Bata in October 1934 and worked in the accounting office in Zlín. She was sent to Singapore in June 1939 in the same function. Sometime between June 1940 and July

1941, she married another Bata employee, Břetislav Sokol (see below). She was evacuated from Singapore on 1 February 1942 and lived in Jubilee Grove, Nainital. After the war, both she and Břetislav worked and lived in Singapore, later in Rhodesia (Zimbabwe) and eventually settled in Canada.

Jedovnický, Stanislav (b. 1916) was born in Ostrovánky near Kyjov, joined Bata in August 1931, graduated from the Bata School of Work and worked as a seller. In August 1939, he was sent to Singapore as an accountant. He joined the SSVF there. During the Japanese Occupation, in December 1943, he was interned at Changi Prison under number 3576 and lived in cell 4.4.11. In 1944, he was transferred to the Sime Road internment camp, where he was in hut #114. After the liberation, in October 1945, he sailed to India for recovery. There is a record from August 1952 of him – together with his wife, Josefa, and two sons, Stanislav and Ivan – travelling on the Dutch ship *Willem Ruys*, from Southampton to Colombo in Ceylon (Sri Lanka). He registered "purchasing agent" as his occupation. After several years in Indochina and India, he emigrated to Australia in 1957, where his family settled.

Jugas, Antonín (b. 1901) was trained as a cabinet maker and joined Bata in December 1923. Prior to moving to Singapore in May 1938, he worked as head of a shop in Penang from 1934. His new position in Singapore was as head of the sales department, and after the death of the Singapore director Václav Rojt in July 1941, he took over the director's position. His wife and son were evacuated on 1 February: his son Milan reached Sydney on 4 February 1942, on board the *Bontekoe*, while his wife arrived in India and was accommodated in Jubilee Grove, Nainital. Jugas was interned in December 1943 at Changi Prison under number 3373 and lived in cell 4.4.26. In 1944, he was transferred to the Sime Road internment camp and put in hut #114. After the war, he visited Zlín in September 1946. He continued to lead the Singapore branch of Bata until 1962, when he retired to Australia. He died there. His son Milan married Líba Starobová in Calcutta in the 1950s, and they eventually settled in Sydney.

Koblížek, František (b. 1915) was trained as a shoemaker, joined Bata in 1931, graduated from the Bata School of Work and became a seller. In August 1938, he left for Singapore as a store master. During the war, he joined SSVF, where he served as Private #12948. He managed to evacuate to India, where he married Anna Rojtová – daughter of the deceased director of Bata Singapore, Václav Rojt – in December 1942. He lived in Batanagar after the war. There is a record from September 1952 of him, along with wife, Anna, and daughter Božena, on Board *Carthage* from Southampton to Singapore; he registered "manager of Bata" as his occupation. He lived and worked in Singapore and Malaysia.

APPENDIX I

Koš, Viktor (b. 1911) was born in Ždánice near Kyjov and joined Bata in February 1931 as a controller. In June 1938, he was sent to Batanagar as head of the control department. His son Pavel and his wife joined him a little later. Before June 1940, they were already living in Singapore, where a daughter Jaroslava was born. During the war, Koš joined the LDC. His wife and two children were evacuated to India on 1 February 1942 on board the *Empress of Japan*. They were provided shelter in Petersfield School, Nainital. Koš attempted evacuation later, boarded *Mata Hari* that left Singapore on 12 February but was captured by the Japanese three days later. Koš was interned in Sumatra, where he met Červinka and Zelníček – two of the survivors from *SS Redang*. All three were released after several weeks in the internment camp and went on an adventurous journey through Sumatra to Medan, where they stayed for the rest of the war, with the help of the local Bata branch. Together with Červinka, he sailed to India in October 1945 for recovery. Koš continued to work for Bata in Singapore for several years, then moved to Bata in London, before eventually being sent to Canada in 1963. He died there in 1995. His son Pavel lives in England, his daughter Jarmila in Canada.

Kožušníček, Rudolf (b. 1910) was born in Křelov near Olomouc, joined Bata in October 1927, and worked in its shops in Luhačovice, Olomouc and Hodonín. Upon his return from military service in 1933, he worked as a correspondent and was sent on a business trip to India in January 1935. In November 1936, he sailed to Saigon to be an accountant for the group of Bata stores in Indochina. Before World War II, he moved to Singapore, where he joined SSVF on 1 January 1941 and served as Private #13774. During the Japanese invasion, he was wounded in battle. In December 1943, he was interned at Changi Prison under number 3374, in cell 4.4.27. In 1944, he was transferred to the Sime Road internment camp, hut #114. There is a record from May 1947 indicating that he and his wife, Dobromila, sailed on *Franconia* from Southampton to Bombay, from where they continued to Singapore. He worked in Singapore until 1963. In February 1964, he moved to Sydney and eventually died in Australia.

Kvapil, Ladislav (b. 1913) was employed by Bata in Singapore before October 1939, when he was reported to have attended the celebration of the anniversary of Czechoslovakia at the Cenotaph. He was evacuated from Singapore on 12 February 1942, on board the *MV Empire Star* to Batavia (Jakarta), where he disembarked and continued on *Deucalion* (along with Mr and Mrs Staroba, his Bata colleague stationed in Java at the time) to Fremantle, Australia, arriving on 2 March 1942. He settled there and later changed his name to "Larry Kent".

Lachs, Erich (b. 1904) was born in Přerov, joined Bata in February 1932 and worked as a supply manager. In December 1938, he was sent to Singapore

APPENDIX I

as head of production and sales of stockings. While in Singapore, he left the company and started to work for Thomas Cook. Together with his wife and two children (son Petr and daughter Margaret), he evacuated on 10 February 1942 to Durban, South Africa. From there, they proceeded through Cape Town to London. He was employed again by Bata's export company Kotva in Zlín in October 1945, but his contract was terminated in February 1946, supposedly because he was still engaged in some work for "competitors". Later he lived in Maroubra, Australia.

Lebloch, Oldřich (b. 1914) was born in Moravský Žižkov near Hodonín and joined Bata as an apprentice in August 1928. He graduated from the Bata School of Work and, two years later, worked in the sales department – first as a controller of the shops and later as a seller-chiropodist in Litoměřice. In February 1934, he left for Hong Kong to become deputy head of a shop before working as head of warehouse storage. He returned to Czechoslovakia for his military service, after which he went back to Hong Kong in March 1938 as a regional controller. In January 1939, he moved to the Philippines as a head of store in Manila. There, he married a Filipina and lived in Singapore before April 1941. In December 1943, he was interned at Changi Prison under number 3375, in cell 4.4.18. In 1944, he was transferred to the Sime Road internment camp and occupied hut #114. After the war, he sailed to India for recovery. He applied for British citizenship in Singapore in September 1949. There is a record of him in January 1951, travelling on a ship – *Chusan* – from London to Singapore; he gave "seller at Bata" as his occupation. Later he settled in England and died there.

Martinec, Břetislav (b. 1903) was trained as a miller and joined Bata in June 1930, before he was sent overseas as a team leader in the construction department. He was later dispatched to India, where he married Marie Svobodová in Calcutta in 1935. In February 1938, he was sent to Batavia (Jakarta) as a builder. At that time, he had one child. He lived in Singapore before June 1940. His wife was evacuated on 1 February 1942 to India, where she was sheltered at Edwinstown House, Nainital. In December 1943, Martinec was interned at Changi Prison under number 3509. In 1944, he was moved to the Sime Road internment camp and put in hut #114. After the war, he worked for Bata in London and eventually died there.

Matuš, Emil (b. 1903) was trained as a clockmaker and joined Bata in August 1928 as a mechanist. It was in this role that he was sent to Batanagar in November 1936. By January 1940, he was already living in Singapore. He joined the SSVF, served there as Private #13781, and fought in the Battle of Singapore as a machine gunner. In December 1943, he was interned at Changi

Prison under number 3376, in cell 4.4.26. In 1944, he was transferred to the Sime Road internment camp, hut #114. He stayed in Malaya after liberation and in the 1960s, was director of the Bata factory in Klang. He retired in Australia, where he died in December 1985.

Mizia, Alfred (b. 1914) was born in Prostřední Suchá near Fryštát na Moravě, joined Bata in August 1929, graduated from the Bata School of Work and worked there as a supply manager from 1930. In August 1933, he moved to the Bata flagship store on the Wenceslau Square in Prague. In June 1938, he was sent to Singapore as a supply manager. He joined the SSVF there. As a family, he and his wife, Růžena, as well as his daughter Iva (b. 1936) and newly born son Alfréd (March 1941) decided not to evacuate. They stayed in Singapore throughout the war. In December 1943, they were interned in Changi Prison: Mizia under number 3377 in cell 4.4.27, later moved to the Sime Road internment camp, first at hut #114, then hut #30. Růžena, under number 3428, and their children, Alfred Raymond (3433) and Iva (3432), were at Changi room A.2.PS. In October 1945, he left for India to recover but returned to Singapore where he stayed until the 1950s or later. Růžena founded and ran a kindergarten called 'Sunny Way' in Singapore. They eventually settled in Australia.

Mráz, Jan (b. 1914) was born in Mutěnice near Strakonice and trained as a knitter. He joined Bata in May 1937 as a deputy director of a stockings workshop in Třebíč. In August 1937, he was sent to Singapore as a stockings seller. He joined the SSVF in March 1938, serving as Private #12949. Like Antonín Čepka (mentioned above), he was first attached to the Singapore Royal Engineer Volunteers (SREV), which was later reorganised; Mráz subsequently served in the Bomb Disposal Unit under the command of Charles Kinahan. During the Japanese Occupation, in December 1943, he was interned in Changi Prison under number 3378 and placed in cell 4.4.25. In 1944, he was moved to the Sime Road internment camp, in hut #114. Following a recovery trip to India, he returned to Czechoslovakia, to his hometown of Mutěnice in 1946. He remained in Czechoslovakia.

Myšák, František (b. 1916) joined Bata in May 1932, graduated from the Bata School of Work and then worked as a seller-chiropodist. In May 1939, he was sent to Singapore as a chiropodist instructor. He joined the LDC, where he served under #179. On 11 February 1942, he was evacuated to India. After the war, he settled in Australia.

Němec, Silvestr (b. 1919). Born in Vémyslice, he joined Bata in September 1936 as a seller. In December 1938, he was sent to Singapore as a chiropodist.

He joined the SSVF and served as Private #13779. He saw action in the Battle of Singapore, was injured on 11 February 1942 and went missing before 15 February 1942. He was last seen in the Pasir Panjang battle. He was declared dead by authorities in July 1947. His name is engraved on the Kranji War Memorial in Singapore, on the war memorial in Zlín, as well as on a memorial in his hometown.

Plhoň, Klement (b. 1890) was born in Bořitov near Černá Hora and trained as a shoemaker. He joined Bata in August 1925, before going overseas and working as head of supply. In August 1939, he was sent to Singapore as a production organiser. During the war, he joined the LDC, where he served under #344. His wife and son Zdeněk were evacuated to India on 1 February 1942. Plhoň attempted to evacuate on the *SS Redang*, which was attacked and sunk by the Japanese on 12 February 1942. He did not survive. His name is engraved on the Kranji War Memorial in Singapore and on the war memorial in Zlín.

Pospíšil, Karel (b. 1910) was born in Přerov, trained as a seller and joined Bata in March 1934 as an arranger in the shop in Přerov. In April 1938, he was sent to Singapore in the same role but later became a manager on a rubber plantation. During the Japanese Occupation, he was interned under number 3363 at the Sime Road internment camp, at hut #114. His wife, Jarmila, and daughter Alena were evacuated on 1 February 1942 to India, where they were provided asylum in Nainital. After the war, Karel again worked on the Bata rubber plantation at Bukit Tiga, Johore, and applied for British citizenship in Malaya in July 1950. He later lived in England.

Řehoř, František (b. 1920) was trained as a seller and joined Bata in that role in 1935. In December 1938, he was sent to Singapore as a seller-chiropodist. He had major conflicts with the director, Rojt. After World War II began in Europe, he joined the Czechoslovak legions in France and later served as a pilot with the Royal Air Force (RAF), squadron 310. He went missing during a mission at the end of August 1944, probably shot down above the Channel. His name is engraved on the war memorial in Zlín.

Rojt, Václav (b. 1885) was born in Domažlice and became head of the planning department at Bata in 1910. During the World War I, he oversaw the production of the whole factory in Zlín. In the 1930s, he helped the company expand its overseas markets and was eventually appointed Director of the Singapore branch in April 1939. He died in July 1941 and was buried at the Bidadari cemetery. His daughter Anna (b. 1916), nicknamed Anička, was evacuated to India on 1 February 1942 and provided shelter in Nainital. In

December 1942, she married František Koblížek (see above) at the Batanagar Chapel of St Wenceslau. Their daughter Božena lives in Australia.

Šebová, Vlasta (b. 1920) joined Bata in 1934, graduated from the Bata School of Work and later worked as a chiropodist. In May 1939, she was sent to Singapore in the same position. In April 1941, she married George Tarry. She was evacuated on 1 February 1942 to India but continued to London while her husband George attempted to evacuate on *Giang Bee*. He survived its sinking on 13 February 1942 and was picked up by *HMS Tapah* which was later captured by the Japanese. He was interned in Palembang in Sumatra, later in Changi Prison in Singapore. After liberation in October 1945, George travelled to England on board the *Sobieski*. Both returned to Singapore in 1946. George died there in November 1947 of a heart attack.

Smržák, Oldřich (b. 1913) was born in Uhřice in central Moravia, joined Bata in August 1927, graduated from the Bata School of Work and worked as a handler before departing for Singapore in August 1938. His new position in Singapore was as head of shoe production. He died together with several other colleagues during an attempted evacuation on board the *SS Redang*, which was sunk on 12 February 1942. His wife, Miroslava, and daughter Oldřiška were successfully evacuated on 1 February 1942 and arrived in India, where they were provided asylum in Petersfield School, Nainital. Widowed Miroslava was remarried to a Batanagar-based Bata employee, Rudolf Šícha. They later emigrated to Australia where, in 1962, they applied for citizenship. At that time, they were known to have two sons, George Charles and Rudolf. The name of Smržák is engraved on the Kranji War Memorial in Singapore (misspelled as "Smrzakova O.") and on the war memorial in Zlín.

Sokol, Břetislav (b. 1910) was born in Chlumec nad Cidlinou, trained as a merchant, and joined Bata in March 1927 as a worker in the rubber factory. From November 1933 to January 1936, he was stationed in the Bata factory in East Tilbury, England. In August 1937, he was sent to Batanagar as an instructor, and from May 1939, worked as a leader in the company's factory in Klang, Malaya. He married his colleague Marie Janečková (see above) before the war. In December 1943, during the Japanese Occupation, he was interned at Changi Prison under number 3577, in cell 4.4.11. In 1944, he was transferred to the Sime Road internment camp, where he was placed in hut #114. After the war, both he and Marie worked lived in Singapore, later in Rhodesia (Zimbabwe) and eventually settled in Canada, where Břetislav died.

Soural, Jan (b. 1914) joined Bata in April 1932, graduated from the Bata School of Work and worked as a chiropodist. In May 1939, he was sent to Singapore as deputy head of a shop. He was successfully evacuated to India where he worked for Bata in Batapur (Pakistan). After the war, he returned to Singapore and is recorded to have also worked at East Tilbury, where he was granted British citizenship. There is a record of him, together with his wife, Elaine, and their daughter Růžena, travelling on *Strathedem* from London to Brisbane in July 1955. He died in 1991 in Bristol.

Štásek, Josef (b. 1913), who was trained as a butcher, joined Bata in 1931 as a seller. In April 1937, he was sent to Singapore to become head of the central warehouse. There, he joined the SSVF, where he served as Private #12947. He died before the war, after contracting typhus in Saigon (Ho Chi Minh City) in 1941.

Strangfeld, Josef (b. 1904), who was trained as a cabinet maker, joined Bata in July 1927. He progressed up the hierarchy to become chief of supplies at the Zlín factory and subsequently director of a factory in France. In 1935, he became head of the Dům služeb ("House of Services") of Bata in Prague – the most prestigious company store in the world. In November 1937, he was sent to Singapore as a sales organiser. He died while attempting an evacuation on board *SS Redang* which was sunk by the Japanese on 12 February 1942. His wife, Anastázie, successfully evacuated to India on 1 February, and was accommodated in Edwinstown House, Nainital. His name is engraved on the Kranji War Memorial in Singapore and on the war memorial in Zlín.

Straussler, Eugen (b. 1908) was born in Podmokly near Děčín, studied medicine at the university and in 1932, got a job as an external doctor at the Bata Hospital in Zlín. In April 1939, he departed for Singapore with his wife, Marta, and sons Petr and Tomáš who later became famous as playwright and screenwriter Tom Stoppard. Eugen died during an attempted evacuation, probably on board *SS Redang* on 12 February 1942. His family was evacuated to India on 1 February and sheltered in the Petersfield School, Nainital. His wife, Marie, then managed a Bata shop in Darjeeling. After the war, she was remarried to a British officer, Kenneth Stoppard and they settled in England. Eugen's name is engraved on the Kranji War Memorial in Singapore.

Vaněk, Alois (b. 1905) was born in Osek near Lipník nad Bečvou and trained as a tailor. In September 1924, he joined Bata as a factory worker and was later promoted to work in the procurement department. In January 1939, he was sent to Singapore as a purchasing agent, together with his wife, Františka, who worked in the accounting team at Bata for three years, and their child. While in Singapore, he got into conflict with the management and left the company. After that, he worked as an independent businessman. His wife and child evacuated on 6 February for India, while Vaněk reached Fremantle, Australia, on the ship *Gorgon* on 20 February 1942. He managed to obtain a visa and joined his family in India where his other child was born. In India, he was offered a job with Bata. In December 1943, he applied to join the Czechoslovak international army but was turned down on the grounds of health problems and the need to care for his wife. After the war, they returned to Czechoslovakia. From May 1946 to 1948, he worked at Bata in Zlín, then moved to work for its branch Exica in Bratislava. He and his family remained in Czechoslovakia.

Varmuža, Josef (b. 1912) was born in Olomouc, trained as a merchant, and joined Bata in May 1937 as an arranger at the advertising department. In August 1939, he was sent to Singapore as an advertising manager. During the Japanese Occupation, in December 1943, he was interned in Changi Prison under number 3382, in cell 4.4.27. In 1944, he was transferred to the Sime Road internment camp, where he was placed in hut #114, then hut #30. After the liberation, in October 1945, he sailed to India for recovery. In February 1950, he applied for British citizenship in Singapore. During the 1960s, he worked as a sales director in Klang. He retired to Canada, where he died in 2000.

Vašica, Jan (b. 1912) was born in Jasenná near Zlín, joined Bata in July 1927, graduated from the Bata School of Work, and later worked in the warehouse and in procurement. In August 1939, he was sent to Singapore to help with procurement and worked in the department under Jaroslav Adamík. His wife, Božena, and daughter (also Božena) were evacuated to India on 1 February 1942 and lived in Bombay during the war. In 1947, Vašica participated in the rally of the Sokol association in Zlín. He later settled in the United States.

Vítek, Karel (b. 1912) joined Bata in August 1929, graduated from the Bata School of Work and worked as an accountant. In August 1939, he was sent to Singapore in the same position. Together with Silvestr Němec and Rudolf Janeček, he joined the SSVF, where he served as Private #13777. He was wounded in battle and captured by the Japanese. In March 1945, he died of malaria and beriberi in the POW camp in Labuan on Borneo. His name is engraved on the Kranji War Memorial and on the war memorial in Zlín.

Vrla, Ladislav (b. 1911) was born in Kvítkovice near Uherské Hradiště and later lived in Napajedla. He joined Bata in 1926, graduated from the Bata School of Work and worked as a factory worker, then as a supplier. In that position, he was sent to Singapore in August 1939. His wife, Marie, who had worked at Bata as a tailor since 1926, was evacuated to India on 6 February 1942. Vrla also managed to escape there. In Calcutta in June 1943, he signed up for the Czechoslovak international army. While in India, he quit the Bata company in January 1944 and started to work in Lahore for another Czech factory, Janda, that was providing supplies to the army. After the war, he lived in Dakar (Senegal) and later settled in Australia.

Vyhnálek, Josef (b. 1917) was born in Nekoř, near Jamné nad Orlicí, and joined Bata in September 1931. He graduated from the Bata School of Work and worked in a factory before becoming a supply organiser and regional controller of the shops. From 1934 to 1937, he worked as a seller-chiropodist in the shops of Zlín, Louny, Mělník, Brno and Mladá Boleslav. In May 1939, he was sent to Singapore in that role before he was promoted to deputy head of the Bata flagship store on North Bridge Road. He joined SSVF where he served as Private #13797. He fought in the Battle of Singapore and was captured by the Japanese on 13 February 1942 around Pasir Panjang. As a POW, he was sent to work camps in Burma and Borneo. After liberation, he travelled first to London at the end of 1945, then decided to return to Zlín, where he was re-employed in March 1946 and worked in Bata's Exica branch in Bratislava. He stayed in Czechoslovakia.

Vytopil, Karel (b. 1910) was born in Brno and worked for Bata from 1927 to 1930 as a seasonal worker before being offered a permanent job in September 1934 as a regional controller of the shops. He left for India in 1935, and in September 1939, was sent to Singapore as director of the sales department. When the war in the Pacific started, he was with his wife, Júlie, and their three children in Batavia, where they lived until the war was over. He worked again for Bata in India in 1946, and later in East Tilbury (1953), Gweru in Zimbabwe (1954) and in the 1960s, in the United States and Canada. He retired in Sydney, where his family is still living today.

Wakerman, František (b. 1921). His original surname was Blažek, but he changed it to Wakerman in the 1930s. He joined Bata in September 1936 as a seller-chiropodist. It was in this role that he was sent to Singapore in December 1938 – in the same group as Silvestr Němec. He was relocated to Klang where he joined the LDC. As the Japanese were advancing south through Malaya, he retreated to Singapore and joined the police force as a volunteer. A few days before the capitulation, he captured a Japanese spy near Bukit Timah. He managed to evacuate on 13 February 1942 to Batavia (Jakarta) and then continued via Ceylon to India. There, he joined the British army and was attached to the Berkshire Regiment, where he served for two years, after which he entered the Military Academy. Consequently, he was with the Sussex Regiment in Madras (Chennai). He participated in the fighting in Burma and for Malaya's liberation and was promoted to the rank of Captain. After the war, he worked in Penang and later settled in Singapore, where he married Daisy, a Chinese. They have four children.

APPENDIX I

Zamara, Vilém (Wilhelm) (b. 1909) was born in Vienna but grew up in Kopisty near Most. He joined Bata in February 1932 as a correspondent, then later worked in shops in Dubí as well as Germany and Algeria. In March 1938, he was sent to Singapore as head of the sampling department. He joined the SSVF before August 1938, serving as Private #13019 (some other sources say #13901). He eventually quit the company and worked as a sales representative for various companies, including Remington typewriters. He was captured in Kuala Lumpur and interned at the Sime Road camp under number 3664, in hut #114. After liberation, he travelled to England in October 1945 and then on to Czechoslovakia. In February 1946, he was re-employed by Bata in its export company Kotva and sent to Singapore again in December 1946. A year later, he once again resigned from the company. In the summer of 1948, he applied for British citizenship in Singapore. He died in Canada.

Zapalač, Jaroslav (b. 1911), who joined the Bata company in July 1930, worked as a supply manager. In that position, he was sent to Singapore in December 1938, travelling in the same group as Silvestr Němec. When the war started in the Pacific, he was based in Batavia (Jakarta). On 27 February 1942, he evacuated on *Marella* and arrived in Fremantle, Australia. In 1945, he lived in Melbourne, but it seems he eventually settled in Malaysia.

Zelníček, Vladimír (b. 1912) joined Bata in July 1926. In January 1939, he was sent to Singapore as a purchaser and probably travelled on the same ship as Silvestr Němec. From May 1941, he served with the volunteer force in Penang. He attempted evacuation on *SS Redang* which was sunk. Zelníček survived, was captured and interned in Sumatra. There, he met Viktor Koš (see above) and joined him in the journey to Medan, where he stayed for the rest of the war. He died in 1988.

Zuna, Josef (b. 1921) was born in Prievidza, grew up in Ostřešany near Pardubice, and joined Bata in September 1935 as a factory worker. He graduated from the Bata School of Work and in June 1938, attended a course to become a seller. In December 1938, he was sent to Singapore as a chiropodist, travelling there on the same ship as Silvestr Němec. After the war started in Europe, he returned to France and later to England, where he joined the British army, earning the rank of Sergeant Major. From October 1946, he worked for Bata again at the Kotva export company in Zlín. He travelled to Singapore in November 1947 but was back in Zlín a year later. He quit the company at the end of 1950.

APPENDIX I

Other Czechoslovaks in Singapore

Apelbaum, David (b. 1904), who lived in Kuala Lumpur with his wife, Jarmila, (b. 1905) and son Jiří (b. 1938), evacuated to Singapore when the Japanese started advancing down the Malay Peninsula. Apelbaum was then working as a musician in the Selangor Club and performed in concerts even in the early period of the Japanese Occupation. They were later interned at Changi Prison under number 3411 (Jarmila, in room A.2.PS) and number 3431 (Jiří, in room A.2.PS). When they were moved to the Sime Road internment camp, David was housed in hut #44. After the war, in 1952, he was granted British citizenship and changed his surname to "Apel". He continued to live and work as a musician in Singapore. He died in 1967 during a holiday visit to Prague – his body was transported to Singapore and was buried at the Jewish Cemetery at Thomson Road. Jarmila died in Singapore in 1985. Their son Jiří/George was living in London at that time, and their daughter Ludmila (probably born after the war), in Singapore.

Bachratý, Štěpán (b. 1916) was a Roman Catholic missionary and teacher in Singapore. In December 1943, he was interned at Changi Prison under number 3367, in cell 4.4.19, and later at the Sime Road internment camp in hut #114.

Berg, Pavel (b. 1908) was born in Vienna. He was a salesman and married. He evacuated on 11 February 1942 on board the *Gorgon* and reached Fremantle, Australia, on 20 February. He eventually settled in Melbourne. His wife, Marie Josefa (b. 1909, Brno), was in Czechoslovakia during the war, but later joined him in Australia. He was granted Australian citizenship in November 1948.

Eisinger, Pavel (b. 1876) worked in Kuala Lumpur as a motor engineer. He was captured there and interned at Changi Prison under number 3371. He was recorded to have been hospitalised for some time, then transferred to the Sime Road internment camp in hut #35.

Getreuer, Pavel (b. 1908) was a salesman at Optorg & Co. He and his wife Stella, a doctor, were interned in Changi Prison under numbers 3372 (Pavel, cell 4.4.28, later in Sime Road hut #114) and 1824 (Stella, room A.2.PS). They remained in Singapore after the war. Pavel joined the Optorg company again in 1946 and worked for some time as Deputy Consul in Greece. His name was still mentioned in the Singapore press in 1968. Stella died in Singapore in July 1957.

Chalemová, Margaret (b. 1916) was a housewife who was captured in Cameron Highlands, Malaya, and interned in Changi Prison under number 3665, in room A.2.PS.

APPENDIX I

Kinský, Vojtěch. Together with his wife and two children, Kinský was evacuated to Australia on 10 February 1942. The family settled in Sydney.

Kočí, Bohuslav (b. 1889) was an artist and sculptor who fought in the First World War and was captured in Brody near Lvov. In October 1918, he joined the Czechoslovak Legions in Russia. He is the creator of the sculpture of the unknown soldier in Vladivostok. In 1920, he settled in China, where he created many sculptures and pieces of art – most famous is the statue of Sun Yat Sen in his mausoleum in Nanking. From October 1937, he lived in Malaya and eventually in Singapore. He died in February 1942, while trying to evacuate on one of the ships.

Luley, Josef (b. 1897) was born in Příbor and graduated from a business academy in Prague. Since August 1921, he worked for the Czechoslovak Ministry of Foreign Affairs, serving as a clerk in the embassy in Budapest, later in Albania, and after December 1929, in higher positions at the Czechoslovak consulates in Calcutta and Bombay. In March 1941, he was sent to Singapore from India as a consular agent and was accommodated at the Raffles Hotel. On 6 February 1942, he evacuated to India, where his wife and daughter lived. He later served as a diplomat in Cape Town (May 1942 to February 1943) and in then Jerusalem (March 1943 to April 1946), but he was dismissed from the ministry in 1949. He retired in 1950.

Marischler, Emil (b. 1905) was born in Přerov and graduated from a business academy. At the beginning of the 1930s, he worked for Bata and sailed to the Far East in December 1932 on the legendary voyage of Bata's ship *Morava*. He worked in the company's branch in Batavia but soon moved to Singapore. Due to conflicts with the management, he quit and worked in Singapore as an independent businessman. In March 1941, he signed up for the Czechoslovak international army but eventually did not join it. His wife Ludmila (b. 1906, Přerov) and daughter Marcela (b. 1936) were evacuated on 6 February 1942 to India, while Marischler arrived on *Wang Pu* to Fremantle, Australia, on 1 March 1942. His wife and daughter travelled on board the *Dominion* to join him there in November 1942. In 1950, the family travelled from Bombay to Fremantle on the ship *Strathmore*. He was granted Australian citizenship in 1959 and died in California in 1982.

Mense, Osvald (b. 1881) was born in Uherské Hradiště and worked as an engineer in Singapore. Together with his wife, Elsa (b. 1886, Vienna), he evacuated on board *Tanda* on 6 February 1942 and arrived in Melbourne on 30 March 1942. Their son had Austrian nationality, and was thus interned in Tatura, Australia. In 1946, Mense was granted Australian citizenship.

APPENDIX I

Milner, N. worked for the company Far East Ox. and Aceth Ltd.

Muhlbergová, Josefina (b. 1864) was a Czechoslovak of German origin. Her fate remains unknown.

Muhlstein, Rudolf worked for Far East Ox. and Aceth Ltd. Together with his wife, Gertruda, he evacuated on 6 February 1942 to India. In March 1947, they travelled on *Madura* from Calcutta to Melbourne.

Neuman, Pavel was an employee of the Human Pipe Ltd. His wife and two children were evacuated on 6 February 1942 to India.

Paronová, Pavlína (b. 1933) was a student who was captured in Cameron Highlands, Malaya (possibly attending the Tanglin Boarding School there) and interned in Changi Prison under number 3666.

Paronová, Simona (b. 1932) was a student captured in Cameron Highlands, Malaya (possibly attending the Tanglin Boarding School there) and interned in Changi Prison under number 3667.

Reiser, Rudolf was sent to Singapore in 1935 by the Czechoslovak state company, Export Institution. Soon after, he became an independent sales representative of several private companies. He spoke Czech with a German accent. He cooperated with the Security Control Office as a confidante in matters of Czechoslovak citizens. When the war started, he accepted an offer to become a censor working for the British government. He later passed on that role to Erich Wodak, director of the Škoda company in Singapore. His wife was evacuated on 6 February 1942 to India, Reiser followed her on 11 February. Their two sons were living in London then.

Robitschek, Pavel (b. 1905), who was born in Nové Sedlo, opened the first Bata store in Singapore in 1931, at Capitol Theatre. He later quit the company around the same time as Marischler (see above), probably in 1933. In 1937, he represented the company Nouveaux Co. In September 1937, he entered a long-distance marriage with Alice Trostler (b. 1912, Plzeň). His wife then travelled to Singapore in October 1937 on board *Conte Rosso*. From 1938 to 1940, Robitschek made public appearances on behalf of the Czechoslovak community in Singapore. Together with his wife, he was evacuated on 6 February via Batavia (Jakarta) to Fremantle. He lived in Sydney during the war and was granted Australian citizenship in 1946. He later returned to Singapore. In May 1945, he and his wife flew from Calcutta to Sydney. There are records of repeated entries into Australia in the 1960s and 1970s.

APPENDIX I

Schmidtová, Ilsa (b. 1928) evacuated on 6 February 1942 to Australia and lived in Perth during the war. She later married Josef Granig from Austria.

Sienkievicz "Benny" Wieslaw (b. 1919) was a Czechoslovak of Polish descent, who lived in Český Těšín. In Singapore, he taught at the King's School. He joined SSVF, served as Private #13734 with the Armoured Cars company and later the Bren Carriers platoon (he therefore served with Silvestr Němec.) It seems he also partially worked for Bata as he was remembered by Josef Vyhnálek (see above) as one of the colleagues he fought with in SSVF and was captured two days before capitulation. As a POW, Sienkievicz was sent to a work camp on Borneo where he died in August 1944. (The Jeyes List has two records, "Sinkewic" and "Syncovitch" – a Czech from Bata. It's unlikely that two different men of the same name from Czechoslovakia would be in SSVF, so we can be quite certain that both entries refer to Sienkievicz "Benny" Wieslaw).

Sládek, Klement (b. 1897) registered his occupation as a "showman". He lived in Singapore with his Russian wife, Fanny Vasilyevna (b. 1901). Both were interned in Changi Prison under numbers 3379 (Klement, in cell 4.4.22, later hut #118 in Sime Road internment camp) and 4641 (Fanny, room A.2.PS).

Svobodová, Anna was the wife of a musician who was interned in Shanghai. She was in Singapore in February 1942.

Svrček, Jan (b. 1916) was a Roman Catholic priest, interned in December 1943 at Changi Prison under number 3380, in cell 4.4.19; later at the Sime Road internment camp, hut #114.

Tkáč, Petr was a Roman Catholic priest, interned in December 1943 at Changi Prison under number 3381, in cell 4.4.19; later at the Sime Road internment camp, hut #30.

Vaníček, Karel (b. 1909) was born in Praha and worked for Bata from April 1938 as head of the sampling unit in Hong Kong but quit the company and worked as an independent salesman. He was living in Singapore when the war started. His wife, Anna Marie (b. 1912, Hamburg), worked as a dentist and was evacuated on 6 February 1942 to India. Vaníček left Singapore on 11 February and arrived in Fremantle on 1 March aboard *Wang Pu*. His wife joined him in Australia, arriving on *Madura* in May 1942. Both travelled to India but returned to Australia in November 1944. In December 1944, they applied for Australian citizenship.

Vodák, Bedřich (b. 1905) was born in Uherské Hradiště and worked in Singapore for the company Vodak, Roth & Co. On 10 February 1942, he evacuated to Australia on board *Wang Pu* and settled in Melbourne. In 1947, he was granted Australian citizenship.

Weinstein, Leo. A former motorcycle racer, he worked as a car and motorcycle specialist in Indochina. After the Japanese Occupation, he moved to Hong Kong and then Shanghai, finally reaching Singapore, where he worked as a truck mechanic. He evacuated on 12 February 1942 aboard *MV Empire Star* to Australia, then continued through Cape Town to London, where he arrived in May 1942. Shortly after that, he joined the Czechoslovak international army.

Wodak, Erich (b. 1902) was born in Uherské Hradiště and was a salesman who later represented the Škoda company in Singapore. Together with wife, Emilie, (who may be a sister of Pavel Berg) and a child, he was evacuated to Australia. Erich arrived in Darwin by airplane from Batavia on 13 January 1942, and continued to Sydney a day later. In May 1946, he applied for Australian citizenship. The family later lived in Melbourne.

- Appendix II -
TOOLS FOR RESEARCH

Searching for ancestors is something that many feel drawn to at a certain point in their lives, and in recent years, there's also been a surge of interest in many countries.

While my own journey of discovering my granduncle Silvestr's life has been woven – as one of the threads – into this book, I think what may be useful for those embarking on a similar journey is a summary of the main tools I used as well as some tips from my personal experience:

Family archives

It is best to begin with whatever you can learn from your family members and family archive. These can be letters, personal diaries, certificates of birth, marriage and deaths, contracts of property sale etc. Other useful leads include information about schools, employers, names of relatives or other relevant people.

State and parish registers

These repositories contain records of births, deaths and marriages – dates, places and additional information about other people involved. In many countries, they can be accessed online, sometimes for free as a public service. In Southeast Asia, the situation may be different: besides church records, there may be registers in clan associations or local religious institutions.

In the Czech Republic, these records can go back to the mid 17th century. Earlier records can also be found in the archives, but unfortunately, a religious war in Europe (Thirty Years' War, 1618-1648) destroyed many written records. One challenge of working with older texts is that they are very hard, even impossible, to read and decipher as the script then was very different from today's. In such cases, help can be found online – there are forums where people with skills volunteer to transcribe old records.

APPENDIX II

International websites with databases

Websites like Ancestry.com, FamilySearch.org or FindMyPast.com are useful for ancestral searches, and most will allow you to begin with a free search to see if there's anything of interest. But do note that if you wish to access digital copies, you will need to pay a fee. Also, one of the challenges – as you go further back in history – is that the transcription of names is often inconsistent. As such, you will need to look for variants of the name (which may appear in strange, scrambled forms). But most of these websites usually allow you to look for similar names, which helps. The website I used was findmypast.co.uk.

There are also specialised genealogy portals where you can start building a family tree by entering all known information about your ancestors, then using their online tools to search for others who share common ancestors with you. You may then connect with these remote relatives and tap into what they have already discovered.

National archives

There are state archives in many countries that now allow you to access their records via the internet, as their resources have been digitised. The National Archives of Singapore (nas.gov.sg/archivesonline) is one good example. In the case of Singapore and Malaysia, many relevant documents can also be found in the UK National Archives (nationalarchives.gov.uk), which holds a huge collection related to Britain's former colonies. However, to access these colonial records necessitates a personal visit to London.

In the course of my research, I also delved into the Australian, Canadian and South African archives as some of the Bata Czechoslovaks evacuated to various other countries during World War II. The Czech National Archives was also a great source of information, in particular on the Bata Shoe Company and the history of my granduncle's hometown. Both the city and school chronicles contained unique historical details about his family and the environment in which he was growing up.

Military archives

As Silvestr was a volunteer with the British army, I was also able to tap into various military archives. These include the archives of the Imperial War Museum in London (iwm.org.uk/collections), the database of the Commonwealth War Graves Commission (cwgc.org), and the database of war memorials in the Czech Republic, managed by the non-profit organisation, Association for Military Memorials (vets.cz).

Finally, there are also other related associations that bring together descendants of various military groups. One such association that provided invaluable online information for me was the Malayan Volunteers Group (malayanvolunteersgroup.org.uk). The website also provides contact with their historians who can help further with inquiries.

Newspapers

Historical events are often recorded in contemporary newspapers and magazines. As such, it is possible to search for the names of your relatives there. Although it's quite rare that their names will appear, there is still a chance they may. In my case, this was how I found several mentions of Silvestr in the Singapore newspapers. Again, you may need to search for variants of the name, as spelling may be inconsistent. But even if your ancestors are not explicitly mentioned, these newspaper articles may provide descriptions or details of interesting moments that they were involved in. NewspaperSG, the Singapore newspaper archives (eresources.nlb.gov.sg/newspapers) managed by the National Library Board, has been an incredibly useful tool in my research.

- Bibliography -

PRIVATE COLLECTION

Aster, Karel. Letter to family, 1945.
Bennett, Jack. 'Jeyes List' of the Prisoners of War in Singapore, 1942.
Koš, Viktor. Diary, 1943.
Máčel, Emil with Karel Hrabica, Stanislav Jedovnický, Viktor Koš, A. Procházka a J. Sokol. Personal correspondence, 1992-1998.
Němec family archive. Letter by Silvestr Němec, 1939.
Němec family archive. Post-war correspondence between his parents and governmental institutions both in Czechoslovakia and Great Britain, and with Silvestr's friends and colleagues from Bata: Pavel Ambrož, Matěj Bohman, Antonín Jugas, Josef Vyhnálek and Josef Zuna, 1945-1947.
Plesek, Olek. *Remembering Private Nemec*, 2018.
Plhoň, Zdeněk. Memoir, 2003.
Varmuža, Viktor. Memoir, 1995.
Vyhnálek, Josef. *Report on my stay abroad and wartime resistance*, 1966.

PUBLIC ARCHIVES

Czech National Archive
File of the case of missing Silvestr Němec (*kart. 10092, sign. 453*).

Archive of the Security Forces of the Czech Republic
Personal correspondence, digest of information about several individual Batamen, 2018.

Archive of the Czech Ministry of Foreign Affairs
Correspondence on liberation of interned Czechoslovak citizens in the

Far East, 1944-1945 (*Londýnský archiv 1939-1945 doplňky*).
Correspondence between the exiled Czechoslovak government and the wives of Czechoslovak men interned in Singapore and with the International Red Cross; contains a list of Czechoslovaks living in Singapore before its occupation by the Japanese, 1942-1944 (*Londýnský archiv, kr. 519*).
Correspondence between the exiled Czechoslovak Ministry of Foreign Affairs and the British government on the matter of captured and interned Czechoslovak citizens, 1943 (*Londýnský archiv, kart. 263, sign. 2-78/3*).
Dvořák, V. Testimony on the situation of the Czechoslovak community in Singapore, 1942 (*Londýnský archiv – důvěrný, kr. 177*).
Folder on establishment of a representation of Czechoslovak consulate in Singapore, 1941 (*Londýnský archiv, kr. 162*).
Folder on financial arrangements of a representation of Czechoslovak consulate in Singapore, 1942 (*Londýnský archiv, kr. 162*).
Lachs, E. Testimony on the situation of the Czechoslovak community in Singapore, 1942 (*Londýnský archiv – důvěrný, kr. 177*).
List of Czechoslovak refugees from Malaya and other related correspondence, 1942 (*Londýnský archiv, kr. 519*).
Political report on the situation in East Asia and the German-Japanese military pact, 1937 (*Londýnský archiv 1939-1945 doplňky*).
Reiser. R. Testimony on the situation of the Czechoslovak community in Singapore, 1942 (*Londýnský archiv – důvěrný, kr. 177*).
Report from Singapore, situation in the colony, 1941 (*Londýnský archiv, kr. 162*).
Report on Bata in British India and Singapore, 1939-1945 (*Londýnský archiv 1939-1945 doplňky*).
Report on the Czechoslovak community in northern India, 1941 (*Londýnský archiv – důvěrný, kr. 177*).
Report on the Czechoslovak community in northern India (*Londýnský archiv, kart. 263, 2-74/3*).
Report on the evacuation of Czechoslovak citizens from Singapore, 1942 (*Londýnský archiv – důvěrný, kr. 177*).
Report on the evacuation of Czechoslovak citizens from Singapore, 1942-1944 (*Londýnský archiv 1939–1945 doplňky*).
Report on the opinions of Jan Antonín Baťa (*Londýnský archiv, 2-74/4*).
Report on the situation of the Czechoslovak consulate in Calcutta in relation to Germany, 1939-1945 (*Londýnský archiv 1939–1945 doplňky*).

Czech Military History Institute
Collection of documents 20. *Fond* 3-29, 31-44, 6-13, 13-5, 3-46, 3-47, 19-2, 13-2.
Collection of documents 22. *Fond* 7-1 (contains a report about the consular activities in Singapore in 1941; correspondence about the activities of the Czechoslovak consul's representative in Singapore, 1941-1942;

correspondence of exiled Czechoslovak Ministry of Foreign Affairs on the fate of Czechoslovak citizens in Singapore and British Malaya, 1942-1945; appeal of Bata wives for exchange of prisoners and liberation of their husbands),

Czech archives in Zlín

Bata. *A road to 100% – Advice to Bata sellers*, 1934 (Fond Baťa, a. s., Zlín, sign. II/6 – Osobní oddělení / publikace, kar. 1281, inv. č. 133).

Bata. *Instructions for our Salesman*, 1930s (Fond Baťa, a. s., Zlín, sign. II/6 – Osobní oddělení / publikace, kar. 1281, inv. č. 132).

Baťa, J. A. *A Bible of Decisions* (Fond Baťa, a. s., Zlín, sign I/4 – Hlavní ředitelna, kart. 68, inv. č. 24).

Bata. *The List of Employees Overseas*, 1944 (Fond Baťa, a. s., Zlín, sign. II/2 – Osobní oddělení, kart. volný, inv. č. 74).

Dittrich, K. *A report from the British Malaya*, 1935 (Fond Baťa, a. s., Zlín, sign. X – Prodejní oddělení, kart. 1596, inv. č. 371).

Kocourek, František, *Practical manual for the textbook of Chiropody*, 1943 (Fond Baťa, a. s., Zlín, sign. II/6 – Osobní oddělení / publikace, kar. 1283, inv. č. 144).

Letter from the Bata headquarters in Zlín to its branch in Singapore, 9 January 1939 (Fond Baťa, a. s., Zlín sign. XXVII – Zahraniční společnosti – korespondence, kar. 1876, inv. č. 2).

Personal files of 24 individual Bata workers sent to India and Singapore (Fond Baťa, a. s., Zlín, sign. II/2 – osobní oddělení, kart. 1125, 1070, 297, 1044, 1101, 1106, 1023, 1036, 1106, 1069).

Sedlář. *A report from a business travel to the East*, 1932-1936 (Fond Baťa, a. s., Zlín, sign. III/2 – Nákupní oddělení, kart. 1387, inv. č. 47).

Telegrams sent by the Batamen in the Far East to Zlín after their liberation, 1945 (Fond Baťa, a. s., Zlín sign. XXVII – Zahraniční společnosti – korespondence, kar. 1877, inv. č. 3).

Czech archives in Znojmo

Census in Vémyslice, 1921 (Archivní fond Okresní úřad Moravský Krumlov, kart. 451).

Census in Vémyslice, 1953 (Vém II, kart. 19).

Construction plan for the reconstruction of a barn of Sylvestr Němec, house No. 23, 1923 (Archivní fond Archiv městečka Vémyslice, kart. 12).

Chládková, Michaela and Moučková, Miroslava. Digest of the archives of the town of Vémyslice, 1529-1953 (archivní pomůcka č. 0793, 1997).

Chronicle of the Agricultural School of Vémyslice, 1929-1939 (Archivní fond Lidová škola zemědělská Vémyslice, sg. K-I 615).

Chronicle of Vémyslice, 1923-1971 (Archivní fond Místní národní výbor Vémyslice, Pamětní kniha městyse Vémyslic, sg. K-I 104).

Correspondence on the change of name of the town of Vémyslice, 1925 (*Archivní fond Archiv městečka Vémyslice, kart. 8*).

Notes from the conferences of teachers at the Vémyslice school, 1925-1928 (*Archivní fond Národní škola Vémyslice, Zápisy učitelských porad, kniha č. 147*).

Register of Punishments in Vémyslice town, 1868-1930 (*Archivní fond Archiv městečka Vémyslice, kn. 170*).

Vémyslice school chronicle, 1915-1953 (*Archivní fond Národní škola Vémyslice, Kronika školy Výmyslické, sg. K-I 1036*).

Vémyslice school chronicle, 1928-1935 (*Archivní fond Základní škola Vémyslice, Kronika měšťanských škol, občanské školy ve Vémyslicích, sg. K-I 1037*).

Imperial War Museum, London

Private Papers of 2nd Lieutenant R. Middleton-Smith (Documents 11931).
Private Papers of C.H.G. Kinahan CBE JP DL (Documents 457).
Private Papers of G.W. Hansard (Documents 23404).
Private Papers of J. Innes (Documents 893).
Private Papers of J.R. Hodgson (Documents 7374).
Private Papers of K.B.H. Stevens (Documents 2046).
Private Papers of Lieutenant A.G. MacKenzie CBE MC, 1942 (Documents 208).
Private Papers of Major L.V. Taylor (Documents 899).
Private Papers of Mrs C.E. Craig (Documents 12413).
S.S.V.F. Year Books 1937-1938, 1938-1939, 1939-1940 (LBY 81066).

National Archives, London

Account of Japanese massacre, Alexandra Hospital, Singapore; known survivors and those missing (WO 361/1416).

Ballentine, G.C. (Brigadier, officer commanding). Account of formation and operations of 44th Indian Infantry Brigade in Singapore, July 1941 July-Feb 1942. by (Cab 106/117).

Defence of Singapore; damage and demolitions; photographic interpretation reports, 1945 (WO 208/1528).

Japanese espionage activities in the East Indian Archipelago, Straits Settlements and India. This file is concerned with Japanese intelligence activity and British countermeasures, mainly in the Straits Settlements (Malaya, Singapore) but including neighbouring territories, in the 1930s and early 1940s (KV3/251).

Japanese intelligence activities in Malaya: Accounts of Japanese espionage against Malaya before the fall of Singapore, directed by the Japanese Consulate in that city (KV3/426).

Labour unrest in Malaya: May Day demonstrations, 1939-1940 (CO 273/662).

Liberated Prisoner of War Interrogation Questionnaires, 1946 (WO 344/406).

Malaya: A massacre by the Japanese at Alexandra Hospital, Singapore, 14 February 1942 (WO 361/770).
Malaya Straits Settlements. Malayan Volunteer Force; legislation, 1940 (CO 820/45).
Malaya: Volunteer force training, Jan-Feb 1940 (WO 106/2437).
Malaya: Volunteers for service, Oct-Nov 1940 (WO 106/2450).
Naval Base, Singapore: Opening of King George VI Dock, 1938 (CO 273/640/8).
Notes on the Federated Malay States Volunteer Forces and Lines of Communication organisation in the Malaya Campaign, 1941-1942; includes summary of F.M.S.V.F. war diary, Jan-Feb 1942. (Cab 106/156)
Percival, A.E. (Major-General). Despatch on operations of Malaya Command, 8 Dec 1941 to 15 Feb 1942, a related correspondence (Cab 106/45).
Prisoners of war, Far East. Federation of Malay States Volunteer Force (FMSVF); nominal roll, 1942-1943 (WO 361/2127).
Singapore: Calling up of volunteers for intensive training, 1941 (FCO 141/16269A).
Singapore: Outline narrative by the combined (India and Pakistan) Historical Section on the defence of the island, Feb 1942; includes account by Brigadier A.E. Cumming., 1942 (Cab 106/196).
Singapore Progress: Architectural and Engineering Works Department, later Civil Engineer in Chief's Department: Photographs of Works (ADM 195/114).
War Diaries, Malaya. Brigades: 1 Malaya Infantry Brigade: 2 Loyal Regiment (North Lancashire) (WO 172/147).
War Diaries, Malaya: Brigades: 45 Indian Infantry Brigade: 7/6 Rajput Rifles (WO 172/139).
Internment of enemy aliens, Straits Settlements; St John's Island, Singapore, 1 940 (CO 323/1799/1).
Water Works – water supply from Johore. Published to mark the completion of the reservoir at Pontian Kechil, 1932 (CO 1069/561).
Williams, G.G.R. (Brigadier). Precis by the official narrator, Brigadier J. Blood, of an account of operations of 1st Malaya Infantry Brigade, 8-15 Feb 1942 (Cab 106/155).

National Archives of Singapore

Ong, Mei Weng. *Nanquiao Jigong – The Extraordinary Story of Nanyang Drivers and Mechanics Who Returned to China During the Sino-Japanese War.* (National Archives of Singapore, 2009).
Ong, Y.V. *Memories Unfolded – A Guide to Memories at Old Ford Factory.* (National Archives of Singapore, 2008).
Reflections & Memories of War. Battle For Singapore. Exhibition Catalogue and

Resource Guide, Vol. 1, 2012.
Reflections & Memories of War. Syonan Years 1942-1945: Living Beneath the Rising Sun. Exhibition Catalogue and Resource Guide, Vol. 2, 2012.
Reflections & Memories of War. The Liberation. Exhibition Catalogue and Resource Guide, Vol. 3, 2012.

ACADEMIC PAPERS

Fohlová, Eva. Economic Policy of the Bata company headquarters in years 1939-1942 (*Hospodářská politika vedení Baťových závodů v letech 1939-1942, diplomová práce, Technická univerzita v Liberci, Fakulta přírodovědně-humanitní a pedagogická, Liberec 2008*).

Glabazňová, Jitka. Transformation of the May Day celebrations in Zlín during the interwar Czechoslovakia (*Proměny prvomájových oslav ve Zlíně v období první Československé republiky, bakalářská práce, Masarykova univerzita, Filozofická fakulta, Historický ústav, Brno 2014*).

Hladká, Magdaléna. Baťa's Legacy (*Baťův odkaz, diplomová práce, Univerzita Tomáše Bati ve Zlíně, Fakulta multimediálních komunikací, Zlín 2015*).

Hladká, Magdaléna. Tomáš Baťa as a pioneer and innovator of advertisement (*Tomáš Baťa jako průkopník a inovátor propagace, bakalářská práce, Univerzita Tomáše Bati ve Zlíně, Fakulta multimediálních komunikací, Zlín 2012*).

Hofmanová, Jana. Application of Bata management system into a modern business (*Aplikace Baťovy soustavy řízení do moderní firmy, diplomová práce, Univerzita Tomáše Bati ve Zlíně, Fakulta multimediálních komunikací, Zlín 2012*).

Hrnčířová, Zuzana. Batanagar – Bata factory and life of Czechoslovaks in India in years 1934-1950 (*Batanagar – Baťovy závody a život Čechoslováků v Indii v letech 1934-1950, diplomová práce, Univerzita Karlova, Filozofická fakulta, Ústav jižní a centrální Asie, Praha 2017*).

Končitíková, Gabriela. Education system in the Bata company before 1945 and application of its methods in today's times (*Podnikové vzdělávání ve firmě Baťa a.s. do roku 1945 a využití těchto principů v současnosti, bakalářská práce, Univerzita Tomáše Bati ve Zlíně, Fakulta humanitních studií, Zlín 2015*).

Koubková, Jana. Moravský Krumlov during the Second World War, with emphasise on the first and last days of the German occupation (*Moravský Krumlov za 2. světové války s důrazem na první a poslední dny okupace, bakalářská práce, Masarykova univerzita, Filozofická fakulta, Historický ústav, Brno 2007*).

Kreisinger, Pavel. Czechs and Slovaks in Australia during the first half of 20th century and their participation in WWI and WWII (*Češi a Slováci v Austrálii v první polovině 20. století a jejich účast ve světových válkách, disertační práce,*

Univerzita Palackého v Olomouci, Filozofická fakulta, Katedra historie, Olomouc 2016).

Kurian, Matěj. Political System of Singapore (*Politický režim Singapuru*, bakalářská práce, Masarykova univerzita, Fakulta sociálních studií, Katedra politologie, Košice 2006).

Lepíková, Markéta. Ethnical composition of Singapore population and its specifics (*Etnické složení obyvatelstva Singapuru a jeho specifika*, bakalářská práce, Univerzita Palackého v Olomouci, Přírodovědecká fakulta, Katedra geografie, Olomouc 2011).

Marek, Martin. Bata factories and their management in relation to the Soviet Union in years 1918-1938 (*Baťovy závody, batismus a Sovětský svaz v letech 1918–1938*, disertační práce, Masarykova univerzita, Filozofická fakulta, Historický ústav, Brno 2010).

Martynková, Ivona. Analysis of Bata services and comparison with today's practice (*Analýza služeb firmy Baťa a srovnání se současnou praxí*, bakalářská práce, Univerzita Palackého v Olomouci, Filozofická fakulta, Olomouc 2011).

Matyášová, Judita. Reflections of the term "home" in the memories of the children of Bata employees in India (*Reflexe vnímání pojmu „domov" ve vzpomínkách dětí zaměstnanců firmy Baťa v Indii*, diplomová práce, Univerzita Karlova, Fakulta humanitních studií, Praha 2017).

Mikel, Filip. Selected principles of the financial management of Bata company in 1932-1939 (*Vybrané principy finančního řízení firmy Baťa v období 1932-1939*, diplomová práce, Masarykova univerzita, Ekonomicko-správní fakulta, Brno 2014).

Mikošková, Barbora. Tailored design of shoes for individual customers and application of the physotherapeutic and diagnostic tools (*Design obuvi pro konkrétního zákazníka s využitím fyzioterapeutických a diagnostických poznatků*, diplomová práce, Univerzita Tomáše Bati ve Zlíně, Fakulta multimediálních komunikací, Zlín 2009).

Mohyla, Petr. Bata Inc. – Setting up the working and social standards (*Baťa a.s. – Určování pracovních a sociálních standardů*, bakalářská práce, Univerzita Karlova, Filozofická fakulta, Ústav hospodářských a sociálních dějin FF UK, Praha 2013).

Uhlířová, Martina. Andragogical legacy of Tomáš Baťa (*Andragogický odkaz Tomáše Bati*, bakalářská práce, Univerzita Palackého v Olomouci, Filozofická fakulta, Katedra sociologie a andragogiky, Olomouc 2011).

BOOKS AND PUBLICATIONS

Baroš, Jan (John). *The Fight and Fate of the Batamen in Singapore and Malaya*. Bata Limited, Batawa, 1945.

Baroš, Jan. *Czechoslovaks on the shores of the Ganges River from the beginnings*

BIBLIOGRAPHY

until the recent times, 1946 (Čechoslováci na březích Gangu od prvopočátků až po dnešní dobu, Československé Národní Sdružení v Indii, Batanagar 1946).

Baťa, Jan Antonín. *Building a country for 40 million people*, 2015 (Budujme stát pro 40 milionů lidí, Tisk Zlín, Zlín 1937; nové vydání 2015).

Baťa, Tomáš. *Essays and Speeches*, 2002 (Úvahy a projevy, UTB, Zlín 2002).

Kiat, G.H. *Bata Shoe Co. 20 Years in Malaya.* Singapore, 1951.

Bruton, Peter. *The Matter of a Massacre, Alexandra Hospital Singapore* (1989).

Cooper, Jon. *Tigers in the Park.* The Literary Centre, Singapore 2016.

Dejmek, Jindřich. *Czechoslovak Diplomacy, Vol. 2* (Diplomacie Československa – Díl II., Biografický slovník československých diplomatů 1918-1992, Academia, Praha 2013).

Diamond, Jon. *Images of War: The Fall of Malaya and Singapore.* Pen and Sword Books, Barnsley: 2015.

Kovaříková, Tereza. Motivation in the stores of Bata (*Motivace v prodejnách a domech služby firmy Baťa*, Acta Musealia 2015/1–2).

Kramoliš, Josef. *From Zlín to Singapore* (Ze Zlína až do Singapuru, Srdcem baťovec, Nadace Tomáše Bati, Zlín 2016).

Krutil, Inocenc. The Extraordinary destiny of Bata's exporter – new perspectives on the Bata phenomenon (*Nevšední osudy Baťova exportéra – o Batismu trochu jinak*, Atelier IM, Luhačovice 1995).

Marek, Martin and Vít Strobach. Bata system and the "Jewish question" at the end of 1930s and beginning of 1940s (*Batismus a „židovská otázka"na přelomu 30. a 40. let dvacátého století*, Židé a Morava XVII: kniha statí ze stejnojmenné konference konané v Muzeu Kroměřížska dne 10. 11. 2010).

Marek, Martin and Vít Strobach. Bata system, accelerated modernity and pioneers of work – the personnel management of Bata company and the organised transfers of workers in 1938-1942 (*Batismus, urychlená modernita a průkopníci práce – personální politika Baťova koncernu a řízené přesuny pracovníků v letech 1938–1941*, Moderní dějiny, č. 1, roč. 18., 2010).

Marek, Martin. Business activities of the Bata conglomerate at the end of 1930s (*Podnikatelské aktivity Baťova koncernu na konci třicátých let*, Studia historica brunensia 57, 2010).

Marek, Martin. Planning of the transfers of units of Bata workers (*Projektování transferu baťovských jednotek*, Acta historica Univeritatis Silesianae Opaviensis, 2010).

Marek, Martin. Strategy of the Bata company in 1938-1939 (*Strategie Baťova koncernu v letech 1938-1939*, Hospodářské dějiny, roč. 25, č. 2, Historický ústav AV ČR, Praha 2010).

History of Vémyslice from 1234 to 1947 (*Městečko Vémyslice 1234–1947*, Vémyslice 1947).

Mitchell, Ron. *Baba Nonie Goes to War – The Memoirs of a Singapore Volunteer on the Thai-Burma Railway.* Coombe Publishing, 2004.

Moffatt, Jonathan and Audrey McCormick Holmes. *Moon Over Malaya – A Tale of Argylls and Marines*. The History Press, Gloucestershire: 2014.

Moffatt, Jonathan and Paul Riches. *In Oriente Primus: A History of the Volunteer Forces in Malaya and Singapore*. Coventry, 2010.

Nelson, David. *The Story of Changi Singapore*. Changi Publication Co., 2001.

Pancheri, Paul Gibbs. *Volunteer! The Story of One Man's War in the East*. Self-published, Buckinghamshire: 1995.

Pike, Francis. *Hirohito's War – The War in Pacific 1941-1945*. Bloomsbury, London, 2015.

Pospíšilová Hana and Jaroslav Pospíšil. The pros and cons of Bata disputes (*Rub a líc baťovských sporů*, Kniha Zlín, Zlín 2012).

Procházka, Ivan. Compatriots at the Far East during WWII (*Krajané na Dálném východě během 2. světové války*, Historie a vojenství, 6/1996).

Ramli, Dol. History of the Malay Regiment 1933-1942. *Journal of the Malaysian Branch of the Royal Asiatic Society*, Vol. 38, No. 207, 1965.

Singapore Directory, 1940.

Stanley, Nigel. *Twists of Fate – The Civilian Ordeal in British Malaya 1941-1945*. Self-published, 2020.

Tan, Kevin Y.L. *Marshall of Singapore: A Biography*. Institute of Southeast Asian Studies, 2008.

Thompson, Peter. *The Battle for Singapore*. Hachette Digital, 2005.

Tsuji, Masanobu. *Singapore 1941-1942: The Japanese Version of the Malayan Campaign of World War II*. Oxford University Press, 1988.

Vaňhara, Josef. The story of one man and one city (*Příběh jednoho muže a jednoho města*, Zlínsko od minulosti k současnosti, 1988–1991. 1991, vol. 10, issue 1, p. 5–94).

Zbořil, Zdeněk. The History of Malaysia, Singapore and Brunei (*Dějiny Malajsie, Singapuru a Bruneje*, Nakladatelství Lidové noviny, Praha, 2009).

NEWSPAPERS AND MAGAZINES

The Straits Times, 1931-1942.
Malayan Tribune, 1931-1942.
The Singapore Free Press and Mercantile Advertiser, 1938-1942.
Morning Tribune, 1931-1942.

Zlín periodicals

Svět, 16. 1. 1942, 21. 1. 1942, 6. 2. 1942, 13. 2. 1942, 20. 2. 1942, 17. 2. 1943, 14. 4. 1943, 6. 10. 1943, 2. 2. 1944, 20. 12. 1944, 25. 4. 1945.
Náš kraj, 16. 2. 1942.
Tep nového Zlína, 8. 5. 1946, 7. 8. 1946, 21. 11. 1947.

Zlín, 7. 2. 1938, 19. 4. 1938, 20. 4. 1938, 21. 12. 1938, 17. 7. 1938, 15. 3. 1939, 11. 8. 1939.
Sdělení zaměstnancům firmy T. a A. Baťa, 12. 7. 1924.
Zlínské noviny, 3. 12. 1993

Other Periodicals
Batanagar News, weekly (1939, 1945, 1946).
Vémyslice Newspapers, July 2014.
Prager Presse, 11. 9. 1927.
Kanadské listy, 3/1995, 1/1996 a 11–12/2000.

- Acknowledgements -

I would like to express my sincere thanks and gratitude to the following:

My family for their understanding and support during the years of research and writing.

Mrs Alena Blažejovská for her production of the Czech audio version of my book that was aired on Czech Radio.

Mr Jan Brož for his support throughout the project.

Mr Lukáš Černý for his kindness and support during my research in Singapore.

Mrs Markéta Fajmonová for rescuing unique contemporary documents from Batanagar.

Mrs Rosemary Fell for all her work for the Malayan Volunteer Group, especially during the years when she was its secretary.

Mr Pavel Hajný for his friendship, support and help in the research in Singapore and elsewhere.

Ms Pam Ho for her keen and diligent work in editing the English manuscript of this book.

Mr Arnošt Hrdina for providing material on the history of Vémyslice, including several historical photographs.

Mrs Jana Jůzlová for her all-round help with the preparation of the Czech edition of this book.

Mr Jiří Kramoliš for sharing his rich family archives documenting Bata's early years in Singapore.

Mr Stanislav Krupař for his friendship, keen interest and lending his camera lens.

Mrs Hana Librová for her lifetime work in the field of environmentalism and for being both kind and strict mentor to me and many others.

Mrs Olga Lomová for her valuable comments on the Czech book manuscript.

ACKNOWLEDGEMENTS

Mrs Jana Lutonská for her friendship and support.

Mr Emil Máčel, in memoriam, for his pioneering work on Singapore Batamen.

Mr Tomáš Maleninský for his support and participation in the research in Singapore.

Mr Martin Marek for his valuable advice and suggestions.

Ms Judita Matyášová for her inspiration and for providing several key contacts.

Mr Jonathan Moffatt for his historical research on Singapore volunteers, for his goodwill towards my project and his invaluable, all-round assistance during my research.

Tomáš Němec for his enthusiasm for the whole project and for preparing the Czech edition of this book at Mystery Press publishing house.

Jakub Neradílek for making available the family archive and the documents of František Kocourek, the pioneer of pedicure at Bata.

Mr Jaroslav Olša Jr for his kindness, advice and support of the project.

Mr Jakub Patočka for his friendship, comments on the texts and lending me his scanner.

Mr Michael Pether for his historical research on the evacuations ships and selfless help.

Mr Sebastian Phu for his help in finding period photographs.

Mr Olek Plesek for his friendship and enthusiasm, and for the several years of work he has devoted to mapping Bata in Singapore and Batanagar.

Mr Ivan Procházka for his advice and support, including providing essential documents from his private collection.

Mr Ian Richardson, in memoriam, for valuable advice and for providing some historical documents.

Mrs Pavla Schneuwly for her support and participation in the research in Singapore.

Mrs Mary Anne Schooling for her support and a guided tour through the old areas of Singapore.

Mrs Marta Silvestrová for her kindness and for lending a scanner.

Mr Tiago Solca of Bata Shoe Co Singapore for his hospitality and assistance during research in Singapore.

Mr Pavel and Mrs Věra Stojar for their inspiring passion in the history of Zlín and their help in my research there.

Mr Peter W. Stubbs for his advice and his work on the wartime history of Singapore.

Mr Viktor Šimek for help in my research in Singapore.

Mr Václav and Mrs Eva Šťastný for their kindness and support during my research in Singapore,

Mr Pavel Velev for his help with the visit to Bata in Singapore and his

ACKNOWLEDGEMENTS

support of the publication of the Czech edition of ths book.

Mrs Jane Wakerman for providing pictures from her family archive and a guided tour through old Singapore.

Mr Stephen Walton of the Imperial War Museum for his efforts - albeit ultimately unsuccessful - to locate the original 'Jeyes List' in the British archives.

Mrs Millie Whyte (née Chudarek) for providing family photographs.

Mr Ben and Mrs Pavla Williams for help in my research and for attending the ceremony at Fort Canning Hill.

Mr Tan Ding Xiang for his research on the Alexandra Hospital Massacre and a guided tour of the hospital grounds.

Mr Alvin Ye for providing information and drawings of Tiong Bahru housing estate.

And the many others for expressing their interest, support or contribution to the whole project.